Books, Readers and
Libraries in Fiction

Books, Readers and Libraries in Fiction

Edited by Karen Attar and Andrew Nash

Available to purchase in print or download
for free at https://uolpress.co.uk

First published 2024 by
University of London Press
Senate House, Malet St, London WC1E 7HU

© the Authors 2024

The right of the authors to be identified as authors of this Work has been asserted by them in accordance with sections 77 and 78 of the Copyright, Designs and Patents Act 1988.

This book is published under a Creative Commons Attribution-NonCommercial-NoDerivatives 4.0 International (CC BY-NC-ND 4.0) license.

Please note that third-party material reproduced here may not be published under the same license as the rest of this book. If you would like to reuse any third-party material not covered by the book's Creative Commons license, you will need to obtain permission from the copyright holder.

A CIP catalogue record for this book is available from The British Library.

ISBN 978-1-913739-02-7 (hardback)
ISBN 978-1-913739-03-4 (paperback)
ISBN 978-1-913739-05-8 (.epub)
ISBN 978-1-913739-04-1 (.pdf)
ISBN 978-1-913739-10-2 (.html)

DOI https://doi.org/10.14296/ufnt1799

Dr. Syntax with a Blue Stocking Beauty' (1820).
From *The Third Tour of Doctor Syntax, In Search of a Wife*.
Etcher: Thomas Rowlandson; Publisher: Rudolph Ackermann. The Minnich Collection. The Ethel Morrison Van Derlip Fund, 1966. Public Domain.

Cover design for University of London Press by Hayley Warnham.
Book design by Nigel French.
Text set by Westchester Publishing Services UK in Meta Serif and Meta, designed by Erik Spiekermann.

Contents

List of figures	vii
Notes on contributors	ix
Acknowledgements	xi
Introduction: books, reading and libraries in fiction *Karen Attar and Andrew Nash*	1
1. Reading envisioned in the fourteenth and fifteenth centuries *Daniel Sawyer*	19
2. 'The gay part of reading': corruption through reading? *Rahel Orgis*	41
3. 'Fling *Peregrine Pickle* under the toilet': reading fiction together in the eighteenth century *Abigail Williams*	59
4. Jane Austen's refinement of the intradiegetic novel reader in *Northanger Abbey*: a study in Ricoeurian hermeneutics of recuperation *Monika Class*	75
5. Evaluating negative representations of reading: Ivan Turgenev's *Faust* (1855) *Shafquat Towheed*	95
6. 'I spent all yesterday trying to read': reading in the face of existential threat in Bram Stoker's *Dracula* *Hannah Callahan*	111
7. 'Into separate *brochures*': stitched work and a *new* New Testament in Thomas Hardy's *Jude the Obscure* *Lucy Sixsmith*	125
8. 'A fire fed on books': books and reading in D. H. Lawrence's *Sons and Lovers* *Susan Watson*	145
9. 'I sometimes like to read a novel': books and reading in Victorian adventure romance *Andrew Nash*	163

10. When it isn't cricket: books, reading and libraries in the girls' school story   181
Karen Attar

11. The body in the library in the fiction of Agatha Christie and her 'Golden Age' contemporaries   203
K. A. Manley

12. 'Very nearly magical': books and their readers in Terry Pratchett's Discworld series   225
Jane Suzanne Carroll

Index   241

List of figures

3.1 Auguste Bernard d'Agesci, *Lady Reading the Letters of Heloise and Abelard*, circa 1780, oil on canvas. The Art Institute of Chicago. CC0 designation. 63

7.1 *Jude the Obscure*: Chapter One. Autograph manuscript. Hardy, Thomas (British, 1840–1928). 436 pages. Ink on paper, 26.5cm × 29cm, circa 1894, published 1895, p. 156. Quoted from the manuscript by permission of The Fitzwilliam Museum, Cambridge. MS 1-1911. 129

7.2 *Jude the Obscure*: Chapter One. Autograph manuscript. Hardy, Thomas (British, 1840–1928). 436 pages. Ink on paper, 26.5cm × 29cm, circa 1894, published 1895, p. 157. Quoted from the manuscript by permission of The Fitzwilliam Museum, Cambridge. MS 1-1911. 129

7.3 *Jude the Obscure*: Chapter One. Autograph manuscript. Hardy, Thomas (British, 1840–1928). 436 pages. Ink on paper, 26.5cm × 29cm, circa 1894, published 1895, p. 157. Quoted from the manuscript by permission of The Fitzwilliam Museum, Cambridge. MS 1-1911. 130

7.4 The Epistle to the Colossians as a separate brochure. Photograph: Lucy Sixsmith. 131

7.5 Stitched work. Photograph: Lucy Sixsmith. 131

7.6 'Twice as understandable'. Photograph: Lucy Sixsmith. 136

Notes on contributors

Karen Attar is Curator of Rare Books and University Art at Senate House Library, University of London, and a former Fellow of the university's Institute of English Studies. She has published widely on aspects of library history, book collecting and librarianship. Her main publication is the third edition of the *Directory of Rare Book and Special Collections in the United Kingdom and Republic of Ireland* (2016). Girls' school stories are a hobby.

Hannah Callahan studied literature and printmaking at Bennington College, and received her Masters degree in Library and Information Science at Simmons University. She has a background in rare books and bibliography and is a librarian and independent researcher based in Minneapolis, Minnesota.

Jane Suzanne Carroll is an Ussher Associate Professor in Children's Literature in the School of English at Trinity College Dublin. Her teaching and research interests centre on landscape, spatiality and material culture in children's fiction. She is the author of *Landscape in Children's Literature* (2012) and *British Children's Literature and Material Culture: Commodities and Consumption, 1850–1914* (2021).

Monika Class is an associate professor of English literature at Lund University. Her research investigates the transformative potential of reading experiences in Britain from the eighteenth to the twenty-first centuries from the perspective of embodiment. As the Principal Investigator of the research group 'The Visceral Novel Reader' (DFG 422574378), she is working on a book manuscript under the same title and also on water poetry from the British Isles published between 2000 and 2024.

K. A. Manley is a retired librarian and co-convenor of the Seminar on the History of Libraries at the School of Advanced Study, University of London. His recent books include *Books, Borrowers, and Shareholders: Scottish Circulating and Subscription Libraries before 1825* (2012) and *Irish Reading Societies and Circulating Libraries Founded before 1825* (2018).

Andrew Nash is Reader in Book History and Director of the London Rare Books School in the Institute of English Studies, University of London. He has written, edited or co-edited books on Scottish literature, Victorian literature and the history of the book, including the final volume of *The Cambridge History of the Book in Britain* (2019) covering the twentieth century and beyond. He is a past editor of the *Review of English Studies*.

Rahel Orgis works as a scientific collaborator at the University Library, Bern. She is the author of *Narrative Structure and Reader Formation in Lady Mary Wroth's* Urania (2017) and co-editor of *Fashioning England and the English: Literature, Nation, Gender* (2018). Her articles on early modern prose fiction and drama have appeared in *Renaissance Studies, ELR, Sidney Journal* and *SPELL*. She is currently researching the development of narrators in early modern fiction.

Daniel Sawyer is a departmental lecturer in English literature and manuscript studies at Oxford. He studies poetry, manuscripts and editing, focusing on the period 1100 to 1500. His latest book is *How to Read Middle English Poetry* (2024), and he is currently writing a new account of poetic innovation in early English.

Lucy Sixsmith completed her PhD thesis, 'Handling Bibles in the Nineteenth Century', at the University of Cambridge in 2023. She has published work in *Book History, Cambridge Quarterly* and *Textual Practice*.

Shafquat Towheed is Senior Lecturer in English and Director of Research for the School of Arts and Humanities at The Open University. He has published extensively on nineteenth- and twentieth-century literature, particularly on the history and practice of reading. His most recent publication (with Corinna Norrick-Rühl) is *Bookshelves in the Age of the COVID-19 Pandemic* (2022). He is Vice President of the Society for the History of Authorship, Reading and Publishing (SHARP).

Susan Watson read English at Cambridge and completed a PhD in creative writing at Goldsmiths, University of London. Her thesis consisted of a collection of poems and lyric essays that respond to and pursue a dialogue with the work of other writers, particularly D. H. Lawrence and Virginia Woolf. The critical component of her research was a study of the work of the poet Anne Carson, who also writes about other writers.

Abigail Williams is Professor of English Literature and Lord White Tutorial Fellow, St Peters College, University of Oxford. Her publications include *The Social Life of Books: Reading Together in the Eighteenth-Century Home* (2017) and *Reading It Wrong: An Alternative History of Early Eighteenth-Century Literature* (2023).

Acknowledgements

This book has its origins in an online conference, entitled The Reader in the Book: Books, Reading and Libraries in Fiction, held at the Institute of English Studies in 2021. We would like to thank all the participants of that event – some of whose work is represented here in revised and much expanded form – for helping shape the lines of enquiry that have led to this book. We gratefully acknowledge the support of the administrative staff of the Institute of English Studies, especially the Institute Manager, Dr Eleanor Hardy, whose practical and intellectual advice helped considerably in the evolution of the volume. We would also like to thank the press's anonymous readers for their careful reading of the manuscript and invaluable suggestions for improvement. Finally, we are grateful to the staff of the University of London Press, especially Emma Gallon, for their enthusiastic and patient support at all stages of the project.

This book is dedicated to the memory of our two sets of parents.

Introduction: books, reading and libraries in fiction

Karen Attar and Andrew Nash

A small breakfast-room adjoined the drawing-room, I slipped in there. It contained a bookcase; I soon possessed myself of a volume, taking care that it should be one stored with pictures.

I returned to my book – Bewick's History of British Birds*: the letterpress I cared little for, generally speaking; and yet there were certain introductory pages that, child as I was, I could not pass quite as a blank. . . . Each picture told a story; mysterious often to my undeveloped understanding and imperfect feelings, yet ever profoundly interesting . . . With Bewick on my knee, I was then happy: happy at least in my way. I feared nothing but interruption and that came too soon.*

'You have no business to take our books. You are a dependent, mamma says; you have no money . . . Now, I'll teach you to rummage my book-shelves: for they are mine'.

. . . the volume was flung, it hit me, and I fell, striking my head against the door and cutting it. The cut bled, the pain was sharp: my terror had passed its climax; other feelings succeeded.

'Wicked and cruel boy!' I said. 'You are like a murderer – you are like a slave-driver – you are like the Roman emperors.'

I had read Goldsmith's History of Rome, *and had formed my opinion of Nero, Caligula, &c. Also I had drawn parallels in silence, which I never thought thus to have declared aloud.*[1]

The above extracts from one of the best-known fictional encounters with a book establish several features about the representation of books, reading and libraries in fiction that the chapters in this volume seek to address. The opening chapter of *Jane Eyre* (1847) has been subjected to numerous critical analyses.[2] Its richness lies not only in the way it immediately links the act of reading with the construction of narrative identity, establishing a motif that will be sustained throughout the novel, but in the way it captures in a short space the 'where', 'why', 'what' and 'how' of books and reading. For Jane, taking possession of a book and reading it is at once transgressive, escapist, empowering and dangerous. Her encounter with Bewick's *History of British Birds* excites both her desire for knowledge – the 'introductory pages' are not wholly rendered 'blank' by her page skimming – and her imagination: the adult Jane links the childhood experience to both her 'understanding' and her evolving 'feelings'. Yet the materiality of the book is also important. Jane's interest in the pictures is contrasted, not to the words and their meaning, but to the typography – the 'letterpress' – the physical marks that her eyes encounter on the page. Then, as the victim of John Reed's abuse, the book as a physical object takes over the scene. John's hurling of it is a barbaric expression of his right of ownership over books he himself has never read. Books are a marker of class division, yet the extent of the family library – confined to a small breakfast room – renders John's snobbish pronouncement about 'gentlemen's children' (ch. 1, p. 42) redundant. Finally, the scene demonstrates how Jane has access to the most transformative aspect of a book – its contents. She is able to combat John's violence with her learning, hurling back words culled from her reading, the ideas already reimagined in relation to her own life and subjugation.

Fictional encounters with books, then, involve and signify more than just reading. The chapters in this volume pick up on these and other associations of books, reading and libraries as they are depicted in a selection of fictional narratives from the medieval period to the twenty-first century. Although the volume has a wide chronological span, it is not designed as a historical survey of the topic – a vast undertaking – but instead offers a set of case studies that, while focused on individual authors and genres from specific periods, can prompt ways of thinking across history and across different kinds of writing. The authors deploy or reference a variety of critical approaches, including intertextuality, hermeneutical phenomenology, information literacy, and the history of the book and reading. Each chapter is alert to the significance of literary form and how fiction, by referencing and performing acts of reading, 'stages its own metafictional debates', as Abigail Williams puts it in her contribution. Two distinctive features emerge. Firstly, the chapters repeatedly show how

INTRODUCTION: BOOKS, READING AND LIBRARIES IN FICTION   3

fictional encounters with books involve more than just the processes and consequences of reading. The various ways in which characters use and interact with books – from falling asleep with them to destroying and creatively reusing them for different purposes – forms a hitherto unrecognised or underappreciated part of fictional narratives. Secondly, and relatedly, the chapters demonstrate how attention to bibliographical forms and the material parts of books, as these are depicted in fictional works, reveals new ways of thinking about literary form and the social and ideological aspects of narrative.

Any study of the representation of books and reading within works of fiction must engage with two related fields or topics of enquiry: the history of reading and intertextuality. Scholarly interest in the history of reading takes as its focus historical evidence of the reading habits of real people, sometimes to indicate reception of a work, often to shed light on an intellectual's thought processes.[3] The essays assembled in the path-breaking collection *The Practice and Representation of Reading* address different 'modes of reading that obtained in the past' in an effort to map not only how reading was practised but 'the meanings attached to it'.[4] Documentary evidence of readerly engagement with texts through marginalia, records of ownership, and personal testimonies, have allowed scholars to discuss individual and group interactions with books and libraries, and the manner of reading. The need to move beyond documentation to consider the 'meanings attached' to reading offers a route into this wider field for studies of fictional representations of books.[5] Portrayals of imagined readers and reading do not simply reflect, amplify, or distort contemporary cultural anxieties or moral debates, they form part of those anxieties and debates themselves. Works of fiction mediate and interpret books, libraries and the act of reading to their own readers, creating a form of reception theory. While this volume does not concern itself directly with actual readers, the relationship between historical attitudes towards books and reading and their treatment in fiction is a central concern, as, for example, in Rahel Orgis's examination of the depiction of women's reading programmes in two early modern texts in relation to historical evidence of women's book ownership and libraries, and Shafquat Towheed's discussion of Ivan Turgenev's novella *Faust* (1855) in the context of critical discourse on the rise of literacy and popular reading in the 1850s.

Encounters with books, reading and libraries as discussed in this volume are connected to, but nevertheless distinct from, the matter of literary allusion and intertextuality. At the very end of *Jane Eyre*, the narrating heroine likens St John Rivers to 'the warrior Greatheart', sealing the evident structural parallel Jane has built between her own narrative and Bunyan's *Pilgrim's Progress* (1678). As Sandra M. Gilbert notes, in her use of Bunyan Brontë was 'typical of many nineteenth-century novelists who – from Thackeray to Louisa May Alcott – relied on his allegory to give point and structure to their own fiction'.[6] Jane encounters and names many books during the course of her narrative, but while she has evidently read it, *Pilgrim's Progress* is not one of them. Quotation, allusion, parody and structural parallels between texts are the substance of intertextuality and intertextual criticism. The chapters in this volume touch inevitably on such matters but the immediate concerns are both more specific and more wide-ranging. Two further examples of texts that allude directly to *Pilgrim's Progress* illustrate the point. Alcott's *Little Women* (1868) parades its debt in the author's preface, with its adaptation of Bunyan's famous exhortation 'Go, then, my little book', and in its opening chapter, explicitly headed 'Playing Pilgrims'.[7] The March sisters had played at the events of Christian's journey towards salvation when they were younger; now they are instructed by their mother to 'begin again, not in play, but in earnest' (ch. 1, p. 18). Their subsequent progress in life is framed in terms of Bunyan's allegory as the chapter headings – 'Beth Finds the Palace Beautiful', 'Amy's Valley of Humiliation', 'Meg Goes to Vanity Fair' and so on – make clear. The Christmas gift of individual copies of a book – conceivably *Pilgrim's Progress* but more likely the New Testament – bound in different colours is to serve as their 'guide'. Yet although Mrs March, in a letter, notes approvingly of the 'well-worn cover' of Jo's 'guide-book' (ch. 12, p. 101), the sisters' embrace of their gift books assumes subtextual importance. Leaving aside the identity of the text, its status as a possession is subordinated to its assumed influence on their moral education.

John Buchan's *Mr Standfast* (1919), while equally explicit in its debt to Bunyan's allegory in its title and narrative structure, works differently.[8] In Buchan's novel the physical copy of *The Pilgrim's Progress* that Richard Hannay is forced to acquire so that he can decipher codes and interpret letters from his contacts serves a dual narrative purpose. While the content of 'the honest old story' acts as a spiritual guide for Hannay in his equally 'earnest' wartime mission, the book itself is one of his 'working tools', one that supports the mechanics of the adventuring, or spy, genre.[9] Reading and bibliographical form assume a vital importance in the unfolding of the story's codes. Hannay knows that his room has been rifled when he notices his bookmark has been removed, and he is careful to acquire the same edition as his contacts – 'the one in the *Golden Treasury* series' – so that lineation and pagination match up.[10]

The chapters in this volume are concerned with similar encounters with the material book and intratextual depictions of actual reading, moving beyond the immediate theoretical implications of intertextual allusion to consider how such encounters contribute to genre conventions and refract social, cultural and ideological discourses on reading. In this context, the text that inevitably looms large is *Don Quixote* (1605–15), the quintessential symbol of the misguided reader who 'became so convinced in his imagination of the truth of all the countless grandiloquent and false inventions he read that for him no history in the world was truer'.[11] Depictions of actual books and reading in *Don Quixote* form only a small part of the narrative. When the priest and the barber encounter Quixote's library, containing 'more than a hundred large volumes, very nicely bound, and many other smaller ones', most of these makers of 'mischief', as they are referred to, are flung out of the window by the housekeeper and later burned.[12] *Don Quixote* – like many of the narratives it inspired – is concerned more with the consequences of reading that has already taken place, underpinning Cervantes's immediate intention of parodying medieval romance and questioning literary form.[13]

As has been shown, the influence of *Don Quixote* on literature of the long eighteenth century was pervasive.[14] In particular, the image of the female reader who 'reads in the wrong way, and chaotically and corporeally reproduces her reading' became a recurrent character type.[15] In such novels the activity of reading as well as the nature of the books consumed becomes important. Scholarly accounts of women readers in the period have discussed fictional representations alongside contemporary discourse on reading, such as that contained in conduct books and historical evidence of actual reading practices. Jacqueline Pearson, for example, has shown how discourse on women's reading – especially of novels and romances – was frequently associated with danger and sexual transgression, and how fictional female readers – like Cervantes's Quixote – were portrayed as dangerously inclined to over-identify with characters and situations, and to confuse story with reality.[16] However, the dominant view that women readers were in need of discipline and guidance in their choice of reading has been challenged by critics like Joe Bray, who argues that fiction of the late-eighteenth and early nineteenth centuries 'frequently represents the female reader not as passive and impressionable, but rather as active and creative'.[17] Maria Edgeworth's *Belinda* (1801) is a case in point. The eponymous heroine, who reads both for education and personal pleasure, confidently asserts in the face of pressure from the pointedly named Mrs Freke, that 'I read that I may think for myself.' Mrs Freke maintains that books 'spoil the originality of genius' and 'when one has made up one's opinions, there is no use in reading'.[18] For Belinda, however, reading is a way of negotiating the world around her on her own terms. Several chapters in this volume add to this revisionary scholarship by reassessing the identification of the female reader as quixotic misreader in texts spanning the mid-seventeenth to the mid-nineteenth centuries. In her reading of prose narratives by Margaret Cavendish and Delarivier Manley, Rahel Orgis shows how in each text what superficially looks like an endorsement of early modern commonplaces regarding the dangers of reading turns out to be a more complicated comment on received ideas. Reading the narratives against contemporary discourses on reading and conduct, Orgis shows how the acquisition of knowledge through reading affords agency to these women readers, enabling them to resist the dangers arising from the 'ideal' reading programmes imposed upon them by patriarchal societies. One of the striking findings of this chapter is the way Cavendish's heroine identifies different kinds of books as valuable for her learning, among them mathematical books – 'to demonstrate truth by reason' – and play books – for 'discover[ing] and express[ing] the humours and manners of men'. The selection is perhaps surprising, yet as Orgis further shows, play books and play-going could be identified in contemporary discourse as sound educational source material rather than morally dangerous activities. Abigail Williams picks up on this point in her chapter, which discusses instances of communal reading in a selection of eighteenth-century novels. Showing how the valorisation of reading in sociable domestic settings can be understood in the context of moral arguments about the dangers of solitary reading, Williams concludes with an analysis of the famous depiction of domestic performance in Jane Austen's *Mansfield Park* (1814), demonstrating how Sir Thomas Bertram's disapproval at his family's attempt at amateur theatricals neatly frames the period's moral concerns about how to read at home.

Both of these chapters show how intratextual depictions of reading provoke a self-referential engagement with fictional forms. As Kate Flint argues, 'representations of reading act as a comment on the status of the text in which such a reference is found' and 'emphasizes the compliance, or otherwise of this text with established conventions concerning both fictional form and the response of readers'.[19] In her discussion of Cavendish in particular, Orgis considers the implications of the text's negotiation of its own genre characteristics. The heroine's choices and preferences in reading are complicated by their relation to the genre of the text in which she is emplotted. Monika Class also explores this theme in her discussion of one of the best-known depictions of what she terms the 'intradiegetic novel reader': Austen's *Northanger Abbey*, published in 1818 but written in the late 1790s. Austen's defence of novels and her refusal to undermine her own composition by presenting a negative portrayal of novel-reading are explored through the framework of hermeneutical phenomenology. Class shows how, in contrast to earlier eighteenth-century depictions of

INTRODUCTION: BOOKS, READING AND LIBRARIES IN FICTION   7

novel-reading, Austen departs from the dominant pathologisation of quixotism by integrating novels into a respectable part of character formation.

Fiction of the Victorian period was equally preoccupied with the image of the woman reader. Along with *Jane Eyre*, Maggie Tulliver in George Eliot's *The Mill on the Floss* (1860) and Isobel Archer in Henry James's *The Portrait of a Lady* (1891) are among many works that depict central female characters as readers.[20] As Carla L. Peterson has shown, the motif of reading in such novels is central to the creation of character. For orphaned or outcast protagonists like Jane Eyre, reading represents 'as it did for earlier cultures, an attempt to discover their true identity, to trace origins and genealogy'.[21] Jane's consumption of 'such books as came in my way' (ch. 13, p.155) – from the opening encounter with Bewick's *British Birds*, *Gulliver's Travels*, Arabian Tales, the Bible, Schiller, the German grammar and dictionary which she uses to teach herself the language, Walter Scott's 'Marmion' and 'the abundant harvest of entertainment and information' she discovers in the 'volumes of light literature, poetry, biography, travels [and] a few romances' (ch. 11, pp.134–5) contained in the one unlocked bookcase in Rochester's library – form a programme of self-education and a process of self-realisation. The parting image of her reading is one of empowerment and harmony with the blind Rochester, who 'saw books through me . . . Never did I weary of reading to him' (ch. 38, p.476).

Unlike Jane, for whom 'the finding of self through the reading of books is an achievable goal', as Peterson avers, Isobel Archer's reading in *The Portrait of a Lady* can be viewed as the opposite of self-realisation.[22] Like Jane, Isobel's reading is furtive: her reading room is 'a mysterious apartment which lay beyond the library' – a sanctuary in which she deliberately isolates herself from the outside world, refusing to look out of the door that opens onto the street 'for this would have interfered with her theory that there was a strange, unseen place on the other side'.[23] Also like Jane, her choice of books is eclectic – Browning, George Eliot, the *Spectator* and German philosophy – but, the narrator suggests, her 'uncontrolled use of a library full of books' is 'laid in the idleness of her grandmother's house' (ch. 3, p.40). Unguided reading fails to equip this pretty young woman for an education in life – especially the fashionable life of London and Florence. Her love of knowledge has 'a fertilising quality and her imagination was strong' (ch. 3, p.38), but like the quixotic readers of earlier periods, she mistakenly bases her knowledge of the world on what she reads, eager to discover whether life in England 'corresponded with the descriptions in the books' (ch. 6, p.73). As the novel progresses, and her determined attempt to shape her own destiny falters, Isobel's appetite for reading declines. She becomes the portrait of a distracted, impotent reader, 'fretting the edge of her book with a paper-knife' (ch. 29, p. 333).

Fictional readers in nineteenth-century novels, quixotic or otherwise, are not, of course, exclusively female. In Stendhal's *Le Rouge et le Noir* (1830), Julien Sorel's 'mad craze for reading' (as it appears to his illiterate father) moulds his ambitions and his love affairs, his 'manual of conduct' initially consisting of Rousseau's *Confessions* and the exploits of Napoleon in *Le Mémorial de Sainte-Hélène*. Julien comes to view his life as a novel he has composed himself: 'At last, he said to himself, my romantic story reaches its conclusion, and the credit is in the end all mine.'[24] In the French tradition, however, the novel most associated with intratextual reading is Gustave Flaubert's *Madame Bovary* (1857), the depiction of a female Quixote whose excessive and uncontrolled reading leads her to confuse fiction with reality and to die disillusioned by her impossible aspirations.[25] Flaubert's text was influential enough for Mary Braddon to rework the essential details of the plot in her sensation novel *The Doctor's Wife* (1864). Both works raise the issue of negative representations of reading, a topic explored by Shafquat Towheed in his chapter on Ivan Turgenev's *Faust*, a novella published two years before *Madame Bovary*. Picking up on earlier chapters in the volume, Towheed is concerned with the inherent paradox arising from the depiction within works of fiction of negative responses or resistance to reading fiction. As his close analysis of Turgenev's text demonstrates, such questions turn on the 'how' as much as the 'what' of reading. Placing the work within the context of the cultural anxieties and moral panics surrounding rising literacy and the growth of the reading public in Britain and Russia in the 1850s, Towheed shows how reading skilfully and critically were afforded a new prominence, one circumscribed by increasing prohibition and control.[26]

Hannah Callahan's chapter on Bram Stoker's *Dracula* (1897) picks up on the topics of literacy and critical reading. Building on a recent strain of criticism, Callahan argues that *Dracula* is as much a novel about books, information and reading as it is about vampires. Like readers today, the characters in *Dracula* are confronted with a bewildering array of information in different documentary forms. Written forms of communication are essential but open to misuse. Drawing on modern rubrics of information literacy, Callahan shows how the text challenges the characters' easy confidence in the authority of books and written records and promotes socially conscious forms of reading and dissemination of knowledge. The narrative form of *Dracula* makes the novel especially conducive to this approach. Constructed as an archive of documents and letters, it demands

INTRODUCTION: BOOKS, READING AND LIBRARIES IN FICTION   9

that readers outside the text employ a critical awareness about information equal to that of the readers inside the text.

Other chapters in the book are similarly concerned with connections between reading, interpretation and the material form of books and documents. In his chapter on envisioned reading in late medieval dream narratives, Daniel Sawyer shows how the tradition of reading followed by visionary experience often involves an active engagement with the material book. Portrayals of embodied reading and the physical identification of reader and book encourages us to 'imagine a material quality of the book described'. The depiction, for example, of a world of 'flexibles quires' in Henryson's *The Testament of Cresseid* and of 'notes and scraps of written material' at the conclusion of *The Kingis Quair* (attributed to James I of Scotland) allows Sawyer (like Callahan) to link the depiction of fluid, mobile reading, engineered by these different material forms and transformed into dream visions, to modern platforms of reading and consuming information.

The materiality of the book is central to Lucy Sixsmith's chapter, which explores Sue Bridehead's New Testament in Thomas Hardy's *Jude the Obscure* (1895). As a book made up of books, the Bible's history as a material object is conspicuously fluid. Sue has recreated her own New Testament by cutting up a bound volume and rearranging the separate 'books' into their chronological order of composition. Situating her discussion within the context of Victorian Bibles as material objects, Sixsmith argues that this apparent act of destruction, easily dismissed as sacrilege, can be viewed conversely as constructive in various ways. *Jude* is 'a novel full of books and reading', and Sue's creative engagement with the material and intellectual form of her Testament forms part of the work's preoccupation with class and education. Excluded from the college walls of Christminster (that is, Oxford), her cutting and rearranging of the volume can be viewed as an alternative form of Bible translation, a stark alternative to Jude's scholarly Greek text. Sixsmith's own reconstruction of Sue's reconstruction shows what can be gained by taking seriously the manual and intellectual work involved in Sue's remaking. What characters *do* with books, to invoke Leah Price, is as important a signifier as actual reading.[27]

Sawyer makes a pertinent observation in his chapter when he notes that 'the word *read* and its cognates do not, in their origins, assume contact with writing. They originate in a verb for interpretation and counsel'. In her chapter on D. H. Lawrence's *Sons and Lovers* (1907) Susan Watson shows how depictions of reading – especially communal or shared reading – are linked to the interpretation of character. The realist strain in this early Lawrence novel is evident in the way reading serves as a signifier of class or social status. As Watson notes, *Sons and Lovers* can be read in the context of self-education movements of the late nineteenth century. Her chapter moves beyond this, however, to show how the reading of books is presented not only as an index to individual characters, but as an index to the relationships between them. Episodes where one character reads aloud to another are a staging of the way each character reads or interprets the other; and in the interiority of Lawrence's narrative, they become an indication of their receptivity towards each other's personality.

The final four chapters in the book are concerned with individual genres. Each chapter demonstrates how the depiction of books and reading contribute to genre characteristics as much as they are conditioned by them. Andrew Nash's account of Victorian adventure fiction shows how books and reading have surprisingly important functions in a genre that explicitly rejects the domestic environment for outdoor activity and rhetorically elevates oral forms of storytelling above the printed word. Elements of the discussion pick up threads from other chapters: Robert Louis Stevenson's association of reading with dreams, for example, can be linked to Daniel Sawyer's discussion of envisaged reading in medieval dream visions, and the function of books and texts as clues to mysteries can be compared to detective fiction, the subject of Keith Manley's chapter. Most strikingly, as in Lucy Sixsmith's account of Sue Bridehead, the discussion shows how a concern with the materiality of books and texts underpins the most salient aspects of the genre: in Haggard's case the textual instantiation and recycling of myth and legend, in Stevenson's the complexity of duty and moral action.

Karen Attar's chapter on the twentieth-century girls' school story is also concerned with a genre which in its setting and valorisation of community activity would appear on the surface to be inhospitable to reading. Attar shows how one of the most successful and prolific writers of such stories turns reading into a social activity to render it acceptable within the genre. Tropes of misreading, of identification and over-identification with characters, of the importance of guidance when reading, and of the differentiation between good and bad books exist in Elinor Brent-Dyer's Chalet School series as in earlier books for adults, with one important twist. Brent-Dyer expects and invites her child readers to identify with the heroines of her books, and uses her characters' reading as an educational guide of what and how to read – with an eye to the adult approvers and purchasers of the books she is writing.

Keith Manley's encyclopaedic chapter on 'Golden Age' detective fiction traces the many ways in which books and libraries fuel the plots of Agatha Christie and her contemporaries.[28] Manley shows how the library is more than just a convenient setting for the bodies of crime fiction – a way of upsetting the ordered rhythm of life in the average village (the ubiquitous setting for so many detective novels of the period). As repositories of knowledge, the contents of libraries can aid the detective in unlocking the secret to a crime. More intricately, it is the library's sense of order that adds to its richness as a tool in a genre that turns on deception and disclosure. As Manley shows, in several examples it is the disruption of this order that offers the clue to the crime – a hidden murder weapon, a misplaced volume, a disguised safe or secret passage.

The concept of the library is critical to Jane Suzanne Carroll's account of Terry Pratchett's Discworld Series, a chapter that brings this volume full circle in its treatment of fantasy narratives. Pratchett's use of precise bibliographical terminology and library typology to describe 'L-space', a quantum space wherein all books and book collections are connected, signals 'the power of books to manipulate the fabric of reality'. As Carroll argues, images of movable type and the making of books underline how books (and knowledge) are 'not immutable or permanent but are composed of moving parts', and so 'open to the possibilities of various, varied, and variable readings'. The mutable nature of books discloses the complexity of authority, truth and power in Pratchett's fictional universe.

In different ways, then, the final two chapters emphasise the importance of the library as a theme within fiction. The portrayal of libraries in literature is a vast subject, and this volume only touches the surface.[29] Nevertheless, a concluding discussion of the topic is warranted here as a means of addressing some of the areas not covered in the volume. The physical edifice of the library has proved an especially rich resource for works of fiction. Libraries are ideal places in which to set mysteries because the buildings, like the Bodleian Library noted by Manley, may well be familiar landmarks, yet much of what goes on inside them is arcane. The very buildings are impenetrable to many, privileging those of a particular gender or class, and the book stacks inaccessible to all, allowing the imagination to run rife. When Adam Appleby, the comic hero of David Lodge's *The British Museum Is Falling Down* (1965), becomes trapped in the stacks – the 'entrails' – of the museum library, he discovers a 'dark underworld, heavy with the odour of decaying paper'. The 'civilised spaciousness' of the reading room, which instils in scholars 'a quiet confidence that wisdom was at their fingertips', is contrasted to 'this cramped and gloomy warren' which hides behind the library's illusion of order.[30] The reading room in the old British Museum Library has been widely fictionalised.[31] In Lodge's novel it becomes a 'huge womb' within which scholars 'curled themselves', fetus-like, 'more tightly over their books' – an apt metaphor, for Appleby, a young Catholic, spends the novel despairing over the possible pregnancy of his wife.[32] The image contrasts with that conjured up by Marion Yule in George Gissing's *New Grub Street* (1891), who likens the readers trapped in their endless pursuit of learning as 'hapless flies caught in a huge web, its nucleus the great circle of the Catalogue'.[33]

The same features of entrapment, exclusivity and arcaneness render libraries a rich setting for ghost stories.[34] In Margaret Oliphant's 'The Library Window' (1896), the narrator, who claims to 'see all sorts of things' while reading her book, perceives a male scholar working in a library through a window that appears from the street to be bricked up.[35] The spectral library and the scholar emerge as an exclusive domain out of reach of the unnamed girl who is spending her summer without her parents in a university town modelled on St Andrews. Academic settings pervade the stories of M. R. James, which are densely populated by references to books and libraries. 'The Tractate Middoth', one of his *Ghost Stories of an Antiquary* (1904), is based around a book in the stacks of Cambridge University Library, containing a will; a library assistant encounters a ghost when going to fetch the book for an enquirer. Two barriers are at play here: limited access to the stacks, and, as Patrick J. Murphy has emphasised in his analysis of the story, women's restricted access to the University Library at all.[36] Another tale, 'Casting the Runes', features the reading room of the British Museum Library, in which a vengeful writer hands a scholar a cursed piece of paper. (It is a sign of the murderer's depravity that he tears a picture roughly from Bewick to send his intended victim as a warning; Harrington sells the copy of the book, with the mutilated page, after the murderer's death.[37]) In our own day, Sean O'Brien, who has openly set several short ghost stories in his collection *The Silence Room* (2008) in an amended version of the Newcastle Literary and Philosophical Society Library, refers to this library's redolence of M. R. James in the way it seems to float free in time, with its spiral staircase and mysterious doors and byways.[38]

The depiction of books and libraries as a threshold to a dream or fantasy world has a long history, as Daniel Sawyer's chapter on the late medieval period demonstrates. It is a common trope in children's fantasy fiction, as, for example, in Michael Ende's *Die unendliche Geschichte* (1979), translated as *The Neverending Story* (1983), where the protagonist Bastian Balthasar Bux steals a book from a second-hand bookshop and is drawn into its adventures which become the beginning of his.[39] A classic earlier example is *Lilith* (1895), the late masterpiece of George MacDonald, widely considered the father of modern fantasy. In this work, subtitled 'A Romance', the doorway between worlds is an ancient library 'whose growth began before the invention of printing', and whose space is visited by the ghost of an old librarian, Mr Raven.[40] Raven (who assumes the form of a bird in the fantasy world), moves between realms via a vault containing the oldest and rarest books, the door to which is disguised by a line of book backs made out of volumes that were 'lost beyond hope of recovery.'[41] On top of one of the shelves, fixed and seemingly unmoveable, lies a mutilated manuscript book written on parchment and bound in limp vellum. It is this volume, which has been cut through diagonally to complete the illusion of the book-backed door, that lures the narrator, Mr Vane, into the other world. The half-book obviously represents the liminal space between two worlds. What fragments of its contents Vane can detect from the turning up of one corner make no 'sense' to him, yet they awaken in him 'impossible' feelings, 'new in colour and form'.[42] As Stephen Prickett points out, there is a suggestion that 'all books span this gap between external and internal worlds',[43] yet it is significant too that the volume is a manuscript book sitting atop a row of printed volumes, forming a bridge between two worlds of book production.

If books and libraries are an essential dynamic in much fantasy fiction, references are sparser in science fiction (for all the difficulty in defining the genre).[44] Active hostility towards books is a token of the dystopian world of the genre. The threatening power of the written word is evident from desire to annihilate it, whether by systematically burning physical volumes in Ray Bradbury's American classic *Fahrenheit 451* (1953)[45] – ultimately hearteningly ineffectual, as rebels memorise the contents of books to keep them alive – or more subtly by narrowing vocabulary and hence gradually rendering the content incomprehensible, as Syme explains in George Orwell's *Nineteen Eighty-Four* (1949):

> By 2050 – earlier, probably – all real knowledge of Oldspeak will have disappeared. The whole literature of the past will have been destroyed. Chaucer, Milton, Byron – they'll exist only in Newspeak versions, not merely changed into something different, but actually changed into something contradictory of what they used to be.[46]

It is not the mere absence of books, but their systematic eradication, which renders these worlds so bleak and depraved. Be the settings humdrum or bizarre, the presence of books and libraries in fiction emphasises how integrated they are in society. And while certain titles may be unedifying, and untaught readers may read uncritically, books and reading are ultimately ennobling and redemptive. The new dimensions they open to readers are seldom as overt as they are in fantasy fiction but are nonetheless real. In fiction as in life, books, reading and libraries are integral to our humanity.

Notes

1. Charlotte Brontë, *Jane Eyre*, ed. by Q. D. Leavis (London: Penguin, 1966), ch. 1, pp. 39–43. Further references are in the text.

2. Studies of reading and allusion in *Jane Eyre* that offer a sustained analysis of the opening chapter include Mark M. Hennelly, Jr, 'Jane Eyre's Reading Lesson', *English Literary History*, 51(4) (1984), 693–717, and Catherine J. Golden, *Images of the Woman Reader in Victorian British and American Fiction* (Gainesville: University Press of Florida, 2003), pp. 51–9. For a more general discussion of Brontë's relationship with books as physical objects and their representation in her work, see Barbara Heritage, 'Authors and Bookmakers: *Jane Eyre* in the Marketplace', *Papers of the Bibliographical Society of America*, 106(4) (2012), 449–85.

3. See, for example, Samuel Taylor Coleridge, *The Collected Works of Samuel Taylor Coleridge*, vol. XII: *Marginalia*, ed. by H. J. Jackson and George Whalley (London: Routledge and Kegan Paul, 1999); William Coolidge Lane, *The Carlyle Collection: A Catalogue of Books on Oliver Cromwell and Frederick the Great Bequeathed by Thomas Carlyle to Harvard College Library*, Library of Harvard University: Bibliographical Contributions, 26 (Cambridge, MA: Harvard University Library, 1888); Voltaire, *Corpus des notes marginales. Oeuvres complètes de Voltaire*, ed. by Natalia Elaguina et al. (Oxford: Voltaire Foundation, 2008–18); Ruth Clayton Windscheffel, *Reading Gladstone* (Basingstoke: Palgrave Macmillan, 2008); Michael Wheeler, 'William Gladstone Reads his Contemporaries', in *The Edinburgh History of Reading: Modern Readers*, ed. by Mary Hammond (Edinburgh: Edinburgh University Press, 2020), pp. 136–44.

4. *The Practice and Representation of Reading in England*, ed. by James Raven, Helen Small and Naomi Tadmor (Cambridge: Cambridge University Press, 1996), p. 12.

5. Connections have been made between real readers and fictional representations in such studies as Kate Flint's *The Woman Reader 1837–1914* (Oxford: Oxford University Press, 1995) which contains a chapter on 'Fictional Reading' (pp. 252–73).

6. Sandra M. Gilbert, 'Plain Jane's Progress', *Signs*, 2(4) (1977), 779–804 (p. 784n10). For fuller accounts of the novel's debt to Bunyan, see Barry V. Qualls, *The Secular Pilgrims of Victorian Fiction: The Novel as Book of Life* (Cambridge: Cambridge University Press, 1982), pp. 43–69; Michael Wheeler, *The Art of Allusion in Victorian Fiction* (Basingstoke: Macmillan, 1979), pp. 27–43.

7. For a discussion of the importance of Bunyan's text on American literature generally, see Ruth K. MacDonald, *Christian's Children: The Influence of John Bunyan's* The Pilgrim's Progress *on American Children's Literature* (New York: P. Lang, 1989).

8. For a detailed discussion, see Jeremy Idle, 'The Pilgrim's Plane-Crash: Buchan, Bunyan and Canonicity', *Literature & Theology*, 13 (1999), 249–58.

9. John Buchan, *Mr Standfast* (1919; Harmondsworth: Penguin, 1983), ch. 2, pp. 35, 32.

10. Buchan, *Mr Standfast*, ch. 5, p. 82.

11. Miguel de Cervantes, *Don Quixote*, trans. by Edith Grossman (London: Vintage, 2005), ch. 1, p. 21.

12. *Don Quixote*, ch. 6, pp. 45–52; (quotation on p. 45).

13. See Anthony J. Cascardi, '*Don Quixote* and the Invention of the Novel', in *The Cambridge Companion to Cervantes*, ed. by Anthony J. Cascardi (Cambridge: Cambridge University Press, 2006), pp. 58–79.

14. See Ronald Paulson, *Don Quixote in England: The Aesthetics of Laughter* (Baltimore, MD: Johns Hopkins University Press, 1998).

15. Amelia Dale, *The Printed Reader: Gender, Quixotism, and Textual Bodies in Eighteenth-Century Britain* (Lewisburg, PA: Bucknell University Press, 2019), p. 12.

16. Jacqueline Pearson, *Women's Reading in Britain, 1750–1835: A Dangerous Recreation* (Cambridge: Cambridge University Press, 1999), ch. 7, pp. 196–218.

17. Joe Bray, *The Female Reader in the English Novel: From Burney to Austen* (New York: Routledge, 2009), p. 1.

18. Maria Edgeworth, *Belinda*, ed. by Kathryn J. Kirkpatrick (Oxford: Oxford University Press, 1994), ch. 17, pp. 227. For a discussion of the novel, see Richard De Ritter, *Imagining Women Readers, 1789–1820* (Manchester: Manchester University Press, 2015), pp. 53–71, where Belinda's developing reading is interpreted as a form of 'symbolic labour' and self-fashioning.

19. Flint, *The Woman Reader*, p. 256.

20. For a critical survey of these and other works, see Golden, *Images of the Woman Reader*.

21. Carla L. Peterson, *The Determined Reader: Gender and Culture in the Novel from Napoleon to Victoria* (New Brunswick, NJ: Rutgers University Press, 1986), p. 28.

22. Peterson, *The Determined Reader*, p. 32.

23. Henry James, *The Portrait of a Lady*, ed. by Nicola Bradbury (Oxford: Oxford University Press, 1995), ch. 3, p. 41. Further references are in the text.

24. Stendhal, *Scarlet and Black*, trans. by Margaret R. B. Shaw (Harmondsworth: Penguin, 1957), ch. 4, pp. 36, 40; ch. 34, p. 451. For an account of the centrality of books and reading to Stendhal's major novels, see James T. Day, 'The Hero as Reader in Stendhal', *French Review*, 54(3) (1981), 412–19.

25. See Soledad Fox, *Flaubert and 'Don Quijote': The Influence of Cervantes on 'Madame Bovary'* (Liverpool: Liverpool University Press, 2008), especially the critical comparison between the two works contained in the final chapter.

26. For a discussion of this wider topic in the context of Britain, see Patrick Brantlinger, *The Reading Lesson: The Threat of Mass Literacy in Nineteenth-Century British Fiction* (Bloomington: Indiana University Press, 1998).

27. Leah Price, *How to Do Things with Books in Victorian Britain* (Princeton and Oxford: Princeton University Press, 2012).

28. See also Nicola Humble, 'The Body in the Library: Christie and Sayers', in *Libraries in Literature*, ed. by Alice Crawford and Robert Crawford (Oxford: Oxford University Press, 2022), pp. 128–39.

29. For a recent attempt at comprehensive treatment, see *Libraries in Literature*, ed. by Alice Crawford and Robert Crawford (Oxford: Oxford University Press, 2022). For a study of fictional treatments of the library profession, see Grant Burns, *Librarians in Fiction: A Critical Bibliography* (Jefferson, NC: McFarland, 1988).

30. David Lodge, *The British Museum Is Falling Down* (1965; London: Penguin, 2010), ch. 6, pp. 92–3.

31. Edward F. Ellis, *The British Museum in Fiction: A Check-List* (Buffalo: [n.pub.], 1981). This deals with the entire Museum, not exclusively its library.

32. Lodge, *The British Museum Is Falling Down*, ch. 3, pp. 41–2.

33. George Gissing, *New Grub Street* (London: Oxford University Press, 1958), ch. 8, p. 110.

34. Twelve of these, including M. R. James's 'The Tractate Middoth', have been anthologised in *The Haunted Library: Classic Ghost Stories*, ed. by Tanya Kirk (London: British Library Publishing, 2016).

35. Margaret Oliphant, *A Beleaguered City and Other Stories*, ed. by Merryn Williams (Oxford: Oxford University Press, 1988), p. 291.

36. M. R. James, 'The Tractate Middoth', in *Ghost Stories of an Antiquary* (London: Book Club Associates, 1976), pp. 181–202; Patrick J. Murphy, *Medieval Studies and the Ghost Stories of M. R. James* (University Park: Pennsylvania University Press, 2017), pp. 147–55. For discussion of James's ghost stories and the connection with libraries more broadly, see Darryl Jones, 'M. R. James's Libraries', in *Libraries in Literature*, pp. 114–27; for 'The Tractate Middoth', see pp. 123–7.

37. M. R. James, 'Casting the Runes', in *Ghost Stories*, pp. 203–29.

38. Sean O'Brien, *The Silence Room* ([Manchester]: Comma Press, 2008), p. 201; Sean O'Brien, 'Lit & Phil Library', youtube.com/watch?v=ThhfIfegmgM, accessed 27 December 2023.

39. See Poushali Bhadury, 'Metafiction, Narrative Metalepsis, and New Media Forms in *The Neverending Story* and the Inkwold Trilogy', *The Lion and the Unicorn*, 27(3) (2013), 301–26. For other examples, see Sara Lodge, 'Fantastic Books and Where to Find Them: Libraries in Fairy Tale and Fantasy', in *Libraries in Literature*, pp. 233–44.

40. George MacDonald, *Lilith: A Romance* (London: Chatto & Windus, 1895), ch. 1, p. 2.

41. MacDonald, *Lilith*, ch. 1, p. 4.

42. MacDonald, *Lilith*, ch. 3, p. 18.

43. Stephen Prickett, 'The Idea of Tradition in George MacDonald', in *Rethinking George MacDonald: Context and Contemporaries*, ed. by Christopher MacLachlan et al. (Glasgow: Scottish Literature International, 2013), pp. 1–17 (p. 8).

44. For discussion of what constitutes science fiction, see Adam Roberts, *The History of Science Fiction* (Houndmills: Palgrave Macmillan, 2006), vii–ix; 1–20; Adam Roberts, *Science Fiction*, 2nd edn (London: Routledge, 2006), 1–36.

45. For discussion of literary allusions in *Fahrenheit 451*, see Peter Sisario, 'A Study of the Allusions in Bradbury's *Fahrenheit 451*', *The English Journal*, 59 (1970), 201–5, 212. For a study of twentieth-century destruction of books which prompted the novel, see Matthew Fishburn, *Burning Books* (Basingstoke: Palgrave Macmillan, 2008); *Fahrenheit 451* is discussed on pp. 162–3.

46. George Orwell, *Nineteen Eighty-Four* (1949; London: Penguin, 1989), ch. 5, p. 56.

Bibliography of secondary literature

Bhadury, Poushali, 'Metafiction, Narrative Metalepsis, and New Media Forms in *The Neverending Story* and the Inkwold Trilogy', *The Lion and the Unicorn*, 27(3) (2013), 301–26.

Brantlinger, Patrick, *The Reading Lesson: The Threat of Mass Literacy in Nineteenth-Century British Fiction* (Bloomington: Indiana University Press, 1998)

Bray, Joe, *The Female Reader in the English Novel: From Burney to Austen* (New York: Routledge, 2009)

Burns, Grant, *Librarians in Fiction: A Critical Bibliography* (Jefferson, NC: McFarland, 1988)

Cascardi, Anthony J., '*Don Quixote* and the Invention of the Novel', in *The Cambridge Companion to Cervantes*, ed. by Anthony J. Cascardi (Cambridge: Cambridge University Press, 2006), pp. 58–79

Crawford, Alice and Robert Crawford (eds), *Libraries in Literature* (Oxford: Oxford University Press, 2022)

Dale, Amelia, *The Printed Reader: Gender, Quixotism, and Textual Bodies in Eighteenth-Century Britain* (Lewisburg, PA: Bucknell University Press, 2019)

Day, James T., 'The Hero as Reader in Stendhal', *French Review*, 54(3) (1981), 412–19

De Ritter, Richard, *Imagining Women Readers, 1789–1820* (Manchester: Manchester University Press, 2015)

Ellis, Edward F., *The British Museum in Fiction: A Check-List* (Buffalo, NY: [n.pub.], 1981).

Fishburn, Matthew, *Burning Books* (Basingstoke: Palgrave Macmillan, 2008)

Flint, Kate, *The Woman Reader 1837–1914* (Oxford: Oxford University Press, 1995)

Fox, Soledad, *Flaubert and 'Don Quijote': The Influence of Cervantes on 'Madame Bovary'* (Liverpool: Liverpool University Press, 2008)

Gilbert, Sandra M., 'Plain Jane's Progress', *Signs*, 2(4) (1977), 779–804

Golden, Catherine J., *Images of the Woman Reader in Victorian British and American Fiction* (Gainesville: University Press of Florida, 2003)

Hennelly, Mark M., Jr, 'Jane Eyre's Reading Lesson', *English Literary History*, 51(4) (1984), 693–717

Heritage, Barbara, 'Authors and Bookmakers: *Jane Eyre* in the Marketplace', *Papers of the Bibliographical Society of America*, 106(4) (2012), 449–85

Idle, Jeremy, 'The Pilgrim's Plane-Crash: Buchan, Bunyan and Canonicity', *Literature & Theology*, 13 (1999), 249–58

MacDonald, Ruth K., *Christian's Children: The Influence of John Bunyan's* The Pilgrim's Progress *on American Children's Literature* (New York: P. Lang, 1989)

Murphy, Patrick J., *Medieval Studies and the Ghost Stories of M. R. James* (University Park: Pennsylvania University Press, 2017)

O'Brien, Sean, 'Lit & Phil Library', youtube.com/watch?v=ThhfIfegmgM.

Paulson, Ronald, *Don Quixote in England: The Aesthetics of Laughter* (Baltimore, MD: Johns Hopkins University Press, 1998).

Pearson, Jacqueline, *Women's Reading in Britain, 1750–1835: A Dangerous Recreation* (Cambridge: Cambridge University Press, 1999).

Peterson, Carla L., *The Determined Reader: Gender and Culture in the Novel from Napoleon to Victoria* (New Brunswick, NJ: Rutgers University Press, 1986).

Price, Leah, *How to Do Things with Books in Victorian Britain* (Princeton, NJ: Princeton University Press, 2012).

Prickett, Stephen, 'The Idea of Tradition in George MacDonald', in *Rethinking George MacDonald: Context and Contemporaries*, ed. by Christopher MacLachlan et al. (Glasgow: Scottish Literature International, 2013), pp. 1–17.

Qualls, Barry V., *The Secular Pilgrims of Victorian Fiction: The Novel as Book of Life* (Cambridge: Cambridge University Press, 1982).

Raven, James, Helen Small and Naomi Tadmor (eds), *The Practice and Representation of Reading in England* (Cambridge: Cambridge University Press, 1996).

Roberts, Adam, *The History of Science Fiction* (Houndmills: Palgrave Macmillan, 2006).

Roberts, Adam, *Science Fiction*, 2nd edn (London: Routledge, 2006).

Sisario, Peter, 'A Study of the Allusions in Bradbury's *Fahrenheit 451*', *The English Journal*, 59 (1970), 201–5, 212.

Wheeler, Michael, *The Art of Allusion in Victorian Fiction* (Basingstoke: Macmillan, 1979).

Chapter 1

Reading envisioned in the fourteenth and fifteenth centuries

Daniel Sawyer

A witch steals from her neighbours by sending a magic, self-moving bag to suck milk from their cows at night. Eventually, the community brings her before the local bishop. He has her demonstrate her bag-animating magic for him and orders an assistant to write down the words and actions she uses in her spell. At this point, reading, of a sort, enters the story:

> The bysshop began the charme to rede,
> And as she dede, he dede yndede.
> He seyde and dede everydeyl
> Ryght as she dede, he dede al weyl.
> The sloppe lay stylle as hyt ded wore:
> For hym ne ros hyt never the more.
> 'Why', seyde he, 'wyle hyt nat ryse?
> And Y have do the same wyse
> And seyd the wrdys, lesse ne mo,
> And for my seyying wyle hyt nat go?'
> 'Nay', she seyde, 'why shuld hyt so?
> Ye beleve nought as Y do.'[1]
> (The bishop began to read the charm, and did just as she did. He said and did everything exactly as she had. The bag lay still, as if it was dead: it never rose for him. 'Why', he said, 'will it not rise? For I've acted in the same way, and said the words, no more and no less – will it not travel at my word?' 'No', she said, 'why should it? You don't believe as I do.')

The bishop tells the witch not to do it again but lets her go without punishment.

I take this incident from Robert Mannyng's *Handlyng Synne*, a lively early fourteenth-century moral manual. For the history of imagined reading and imagined books, two facets of the passage hold particular interest: the public, aural, record-keeping quality of the imagined reading, and the practical, salvific, non-fictional thrust of *Handlyng Synne* itself. The poem imagines the bishop reading aloud as part of the recording of process. In his reading of the spell he attempts a speech act, for he tries to use language to make something happen. Thus the moral of the story, as Mannyng interprets it: beyond the right form of words, belief matters; if this holds true even for magic bags, it must be true for Christian practice. *Handlyng Synne* sits beyond fiction's borders. Whatever Mannyng's audience thought of the likelihood of magical milk-stealing bags, they probably understood the story as truthful in its salvific purpose, in saying something about belief. Moreover, the poem, even in a story about belief, stays unconcerned about the inner lives of the bishop and the witch: they are not characters. Not, of course, that premodern writing as a whole lacked fictionality or interiority. Criticism can trace interiority in any period, and scholars have argued for developments in fictionality in and around the twelfth century.[2] I only observe that plenty of imagined reading was imagined in works that, however clever and crafty in other ways – and *Handlyng Synne* is a clever poem – did not strive for fiction. A writer could imagine reading outside fiction, and fiction itself demands careful handling as a category.

Distance in time lends earlier literature a particular power to test categories and concepts. Descriptions of imagined reading in Middle English and Older Scots usefully complicate our ideas about fiction, remind us that reading has long meant more than just one person looking silently upon a book, and show how a book might take a variety of forms and have porous borders. Here, I shall explore one literary-critical touchstone for imagined reading in the period, and then trace what happened when a series of poets turned the idea of reading followed by visionary experience into a tradition. Once it became a recognisable *topos*, imagined reading leading into a vision allowed writers to inflect and position their work through the precise connotations of their language for the physical book and the act of reading; recent and older work exploring this area of vocabulary in the period lets us explore that bookish language.[3] The developing idea of private reading appears in literary accounts. But so do counter-teleological examples of reading imagined in non-private, inhabitable, communal ways. These works show why and how the history of imagined reading might think carefully about the concepts of fiction and of the book, and might avoid stories of assumed progress.

One might call imagined reading in Scots and English at this time unimportant. Latin was the normative written language, and intellectual works in Latin had a carefully worked out set of approaches to reading, recoverable today in manuscript evidence and in surviving overt discussions. Larger-scale histories of reading have mapped out these materials, and have identified major changes in the twelfth and thirteenth centuries: an increasing sophistication of on-page aids and a growth in wide-ranging scholastic reading.[4] Furthermore, besides Latin, the island of Great Britain sat well within French's cultural sphere of influence: England had been conquered by a Francophone Norman dynasty, who had gone on to conquer Wales, while Scotland frequently found itself allied with France against that same dynasty. French consequently persisted as a prestige vernacular. Indeed, it is if anything in this period in particular, roughly from the eleventh century to the fifteenth, that we find Scots and English at their most decentralised, peripheral and non-standardised.[5] One might, then, find good reasons to focus these questions on Latin or French materials.

However, the very peripheral status of English and Scots itself demands attention. It was during this period that writings in these tongues were at their most uncertain and experimental. Genre, voice, fictionality and value were 'in play' in ways they never quite would be again. Writing was both transnational and regional, but rather less national than it has been since. The period therefore offers a vital standpoint from which to encounter writings from later times: less national, less standard, not dominant and not an assumed default. By studying Scots and English in this period we might slide out from underneath some assumptions about fiction, reading and books.

It is in one of the Middle English works long lauded for its quasi-novelistic attention to inner life, Geoffrey Chaucer's *Troilus and Criseyde*, that the period's most often-noted moment of imagined reading occurs.[6] Having come to Criseyde's house, her uncle Pandarus:

> . . . fond two othere ladys sete and she,
> Withinne a paved parlour, and they thre
> Herden a mayden reden hem the geste
> Of the siege of Thebes, while hem leste.[7]
> (Found her sat with two other ladies within a paved parlour; the three of them were hearing a maiden read them the tale of the siege of Thebes, for as long as they liked.)

When Pandarus asks about Criseyde's reading material, she reports that:

> This romaunce is of Thebes that we rede;
> And we han herd how that kyng Layus deyde
> Thorugh Edippus his sone, and al that dede;
> And here we stynten at thise lettres rede –
> 'How the bishop, as the book kan telle,
> Amphiorax, fil thorugh the ground to helle.'
> (We're reading a romance about Thebes, and we have heard how King
> Laius died through his son Oedipus, and all that story; and we've
> stopped here at these red letters: 'How Bishop Amphiaraos fell through
> the ground to hell, as the record can tell.' II.100–5)

Criseyde and her companions are reading together, as we know people commonly did in the fourteenth and fifteenth centuries, and would do in later times too.[8] In modern terms, Criseyde listens and it is the 'mayden', junior to the others present, who reads; to Criseyde, though, they are all reading, and the poem imagines her actively engaged with the material book too, identifying the red ink topical rubric which lets readers track their position, and which the maiden will presumably use to find their place again. I suspect the last two lines quoted suggest that Criseyde reads the rubric out, and so I have imposed quotation marks on them in reproducing them here.

Scholarship's conception of reading must be open to groups, who might relate only intermittently with the physical book. The word *read* and its cognates do not, in their origins, assume contact with writing. They originate in a verb for interpretation and counsel, senses which they kept through Old and Middle English. Etymology is not destiny, but these meanings do persist today: when critics speak of 'a reading' of a work, or when a pundit gives their 'read on' geopolitics, the word's oldest senses sit foremost.

Criseyde's household reading also leads her and Pandarus into questions of gendered bookishness, and perhaps gendered linguistic competence. Both Criseyde's description of a 'romaunce' that 'is of Thebes' and the French form of *Amphiorax* rather than *Amphiaraus* hint that Criseyde's group are reading the *Roman de Thèbes*, a French version of the tale. Pandarus, meanwhile, remarks that of this story 'ben ther maked bookes twelve' ('twelve books have been written', II.108), suggesting that he knows Statius' twelve-book Latin *Thebaid*. Chaucer's characters briefly sketch an awareness of the reading boundaries between Latinity and Francophony, and the hazy borders of history and romance. Later in the poem, Criseyde's reflections on divine power suggest wider and more intellectual reading.[9]

Such moments, though, work as lone allusions and descriptions. What happened when imagined reading became a *topos*, a tradition? In fourteenth- and fifteenth-century Great Britain, dream-vision poems developed a tradition of opening with imagined reading. As each poet reformulates the idea of reading before vision, this line of works offers helpful case studies. Criticism has said much about literary allusion in these passages, but less about the specific wording of the descriptions of reading and of books.

Chaucer seems, in the surviving record, to have invented the idea of describing the reading of a particular book that then affects the ensuing dream.[10] Being Chaucerian, the relevant passages in the *Book of the Duchess* and the *Parliament of Fowls* have been well picked over for their allusions and the roles they play in their respective poems.[11] The *Book of the Duchess* begins with a speaking, narrating figure who cannot sleep:

> Upon my bed I sat upright
> And bad oon reche me a book,
> A romaunce, and he it me tok,
> To rede and drive the night away;
> For me thought it better play
> Then playe either at ches or tables.
> (I sat upright in my bed and asked someone to hand me a book, a romance, to read and drive the night away, because it seemed to me a better amusement than playing either chess or backgammon, and he brought it to me, 46–51.)[12]

Reading for Chaucer's sleepless speaker reveals a social position: though – judging by his uncomprehending conversation with the knight encountered later in the poem – not presented as courtly, he has servants enough to be non-specific about them ('oon'), and to have his reading matter fetched. The book request might have a haphazard tone: the reliance on someone else, the indefinite article, and especially the baggy term *romaunce* hint at this. 'A romaunce' only shakily describes what the speaker in fact receives, which turns out, as the reader relates its plot (62–230), to be Ovid's *Metamorphoses*. The sense of Middle English *romaunce* is a hot potato of a topic, but the word typically means a knightly adventure story, more rarely simply a story or poem, or, more rarely still, a work in French.[13] *Metamorphoses* might be filed under the second of these senses, or under the third in French translation, but it fits the noun a little awkwardly, and Chaucer might have hoped an audience would be piqued and amused by realising that the speaker's haphazardly fetched 'romaunce' is Ovid. That effect would, at least, fit with the way in which the speaker's limited perceptions drive comedy and pathos later in the poem.

24   DANIEL SAWYER

When sleep does come for the poem's dreamer, it brings him and the book together: 'Such a lust anoon me took / To slepe that ryght upon my book / Y fil aslepe' ('at once such a wish to sleep took hold of me that I fell asleep right there, upon my book', 273–5). This is personal, embodied reading. The wording could have a faint metaphorical edge, for to sleep 'upon' something in late Middle English could, somewhat rarely and mostly in the fifteenth century, mean to sleep with an idea in one's head (*MED*, 1(d)). Chaucer's wording might therefore invite that sense too, letting an audience hear both senses: physically sleeping with the book, and being influenced by its contents.[14] The poem's end reprises the same idea: the tolling of midnight by a bell inside the dream wakes the dreamer, who finds himself lying in bed, 'And the book that I hadde red, / . . . I fond hyt in myn hond' ('and I found the book that I had been reading in my hand', 1326, 1329). Again Chaucer's wording emphasises the bodily connection here, but from this and from the earlier mention of the book an audience might also reasonably imagine a portable book. The book can be read in bed, and it can be held in the hand. Aspects of this sound very normal, and we need not downplay ways in which Chaucer's description dovetails with present-day reading in bed. Nevertheless, it does remain part of the studied, mannered dream-vision genre: these passages do not require readers to imagine a plausible, consistent fiction in which Chaucer's book must be one definable size, but they do craft a casual, personal model of reading.

The opening of Chaucer's *Parliament of Fowls* strikes some similar notes:

> Nat yoore
> Agon it happede me for to beholde
> Upon a bok, was write with lettres olde,
> And thereupon, a certeyn thing to lerne,
> The longe day ful fast I redde and yerne.
>
> For out of olde feldes, as men seyth,
> Cometh al this newe corn from yer to yere,
> And out of olde bokes, in good feyth,
> Cometh al this newe science that men lere.
> But now to purpos as of this matere:
> To rede forth hit gan me so delite
> That al that day me thoughte but a lyte.
> (Not long ago, I happened to see a book that was copied in old handwriting, and I read in it all the long day, very fast and eagerly, in order to learn a certain thing. For, as men say, new corn comes from old fields year on year, and, truly, all the new knowledge that men learn

comes out of old books. But now to the point of this discussion: reading
on delighted me so much that the whole day seemed to me just a little
time, 17–28)

Chaucer, like his contemporaries, often invoked old books, and the link
between 'olde bokes' and 'newe science' elaborates on a routine reflex.[15]
Chaucer did not often, though, ask readers to imagine the age of handwriting, and his remark that the book 'was write with lettres olde' makes
readers imagine a material quality of the book described. The scripts
taken as models in book production changed over time in observable
ways – thus the existence of palaeography as a field – and remarks such
as this one in verse, and many others in surviving practical writing, show
that premodern readers themselves knew these changes.[16] Chaucer writes
nothing more precise that would guide the imagination towards a book
copied in a hand modelled on (say) a much earlier and radically distinct
script such as English Caroline minuscule, or merely a book copied in a
hand modelled on an earlier form of a more familiar script. But his remark
on the 'lettres' sets his audience up to envisage books in which every line
makes clear the age of the leaves.

Besides a hint of everyday palaeography, this passage also indicates a
particular kind of reading. It is deeply involved:

To rede forth hit gan me so delite
That al that day me thoughte but a lyte. (27–8.)

To underscore the wholly engrossing, time-swallowing quality of the
reading, 'day' holds the same second-beat position in both of the stanza-
terminal lines:

The lónge dáy ful fást I rédde and yérne
That ál that dáy me thóughte bút a lýte.

The reader ceases only when nightfall cuts off his light source (85–7). The
poem describes an episode of what the history of reading in a later period
might call intensive reading. Having been reading *Somnium Scipionis*,
itself a dream-vision text, the reader falls asleep and dreams a complex,
finely worked vision of artifice, interpretation and debate. The poem's
close takes a different tack to the physicality and specificity of the waking
upon the book in the *Book of the Duchess*. The dreamer moves precisely
not to the book that he was reading: 'I wok, and othere bokes tok me to' ('I
woke, and turned to other books', 695). The *Parliament* ends in reading
unlike that found in the *Book of the Duchess*, reading that is hunting,
multi-codical, and perhaps less physically engaged with the material
page. One poet could make different uses of the sequence of reading and

26   DANIEL SAWYER

then dreaming. So much for Chaucer's initiation of the tradition of books prompting visionary reading. Where did that tradition go?

The next major work to use the book-before-vision *topos* is *The Kingis Quair*. Internal biographical details and the title – an external imposition – strongly suggest that James I of Scotland (1397–1437) wrote this poem, perhaps in the 1420s.[17] The poem begins with its dreamer around midnight:

> Quhen I lay in bed allone waking,
> New partit out of slepe a lyte tofore,
> Fell me to mynd of many diverse thing –
> Of this and that – can I noght say quharfore,
> Bot slepe for craft in Erth myght I no more.
> For quhich as tho coude I no better wyle
> Bot toke a boke to rede apon a quhile.

> Of quhich the name is clepit properly
> *Boece* (efter him that was the compiloure)
> Schewing the counsele of Philosophye . . .
> (When I lay awake and alone in bed, having just woken from sleep a little before, I thought of many different things, of this and that; I can't say why, but I couldn't get to sleep by any earthly method. I knew no better trick than to take a book to read for a while – a book properly titled *Boethius*, after its compiler, that explains the advice of Philosophy [i.e. Boethius' *De consolatione philosophiae*].)[18]

The dreamer reads not just at night, but after sleeping. This passage's account of waking from an earlier sleep might, perhaps, describe the first part of a premodern biphasic sleep pattern.[19] The poem presents reading Boethius as a sustained, time-bound experience. Like the dreamer in the *Book of the Duchess*, the protagonist of the *Quair* – let us call him 'James' – places the book at his head as he returns to trying to sleep, but he also feels the physical toll paid by late-night readers, so that his reading is if anything even more embodied:

> The longe night beholding (as I saide),
> My eyen gan to smert for studying.
> My buke I schet and at my hede it laide
> And doun I lay.
> (Having gazed through the long night (as I said), my eyes smarted from studying. I shut my book and laid it next to my head, and down I lay, 50–3.)

The poem crafts a strikingly close physical identification of reader and book through the return of the same verb, first as a transitive with the book as object ('laide'), then intransitively ('doun I lay'). The pattern of following events differs from those in Chaucer's dream visions; though older criticism sometimes took Scottish poems such as the *Quair* as Northern reflexes of Chaucerianism, they stand rooted in a much wider range of materials than just Chaucer.[20] James lies awake, thinking, rises at Matins, has an eventful day, and only the following night begins to dream a significant dream related to his reading (510–11).

Reading returns, however, at the poem's end: James, still distressed, rises from his dream and goes to his window, where a turtle dove brings him a comforting letter written in gold on a branch (1233–53). The turtle dove sequence happens outside and after the dream but is nevertheless knowingly fanciful. James's imagined response deserves attention:

Ane hundreth tymes or I forther went
I have it red with hertfull glaidnese.
And, half with hope and half with dred it hent,
And at my beddis hed with gud entent
I have it faire pynnit up.
(Before I went any further, I read [the message] a hundred times with heartfelt gladness. I took it and, half in hope and half in fear, with good will, I have pinned it up neatly at the head of my bed, 1255–9.)

Though present-day readers probably outdo them thanks to instant messaging and email, fourteenth- and fifteenth-century readers lived in a world of non-codical reading too, sending notes to each other on parchment scraps, drafting in wax tablets, displaying texts in rooms and above doorways, peering at the graffiti in churches and so on.[21] The *Quair* imagines a courtly, aestheticised offshoot of the same set of practices, inviting present-day historians of reading to keep in mind text and reading beyond the codex.

Further challenges that expand the idea of the book crop up in another Scottish poem, Robert Henryson's *Testament of Cresseid*. Little is known of Henryson's life, and the poem cannot be assigned a date much more precise than the later fifteenth century, but it draws on the same tradition. Henryson has his aged speaker reading *Troilus and Criseyde*:

To cut the winter nicht and mak it short
I tuik ane quair – and left all uther sport –
Writtin be worthie Chaucer glorius
Of fair Creisseid and worthie Troylus.
(To cut and shorten the winter night, I set aside all other amusements and took up a quire written by worthy and glorious Chaucer about beautiful Criseyde and worthy Troilus.)[22]

The *Testament* offers another figure seeking to 'cut' the night, as in earlier versions of the book-and-vision *topos*, but in this case one who selects his reading matter himself, with intention. He picks up a 'quire', and this word, already encountered in the epitextual, retrospectively imposed title of *The Kingis Quair*, now demands attention. Modern codicology uses 'quire' to mean several folded sheets (bifolia) tucked one inside the other. Such groupings are the building block of the manuscript book and the atom of codicology. In Middle English and Older Scots, though, the term had a wider and looser range of meanings. It might indicate a short work (as in *The Kingis Quair*), or an unbound book.[23] Wills, booklists and other writings about books from the period often mention books 'in quires' or simply as 'a quire', and such mentions seem to mean books living without hard bindings, either 'limp bound' in flexible parchment, or loosely gathered as bundles of quires.[24] In fact, most manuscripts that survive do so in much later bindings, and scholars can only rarely prove that a given manuscript had a binding within the period; though twenty-first-century pop culture tends to imagine a weighty tome with a thick wooden hard-board binding when given the phrase 'medieval manuscript', it is possible – plausible – that loosely bound or unbound books were the more common norm, as paperbacks are today. In choosing the word, then, Henryson gestures towards fluid, mobile reading in informally gathered bundles of leaves, not the meditative, devotional contemplation of one great work/book. While criticism has typically taken these lines as a description of reading *Troilus and Criseyde*, 'ane quair' might even mean just one physical group of leaves from a copy of the poem. For the narration of the *Testament* goes on to specify that:

> thair I fand efter that Diomeid
> Ressavit had that lady bricht of hew,
> How Troilus neir out of wit abraid
> (there I found how, after Diomede had taken in that bright-complexioned
> lady [Cresseid], Troilus leapt almost out of his wits, 43–5).

These lines refer to Book V of Chaucer's poem, and so Henryson might well ask readers here to imagine one specific physical part. He will go on to inflect Chaucer's story of Troilus and Criseyde by recounting his own version of subsequent happenings. By invoking the physically looser world of un- and lightly bound books, he can prepare readers for a mythologically looser world of stories open to change in the hands of different poets. Henryson's precise wording for imagined reading in an imaginary book makes up part of his broader artifice.

READING ENVISIONED IN THE FOURTEENTH AND FIFTEENTH CENTURIES   29

Henryson continues writing of Troilus:

Of his distres me neidis nocht reheirs,
For worthie Chauceir in the samin buik,
In gudelie termis and in joly veirs,
Compylit hes his cairis, quha will luik.
To brek my sleip ane uther quair I tuik,
In quhilk I fand the fatall destenie
Of fair Cresseid, that endit wretchitlie.
(I need not recite again his distress, for in the same book worthy
Chaucer has given an account of his [i.e. Troilus'] troubles, in noble
words and gallant poetry, for whoever will examine it. To break my
sleep, I took another quire, in which I found the fateful destiny of
beautiful Cresseid, who ended wretchedly, 57–63.)

The 'uther quair' gives Henryson a pretext to extend on Chaucer's work. The
speaker's ability to take up 'ane uther quair' with ease implies – again,
without needing to posit a consistent, realist setting – a book collection, a
personal library. More importantly, however, this stanza brings the *topos*
of imagined reading before a dream vision into explicit contact with an
early sense of imagined reading in fiction: the first letters of the lines read,
acrostically, 'O FICTIO'. In a study of Henryson's intertextual play, this
acrostic would send criticism off to consider his use of allusion and his
claims to poetic authority and creativity. For a study of fictional reading,
though, 'O FICTIO' asks us to consider just what fiction is, and was.
Fifteenth-century *fictio* does not, of course, indicate quite the same thing
as present-day *fiction*: *fictio* primarily meant (neutrally) shaping or fashioning, or (a little negatively) feigning and fable.[25] The first known written
evidence for its use in Scots and English crops up in the 1490s, soon after
Henryson's writing, in the feigning sense.[26] If Chaucer has been fashioning or fabulating, so can Henryson: 'Quha wait gif all that Chauceir wrait
was trew?' ('Who knows whether all that Chaucer wrote was true?') he
asks as the next stanza begins (64). While *fictio* at this time was not modern fiction, Henryson's witty deployment of it here does show a willingness
to weave into readers' experience an awareness of his own work's construction and its place in literary tradition – and, interestingly, to weave
it in a way open only to reading by eye: a listening audience would have
trouble grasping the acrostic. The *Testament* uses the *topos* of reading
before dreaming to loosen readers' senses of the boundaries of books and
literary works, and to show off its own processes of artful rewriting.

Reading, the book and fiction were all complex, rich ideas in fourteenth-
and fifteenth-century writing. Yet the evidence presented so far might

risk giving a teleological portrait, in which dream visions increasingly dabble in self-referential commentary as time goes on, moving out of religiosity into playful fiction and pointing towards the novel. I therefore close by travelling back earlier in the fifteenth century, to another example of the book-and-vision idea that offers at least as much *mise-en-abyme* as any of these other examples, yet turns the *topos* to ends not fictional but devotional.

The poet John Lydgate enjoyed a long and prolific fifteenth-century career, and positioned himself as part of a nascent Chaucerian tradition; he would later become the namesake of George Eliot's Tertius Lydgate.[27] Lydgate's 'Fifteen Joys and Sorrows of Mary' inherits the concept of the visionary reading opening, but uses it to pursue an unimpeachably devout meditation rather than a fictional purpose.[28] Lydgate draws on the same idea of serendipitous reading becoming vision. He has the poem's visionary reader-speaker reading between midnight and morning to take their mind off the world's troubles. They report that they 'Vnclosyd a book' ('Opened a book', 5), and the verb 'Vnclosyd' suggests, in its effortful litotes and its suggestion of the possibility of firm closing, a more substantially bound manuscript with hard wooden boards and one or more clasps to fasten it shut. The reading is, though, haphazard, or at least providential, rather than precise and directed:

> Of fortune turnyng the book, I fond
> A meditacioun which first cam to myn hond
> (Leafing through the book as fortune led me, I found a meditative work that came to my hand first, 6–7).

At the start of the meditative work, the reader finds a Pietà image of Mary mourning Jesus. Then, as the reading continues, the reader begins a series of perceptive experiences that might or might not be visions:

> Vpon the said meditacioun,
> Of aventure, so as I took heed,
> By diligent and cleer inspeccioun,
> I sauh rubrisshis, departyd blak and reed,
> Of ech chapitle a paraf in the heed.
> (By chance, as I attended with careful and keen scrutiny, I saw, upon this devotional work, rubrics distinguished in black and red, and a paraph at the head of every section, 16–19.)

The poem merges staged reading attention and the reading apparatus expressed on the page through an elegant punning *rime equivoque* on 'heed' (16, 19), and through the subdued pun on reading and the colour red (18). Lydgate probably describes a table of contents here, and at this time tables of contents were not mundane, expected features. In a manuscript culture, when different scribal hands guaranteed that no two copies of the same work would agree in their page or leaf numbering, such tables had to be custom-made and keyed either to the specific manuscripts in which they lived, or (as here) to textual divisions: each 'chapitle', chapter.[29] This potential unfamiliarity explains why Lydgate's description goes into some detail about the apparatus's workings ('Of ech chapitle a paraf in the heed'). Lydgate's account superimposes the table on ('Vpon') the image of Mary, and Martha Rust has suggested in a brief discussion of this passage that he imagines the reader visually imposing a graphically highlighted apparatus onto the text from their memory.[30] Certainly Lydgate does give the 'rubrisshis' the same serendipitous arrival as the image. The picture of Mary comes 'Of fortune ... to myn hond', and he notices the table 'Of aventure', by chance, the haphazardness perhaps lightly pointed up by variation into one of Lydgate's distinctive 'broken-backed' lines, with its second and third beats abutting at his typical metrical caesura ('Of áventúre, | só as Í took héed', x/x/|/x/x/).[31] For this poem's opening, no neat line divides the practical route-finding table of contents from the devotional 'meditacioun' image in looking and reading. Readers encounter both at once, superimposed in imagined sight.

The text adds further layers of vision. In the next stanza, the visionary reader sees someone else depicted in the book, himself praying to Mary.

>   and to that hevenlie queene
> I sauh oon kneele devoutly on his knees;
> A Pater-noster and ten tyme Avees
> In ordre he sayde at th'ende of ech ballade,
> Cessyd nat, tyl he an eende made.
>
> Folwyng the ordre, as the picture stood,
> By and by in that hooly place,
> To beholde it did myn herte good;
> But of entent, leiseer cauht and space,
> Took a penne, and wroot in my maneere
> The said balladys, as they stondyn heere.
> (And I saw someone kneel devoutly on his knees to that holy queen; at the end of each stanza he said a Paternoster and ten Aves, in order, without pausing until he had finished. It did my heart good to behold it, following the order, as the picture stood, by and by in that holy place; but, intentionally, having found opportunity and time, I took a pen and wrote in my style the said stanzas, as they stand here, 25–35.)

Claiming to (re)write the experience of vision in Lydgate's own 'maneere', the poem becomes about devotion but also becomes a transmission of devotion, from the devotee in the imagined book to Lydgate and then on to the poem's readers. This sequence offers as densely and playfully nested a set of envisioned readings as one could ask for, with the most material detail of any of my examples in its discussion of the book itself. It offers these things, though, for a different purpose, presenting itself as something readers can imitate and repeat to further their devotional relationship with Mary.

It is tempting to place these envisionings of books and reading into a historical sequence of growing sophistication and development. Past appreciations have tended to see Chaucer as an urbane, fictionalising writer, whose sophistication in describing envisioned reading flowed on to, and perhaps advanced among, erudite fifteenth-century Scots poets.[32] History prefers linear process, and since the Industrial Revolution it has tended to transpose the paradigm of technical progress onto the arts. Granted, later poets do revise Chaucer's vision, and indeed in Chaucer and elsewhere there appear flickers of reading practices very like our own, such as reading in bed. Neither the revisions nor the glimpses, however, constitute a march towards present-day reading as a *telos*. Rather, these poets' envisioned readings lead in different directions from their Chaucerian origin-point. James I weaves reading more intimately into a rhythm of sleep and wakefulness, and closes his poem with the reading of notes and scraps of written material, not codices. Henryson foregrounds the role of feigning in his own activity and in his literary inheritance, and writes of the world of flexible quires, far looser in organisation and agglomeration than the unitary, fully bound early manuscript we experience or imagine today. Lydgate multiplies the layers of envisioned reading, and extends the *topos* of the envisioned book devotionally, with different aims and little impulse towards fiction. These poems show that diachronic changes in reading have many goals, which may pull against each other; that fiction has its own history; and that the idea of the book can fruitfully shift and multiply beyond the sealed and bound codex.

Though the recurring idea of reading and then dreaming makes up only a corner of the history of imagined reading, it might cast some light on reading's near future. The un-teleological history laid out above should remind us that reading *has* a future, in the first place: reading has not reached a static, completed state, and will change around and underneath those who study its history. Reading's future will mix newly emphasised options from among the reading approaches available since the first writings together with technological affordances which are genuinely new. The high-speed cross-referencing and the flitting quality found in present-day digital reading echo some habits of readers before the rise of the novel. The widespread present-day use of video to discuss books, especially among younger readers, effectively creates a certain kind of group reading, albeit an asynchronous kind.

However, 'a medieval manuscript is not an iPad', and the reading landscape today contains much that is new or at least newly proliferating.[33] Imagined descriptions and images of reading partake in a newly widespread fetishisation of the physical book, for instance, so that the material passion once restricted to eccentrics such as the fourteenth-century bibliophile Richard de Bury now pulses through broadly shared trends such as 'dark academia'.[34] A strong, and in my view related, current of nostalgia can be found in the manner in which poetry is presented when circulated on Instagram.[35] These trends draw on a knowingly inaccurate imagination of past reading. While they involve images of physical codices, they spread on social media platforms which differ profoundly from codices, and for that matter from e-books. E-books, indeed, appear to have reached an equilibrium of only limited success.[36] They might have created something of a distraction from the advent of the ever-changing online *feed*, which has caused much greater changes in reading experiences real and imagined.

A great deal of both reading and reading about reading now takes place on endlessly updated feeds, in what has been tentatively called, adapting a term from film studies, 'binge-scrolling'.[37] Feeds also channel a great deal of present-day discussion of reading, as Sarah Jerasa has observed in the teenaged readers she finds forming communities, and probably canons, on 'BookTok', book-focused parts of TikTok.[38] I do not think that Instagram and TikTok will necessarily persist for decades: online platforms come and go. But I do expect feeds like them to persist, with concomitant habits. Reading and the discussion of reading in the feed are more aural and visual – snatches of poetry come imposed on images, folk-literary-critical opinions arrive as video clips – and a feed makes reading a paratactic succession of experiences, with only a vague sense of algorithmically imposed semi-order. That is, the feed is rather like a dream. In the coming years, addressing different aspects this time around, dreams might once again help us talk about how we read and how we imagine reading.

Notes

1. Robert Mannyng of Brunne, *Handlyng Synne*, ed. by Idelle Sullens, Medieval and Renaissance Texts and Studies, 14 (Binghamton, NY: Center for Medieval and Early Renaissance Studies, 1983), ll. 533–44. In this and other quotations from Middle English and early Scots I have silently modernised uses of thorn (þ), yogh (ȝ), *i/j*, and

u/v for readers' convenience. At points, I have also silently punctuated and capitalised for clarity. All translations are my own.

2. For example, Laura Ashe, *The Oxford English Literary History, vol. I, 1000–1350: Conquest and Transformation* (Oxford: Oxford University Press, 2017), pp. 127–80, 241–98.

3. Pierre Gasnault, 'Observations paléographiques et codicologiques tirées de l'inventaire de la Librairie pontificale de 1369', *Scriptorium*, 34 (1980), 269–75; Jeremy Griffiths, 'Book Production Terms in Nicholas Munshull's *Nominale*', in *Art into Life: Collected Papers from the Kresge Art Museum Medieval Symposia*, ed. by Carol Garrett Fisher and Kathleen L. Scott (East Lansing: Michigan State University Press, 1995), pp. 49–71; Daniel Sawyer, 'Missing Books in the Folk Codicology of Later Medieval England', *The Mediæval Journal*, 7(2) (2019 for 2017), 103–32.

4. For example, *Medieval Literary Theory and Criticism, c.1100–c.1375: The Commentary Tradition*, ed. by A. J. Minnis and A. B. Scott (Oxford: Clarendon, 1988); M. B. Parkes, *Scribes, Scripts, and Readers: Studies in the Communication, Presentation and Dissemination of Medieval Texts* (London: Hambledon, 1991); Paul Saenger, *Space between Words: The Origins of Silent Reading* (Stanford, CA: Stanford University Press, 1997). For corrective commentary on Saenger's thesis, see Daniel Donoghue, *How the Anglo-Saxons Read their Poems* (Philadelphia: University of Pennsylvania Press, 2018), pp. 35–43.

5. Much of the written evidence surviving from the earlier Old English period comes from a time of incipient standardisation in writing, though probably not in speech; see, for instance, Mark Faulkner, 'Quantifying the Consistency of "Standard" Old English Spelling', *Transactions of the Philological Society*, 118 (2020), 192–205.

6. A. C. Spearing, *Criticism and Medieval Poetry* (London: Arnold, 1964), pp. 96–118.

7. *Troilus and Criseyde*, in *The Riverside Chaucer*, 3rd edn, ed. by Larry D. Benson (Boston: Houghton, 1987), ll. II.81–4. All subsequent quotations from Chaucer come from this edition.

8. Joyce Coleman, *Public Reading and the Reading Public in Late Medieval England and France* (Cambridge: Cambridge University Press, 1996); Abigail Williams, *The Social Life of Books: Reading Together in the Eighteenth-Century Home* (New Haven, CT: Yale University Press, 2017); W. R. Owens, 'Reading Aloud, Past and Present', in *The Edinburgh History of Reading: Early Readers*, ed. by Mary Hammond (Edinburgh: Edinburgh University Press, 2020), pp. 297–314.

9. James Simpson, 'Capaneus' Atheism and Criseyde's Reading in Chaucer's *Troilus and Criseyde*', in '*Of latine and of othire lare': Essays in Honour of David R. Carlson*, ed. by Richard Firth Green and R. F. Yeager (Toronto: PIMS, 2022), pp. 67–81.

10. Marshall W. Stearns, 'Chaucer Mentions a Book', *Modern Language Notes*, 57 (1942), 28–31 (p. 31).

11. Piero Boitani surveys the literary aspects of the allusions to books in these passages in 'Old Books Brought to Life in Dreams: The *Book of the Duchess*, the *House of Fame*, the *Parliament of Fowls*', in *The Cambridge Companion to Chaucer*, ed. by Piero Boitani and Jill Mann (Cambridge: Cambridge University Press, 1986), pp. 39–57, which remains a helpful orientation to these works. Chaucer's *House of Fame* is also densely allusive, but does not begin with the reading of a book *before* the vision, so I pass over it here.

12. This passage is part of a section which has less support than most of the rest of the poem in the surviving witnesses, but is on balance probably Chaucerian: Julia Boffey and A. S. G. Edwards, 'Codicology, Text, and the *Book of the Duchess*', in *Chaucer's 'Book of the Duchess': Contexts and Interpretations*, ed. by Jamie C. Fumo (Cambridge: Brewer, 2018), pp. 11–27 (pp. 20–1).

13. Hans Kurath et al., *Middle English Dictionary* https://quod.lib.umich.edu/m/middle-english-dictionary/dictionary, accessed 15 July 2022, henceforth *MED*, *s.v.* 'romaunce n.'

14. *MED*, *s.v.* 'slepen v.', sense 1(d).

15. See, for example, in the Manciple's Tale: *Canterbury Tales*, ll. IX 105–8.

16. Sawyer, 'Missing Books', pp. 114–15.

17. The title *The Kingis Quair* is epitextual, not authorial: an unknown sixteenth-century hand writes, in the sole known copy, 'Heirafter folowis the quair maid be King Iames of Scotland the first, callit the Kingis Quair and maid quhen his maiestie wes in Ingland' ('Next comes the quire made by King James I of Scotland, called *The King's Quire* and written when His Majesty was in England'): Oxford, Bodleian Library, MS Arch. Selden B. 24, f. 191ᵛ.

18. James I of Scotland, *The Kingis Quair*, ed. by John Norton-Smith (Oxford: Clarendon, 1971), ll. 8–17. All subsequent quotations from the poem come from this edition.

19. A. Roger Ekirch, 'Sleep We Have Lost: Pre-Industrial Slumber in the British Isles', *American Historical Review*, 106 (2001), 343–86; for biphasic sleep elsewhere in literature from Great Britain in this period, see Megan Leitch, *Sleep and Its Spaces in Middle English Literature: Emotions, Ethics, Dreams* (Manchester: Manchester University Press, 2021), pp. 99–100. Daniel Wakelin suggested the thought of biphasic sleep in the *Quair* to me (private communication).

20. Kylie M. Murray, *The Making of the Scottish Dream-Vision* (Oxford: Oxford University Press, forthcoming, 2025).

21. Elisabeth Lalou, 'Inventaire des tablettes médiévales et présentation générale', in *Les Tablettes à écrire de l'Antiquité à l'Époque Moderne*, ed. by Elisabeth Lalou, Bibliologia, 12 (Turnhout: Brepols, 1992), pp. 233–88; Heather Blatt, *Participatory Reading in Late-Medieval England* (Manchester: Manchester University Press, 2018), pp. 128–66; Daniel Wakelin, *Designing English: Early Literature on the Page* (Oxford: Bodleian Library, 2018), pp. 157–82.

22. *The Testament of Cresseid*, in *The Poems of Robert Henryson*, ed. by Denton Fox (Oxford: Clarendon, 1981), pp. 111–31, ll. 39–42. All subsequent quotations from the poem come from this edition.

23. *MED*, *s.v.* 'quaier n.'; William A. Craigie et al., *A Dictionary of the Older Scottish Tongue, from the Twelfth Century to the End of the Seventeenth* (London: Oxford University Press, 1937–2002), henceforth *DOST*, *s.v.* 'Quair, Quare, n.'.

24. Sawyer, 'Missing Books', pp. 109–11, 122–3.

25. R. E. Latham et al., *Dictionary of Medieval Latin from British Sources* (London: British Academy, 1975–2013), *s.v.* 'fictio'.

26. *DOST*, *s.v.* 'fictioun, n.'; *OED*, *s.v.* 'fiction n.'; not in *MED*.

27. Bridget Whearty, 'Chaucer's Death, Lydgate's Guild, and the Construction of Community in Fifteenth-Century English Literature', *Studies in the Age of Chaucer*, 40 (2018), 331–7; Judith Johnston, *George Eliot and the Discourses of Medievalism*, Making the Middle Ages, 6 (Turnhout: Brepols, 2006), p. 101.

28. *The Minor Poems of John Lydgate*, ed. by Henry Noble MacCracken, 2 vols, EETS, Extra Series, 107, Original Series, 192 (London: Paul, Trench, Trübner, 1911–34), II, pp. 268–79; subsequent references given as line numbers.

29. Wendy Scase, '"Looke this Calender and then Proced": Tables of Contents in Medieval English Manuscripts', in *The Dynamics of the Medieval Manuscript: Text Collections from a European Perspective*, ed. by Karen Pratt et al. (Göttingen: V&R unipress, 2017), pp. 287–306; Daniel Sawyer, 'Page Numbers, Signatures, and

Catchwords', in *Book Parts*, ed. by Dennis Duncan and Adam Smyth (Oxford: Oxford University Press, 2019), pp. 136–64 (pp. 145–8).

30. Martha Dana Rust, *Imaginary Worlds in Medieval Books: Exploring the Manuscript Matrix* (Basingstoke: Palgrave Macmillan, 2007), p. 20.

31. Maura Nolan, 'Performing Lydgate's Broken-Backed Meter', in *Interpretation and Performance: Essays for Alan Gaylord*, ed. by Susan F. Yager and Elise E. Morse-Gagné (Provo, UT: Chaucer Studio, 2013), pp. 141–59.

32. For Henryson's work, for example, presented as an advance on Chaucer's in a standard literary history, see R. James Goldstein, 'Writing in Scotland, 1058–1560', in *The Cambridge History of Medieval English Literature*, ed. by David Wallace (Cambridge: Cambridge University Press, 1999), pp. 229–54 (pp. 240–1). Goldstein's framing here is both typical of and forgivable in literary-historical writing, and I adduce it as an example only because it is normal, not because I think it egregious.

33. Elizabeth Eva Leach, 'It Might Be Technology, But a Medieval Manuscript Is Not an Ipad', *Elizabeth Eva Leach Blog*, 4 Feburary 2013 https://eeleach.blog/2013/02/04/it-might-be-technology-but-a-medieval-manuscript-is-not-an-ipad, accessed 18 October 2022.

34. Michael Camille, 'The Book as Flesh and Fetish in Richard de Bury's *Philobiblon*', in *The Body and the Book*, ed. by Dolores Warwick Frese and Katherine O'Brien O'Keeffe, Ward-Phillips Lectures in English Language and Literature, 14 (Notre Dame, IN: University of Notre Dame Press, 1997), pp. 34–77. Ana Quiring, 'What's Dark about Dark Academia', *Avidly, Los Angles Review of Books*, 31 March 2021 https://avidly.lareviewofbooks.org/2021/03/31/whats-dark-about-dark-academia, accessed 18 October 2022. Zachary Hines, 'The Secret (Book) History of Dark Academia', *New Chaucer Studies: Pedagogy and Profession* 5.1 (2024), doi:10.5070/NC35062964.

35. Tanja Grubnic, 'Nosthetics: Instagram Poetry and the Convergence of Digital Media and Literature', *Australasian Journal of Popular Culture*, 9 (2020), 145–63.

36. Stephen Kelly, 'Cargo in the Arbor: On the Metaphysics of Books and Scholarly Editions', in *Manuscript Culture and Medieval Devotional Traditions: Essays in Honour of Michael G. Sargent*, ed. by Jennifer N. Brown and Nicole R. Rice (Woodbridge: York Medieval Press, 2021), pp. 84–105 (p. 104).

37. Tina Kendall, 'From Binge-Watching to Binge-Scrolling: TikTok and the Rhythms of #LockdownLife', *Film Quarterly*, 75 (2021), 41–6.

38. Sarah Jerasa, 'BookTok 101: TikTok, Digital Literacies, and Out-of-School Reading Practices', *Journal of Adolescent and Adult Literacy*, 65 (2021), 219–26.

Bibliography of secondary literature

Ashe, Laura, *The Oxford English Literary History, vol. I, 1000–1350: Conquest and Transformation* (Oxford: Oxford University Press, 2017)

Blatt, Heather, *Participatory Reading in Late-Medieval England* (Manchester: Manchester University Press, 2018)

Boffey, Julia and A. S. G. Edwards, 'Codicology, Text, and the *Book of the Duchess*', in *Chaucer's 'Book of the Duchess': Contexts and Interpretations*, ed. by Jamie C. Fumo (Cambridge: Brewer, 2018), pp. 11–27

Boitani, Piero, 'Old Books Brought to Life in Dreams: The *Book of the Duchess*, the *House of Fame*, the *Parliament of Fowls*', in *The Cambridge Companion to Chaucer*, ed. by Piero Boitani and Jill Mann (Cambridge: Cambridge University Press, 1986), pp. 39–57

Camille, Michael, 'The Book as Flesh and Fetish in Richard de Bury's *Philobiblon*', in *The Body and the Book*, ed. by Dolores Warwick Frese and Katherine O'Brien O'Keeffe, Ward-Phillips Lectures in English Language and Literature, 14 (Notre Dame, IN: University of Notre Dame Press, 1997), pp. 34–77

Coleman, Joyce, *Public Reading and the Reading Public in Late Medieval England and France* (Cambridge: Cambridge University Press, 1996)

Craigie, William A. et al., *A Dictionary of the Older Scottish Tongue, from the Twelfth Century to the End of the Seventeenth* (London: Oxford University Press, 1937–2002)

Donoghue, Daniel, *How the Anglo-Saxons Read their Poems* (Philadelphia: University of Pennsylvania Press, 2018)

Ekirch, A. Roger, 'Sleep We Have Lost: Pre-Industrial Slumber in the British Isles', *American Historical Review*, 106 (2001), 343–86

Faulkner, Mark, 'Quantifying the Consistency of "Standard" Old English Spelling', *Transactions of the Philological Society*, 118 (2020), 192–205

Gasnault, Pierre, 'Observations paléographiques et codicologiques tirées de l'inventaire de la Librairie pontificale de 1369', *Scriptorium*, 34 (1980), 269–75

Goldstein, R. James, 'Writing in Scotland, 1058–1560', in *The Cambridge History of Medieval English Literature*, ed. by David Wallace (Cambridge: Cambridge University Press, 1999), pp. 229–54

Griffiths, Jeremy, 'Book Production Terms in Nicholas Munshull's *Nominale*', in *Art into Life: Collected Papers from the Kresge Art Museum Medieval Symposia*, ed. by Carol Garrett Fisher and Kathleen L. Scott (East Lansing, MI: Michigan State University Press, 1995), pp. 49–71

Grubnic, Tanja, 'Nosthetics: Instagram Poetry and the Convergence of Digital Media and Literature', *Australasian Journal of Popular Culture*, 9 (2020), 145–63

Jerasa, Sarah, 'BookTok 101: TikTok, Digital Literacies, and Out-of-School Reading Practices', *Journal of Adolescent and Adult Literacy*, 65 (2021), 219–26

Johnston, Judith, *George Eliot and the Discourses of Medievalism*, Making the Middle Ages, 6 (Turnhout: Brepols, 2006)

Kelly, Stephen, 'Cargo in the Arbor: On the Metaphysics of Books and Scholarly Editions', in *Manuscript Culture and Medieval Devotional Traditions: Essays in Honour of Michael G. Sargent*, ed. by Jennifer N. Brown and Nicole R. Rice (Woodbridge: York Medieval Press, 2021), pp. 84–105

Kendall, Tina, 'From Binge-Watching to Binge-Scrolling: TikTok and the Rhythms of #LockdownLife', *Film Quarterly*, 75 (2021), 41–6

Kurath, Hans and others, *Middle English Dictionary* https://quod.lib.umich.edu/m/middle-english-dictionary/dictionary

Lalou, Elisabeth, 'Inventaire des tablettes médiévales et présentation générale', in *Les Tablettes à écrire de l'Antiquité à l'Époque Moderne*, ed. by Elisabeth Lalou, Bibliologia, 12 (Turnhout: Brepols, 1992), pp. 233–88

Latham, R. E. et al., *Dictionary of Medieval Latin from British Sources* (London: British Academy, 1975–2013)

Leach, Elizabeth Eva, 'It Might Be Technology, But a Medieval Manuscript Is Not an Ipad', *Elizabeth Eva Leach Blog*, 4 February 2013 https://eeleach.blog/2013/02/04/it-might-be-technology-but-a-medieval-manuscript-is-not-an-ipad

Leitch, Megan, *Sleep and Its Spaces in Middle English Literature: Emotions, Ethics, Dreams* (Manchester: Manchester University Press, 2021)

Minnis, A. J. and A. B. Scott (eds), *Medieval Literary Theory and Criticism, c.1100–c.1375: The Commentary Tradition* (Oxford: Clarendon, 1988)

Murray, Kylie M., *The Making of the Scottish Dream-Vision* (Oxford: Oxford University Press, 2022)

Nolan, Maura, 'Performing Lydgate's Broken-Backed Meter', in *Interpretation and Performance: Essays for Alan Gaylord*, ed. by Susan F. Yager and Elise E. Morse-Gagné (Provo, UT: Chaucer Studio, 2013), pp. 141–59

Owens, W. R., 'Reading Aloud, Past and Present', in *The Edinburgh History of Reading: Early Readers*, ed. by Mary Hammond (Edinburgh: Edinburgh University Press, 2020), pp. 297–314

Parkes, M. B., *Scribes, Scripts, and Readers: Studies in the Communication, Presentation and Dissemination of Medieval Texts* (London: Hambledon, 1991)

Quiring, Ana, 'What's Dark about Dark Academia', *Avidly, Los Angles Review of Books*, 31 March 2021 https://avidly.lareviewofbooks.org/2021/03/31/whats-dark-about-dark-academia

Rust, Martha Dana, *Imaginary Worlds in Medieval Books: Exploring the Manuscript Matrix* (Basingstoke: Palgrave Macmillan, 2007)

Paul Saenger, *Space between Words: The Origins of Silent Reading* (Stanford, CA: Stanford University Press, 1997)

Sawyer, Daniel, 'Missing Books in the Folk Codicology of Later Medieval England', *The Mediæval Journal*, 7(2) (2019 for 2017), 103–32

Sawyer, Daniel, 'Page Numbers, Signatures, and Catchwords', in *Book Parts*, ed. by Dennis Duncan and Adam Smyth (Oxford: Oxford University Press, 2019), pp. 136–64

Scase, Wendy, '"Looke this Calender and then Proced": Tables of Contents in Medieval English Manuscripts', in *The Dynamics of the Medieval Manuscript: Text Collections from a European Perspective*, ed. by Karen Pratt et al. (Göttingen: V&R unipress, 2017), pp. 287–306

Simpson, James, 'Capaneus' Atheism and Criseyde's Reading in Chaucer's *Troilus and Criseyde*', in *'Of latine and of othire lare': Essays in Honour of David R. Carlson*, ed. by Richard Firth Green and R. F. Yeager (Toronto: PIMS, 2022), pp. 67–81

Spearing, A. C., *Criticism and Medieval Poetry* (London: Arnold, 1964)

Stearns, Marshall W., 'Chaucer Mentions a Book', *Modern Language Notes*, 57 (1942), 28–31

Wakelin, Daniel, *Designing English: Early Literature on the Page* (Oxford: Bodleian Library, 2018)

Whearty, Bridget, 'Chaucer's Death, Lydgate's Guild, and the Construction of Community in Fifteenth-Century English Literature', *Studies in the Age of Chaucer*, 40 (2018), 331–7

Williams, Abigail, *The Social Life of Books: Reading Together in the Eighteenth-Century Home* (New Haven, CT: Yale University Press, 2017)

Chapter 2

'[T]he gay part of reading': corruption through reading?

Rahel Orgis

> [M]alice enters insensibly in the soule, with sweet words, and under the baites of the adventures which recreate us. What spirit or what innocence soever wee have, as bodyes take, even without our assent, the qualities of what wee feed on; so our spirits put on them, in despight of us, I know not what, of the bookes wee read, our humour is altered ere we be aware; wee laugh with those that laugh, we grow debauched with libertines, and wee muse with the Melancholy; So far, that wee see persons wholy changed after Reading certaine books.[1]

The notion that reading can effectively corrupt a person was a powerful discursive trope in the early modern period and beyond, as illustrated in the above quote from Jacques du Bosc's influential conduct book *L'Honneste Femme*, which circulated in English translations from 1639 until the mid-eighteenth century.[2] It followed that above all youthful or female readers should abstain from entertaining, that is, 'gay', but morally dubious texts such as fanciful romances with 'adventures which recreate us'. At the same time, William St Clair and Irmgard Maassen trace a shift in conduct books away from the traditional advocation of silence for women in the sixteenth century to the valorisation of learned conversation nurtured by education and wholesome reading, to the point where 'In the eighteenth century, advice on reading was to become one of the largest components of English conduct books for women.'[3]

This normative discourse on women's reading in turn informs authors' marketing of their works as they need to navigate the gap between what readers are advised to read and what they do read, and it doubly concerns female authors as both readers and authors, especially if they produce works of potentially harmful genres. Two fictional works that pointedly negotiate this context are Margaret Cavendish's prose narrative 'Assaulted and Pursued Chastity' (1656) and Delarivier Manley's *roman à clef, The New Atalantis* (1709), whose portrayals of female readers have wider implications and constitute critical reflections on women's reading and its effects. Although separated by half a century, both authors similarly emplot their negotiation of conduct-book advice on reading through scenes focused on the development and consequences of a young woman's reading programme.

Cavendish's 'Assaulted and Pursued Chastity' is a combination of romance, travel writing and science fiction, following a nameless virtuous young lady's attempts to escape her princely would-be seducer and later husband, and featuring episodes of imprisonment, cross-dressing, shipwreck, exotic travels, heathen cannibals converted, piracy and epic battles. Early on in this fantastical tale, the imprisoned heroine discusses with the old lady who guards her what kinds of books merit reading, thereby outlining an intriguing idiosyncratic reading programme. Manley's *New Atalantis*, known best for the scandal caused by its fictional representation of the contemporary elite, presents not only one but two reading programmes for a young woman. The *roman à clef* depicts the allegorical characters Virtue and Astraea, who are acquainted with the depravity of notable dignitaries in the island Atalantis, that is England, by the help of Intelligence. In the resulting string of juicy episodes, one recounts the seduction of the young Charlot by her guardian 'the Duke', who purposely designs reading programmes for her to shape her according to his desires. In both texts, what superficially looks like a wholesale endorsement of early modern commonplaces regarding the dangers of reading turns out to be a more complicated comment on received ideas. Cavendish's fictional heroine tries to overcome her romance trials by the acquisition of mathematical and scientific knowledge, and Manley's manipulated female character draws unexpected lessons from her morally dubious reading, which counteract her seducer's intentions. Furthermore, through these scenes of reading within their fiction, both authors engage in a meta-poetic reflection on their own writing, its generic characteristics, potential impact and hence its worth, though not to the same effect. Whereas Cavendish's meta-poetic reflection threatens to undercut the narrative's didactic justification, Manley indirectly valorises her scandalous *roman à clef* as a more effective educational text than the pious reading traditionally sanctioned for young women by conduct books.

'[B]ooks of education and piety'

Two common assumptions underlie Cavendish's and Manley's negotiation of what reading is appropriate for young women's education and pastime, and what consequences reading inappropriate texts may have. Firstly, as du Bosc elaborates, that reading is morally affective and hence potentially dangerous or beneficial to a person.[4] Secondly, that young and/or female readers are especially vulnerable to the influence of reading because 'the Brains of Children are both hot and moist; . . . their Softness doth not only make all things to be easily Imprinted, but the Images also of all sensible Objects to be here very fresh and strong'.[5] It comes as no surprise, then, that the reading primarily recommended for women in the period can be summed up with Manley's phrase, 'books of education and piety'.[6]

The common assumptions outlined above are also addressed in prefaces, which frequently aim to market texts as wholesome for readers and negotiate what genres may be more or less likely to benefit or harm readers. Thus Cavendish specifies in the opening paragraph of 'Assaulted and Pursued Chastity' that: 'In this following tale or discourse, my endeavour was to show young women the danger of travelling without their parents, husbands or particular friends to guard them; for though virtue is a good guard: yet it doth not always protect their persons, without human assistance.'[7] Cavendish refrains from determining the genre of her text, avoiding the problematic designation 'romance', although romance is of course *the* genre that features extensive travelling and virtuous damsels in distress. Instead, Cavendish stresses the text's conservative didactic aim, presenting it as a warning of the danger of rape in the tradition of an exemplum authorised by a Bible episode, but certainly not as an entertaining 'tale' (p. 47). Cavendish's opening hence indirectly endorses the assumptions about the effect of reading mentioned above while trying to evade du Bosc's censure of the type of pernicious books he labels 'Romans' in the French original,[8] translated as 'looser Pamphlets' in 1639 and 'Romances' in 1692.[9]

Manley's *New Atalantis* likewise seems to subscribe to normative assumptions about reading judging by the double reading programme for young women it presents in the story of Charlot: the first programme for a virtuous education, the second for seduction.[10] Charlot's guardian initially intends her 'to be educated in the high road to applause and virtue' (p. 30):

> He banished far from her conversation whatever would not edify, airy romances, plays, dangerous novels, loose and insinuating poetry, artificial introductions of love, well-painted landscapes of that dangerous poison. Her diversions were always among the sort that were most innocent and simple, such as walking, but not in public assemblies: music, in airs all divine: reading and improving books of education and piety. (p. 30)

The list of genres that a young woman should or should not read is conventional. Fiction in the form of romance, plays and novels, and all art to do with love, are out of the question because they are corrupting and 'dangerous'. The only books allowed are educational and pious ones that 'edify' and 'improv[e]' a young woman.

This reading programme, whose effects I will discuss below, resembles the advice found in conduct books like Robert Codrington's, published in 1664, where we read of young women's education that:

> In the first place they are to read Books of Piety, which may inflame their hearts with the love of God; and in this all the faculties of their Memory, Imagination, and of their Reason are continually to be exercised; it cannot be imagined how much this Impression prevaileth even to the conquering of Nature it self, for this will preserve their souls from the contagion and corruption of the world.[11]

Fifty years later, George Hickes even provides an extended list of titles that he recommends for women's reading,[12] in which over two-thirds of the roughly thirty titles are religious, five conduct books and the remaining works focus on morals, the art of conversation and friendship, as well as including, for the 'curious', 'the best Histories and Memoirs'.[13] By contrast, only 'some select Profane Authors, that have nothing dangerous in them for the Passions' are advisable, which ideally should 'give them [young women] a distaste of most Plays and Romances'.[14] Hence, histories are preferable to romances, and moral philosophy is likewise acceptable, whereas caution is needed regarding '*Eloquence* and *Poetry*' as well as '*Musick* and *Painting*', all liable to 'confoun[d] quick and spritely Imaginations too much' and especially 'dangerous' if 'giv[ing] a sense of Love' in a 'polish'd and wrapt up' fashion.[15] Hence the necessity to 'give an orderly Course' to young women's education along the lines of the educational programme designed by Charlot's guardian since 'Prohibition, will but increase the Passion' and 'Musick and Poetry, so they be but Christian, would be the greatest of all Helps, to disrelish all Profane Pleasures.'[16]

While these general ideas about a young woman's ideal reading programme are reprinted in one conduct book after another, with passages travelling almost verbatim from translations of du Bosc's *Honneste Femme* into the early eighteenth century, some conduct books also intimate what studies of early modern women's libraries have confirmed,[17] namely that female readers did not necessarily restrict themselves to 'books of education and piety'. Thus, Codrington's *The Second Part of Youths Behaviour* reiterates du Bosc's condemnation of 'looser Pamphlets', but defines them as 'idle Songs and Ballads' that are to be forbidden.[18] He criticises 'Ladies who learn by heart the Tales of *Parismus*, or *Amadis de Gaule*' instead of studying histories,[19] yet elsewhere claims that concerning romances, 'the most received opinion is, that such Romances that are of a serious, generous, and of a noble Subject, are not only to be permitted, but to be preferred to their observance', singling out Gaultier de Coste, seigneur de La Calprenède's *Cassandra* and the *Arcadia* of Sir Philip Sidney.[20] Moreover, for Codrington even 'going to Stage-playes' is acceptable, though they 'are by divers accounted worse than vanity', as long as women make 'moderate use' of this liberty and refrain from 'daily frequenting', which is 'much to be condemned'.[21]

Analyses of extant records on early modern women's book ownership and reading show that although all women's libraries, as far as they are recoverable, contained a substantial number of devotional and religious books,[22] they also regularly contained works of other genres, such as herbals, medicinal texts, 'work books' (that is, pattern books), conduct books, plays, romances, histories and political treatises.[23] Compared to sixteenth-century collections, the libraries of women in the seventeenth century seem to have grown in size, which generally also entails a greater variety of works.[24] Thus, among Cavendish's contemporaries, Frances Wolfreston (1607–76) owned a large collection of devotional and theological books, but also romances and plays,[25] and Elizabeth Pepys (1640–69) owned a book closet of her own containing several romances in folio that she read and enjoyed, and which served as objects of prestige to be displayed to friends.[26]

'[G]ive me play-books, or mathematical ones'

It is against this background of conflicting convictions, admonishments and realities that Cavendish's female protagonist in 'Assaulted and Pursued Chastity' outlines a rather different ideal reading programme for young women. The scene is surprising in more than one respect. First, the reading programme is not simply imposed by an authoritative figure but negotiated by the heroine herself. This is potentially problematic, since it runs counter to the assumption that young women themselves cannot know what is good for them – or, as Manley puts it in relation to Charlot's 'disgust' at being 'denied the gay part of reading', ''Tis natural for young people to choose the diverting before the instructive' (p. 35). In addition to detailing what women should or should not read, conduct books therefore routinely state that someone 'wise and vertuous' should choose their reading material for them.[27] However, Cavendish's heroine does not conform to this stereotypical view of 'young people', but chooses 'the instructive' over 'the diverting'. Indeed, she echoes conduct books, insisting that she only desires to receive books 'if they were good ones', because otherwise 'they are like impertinent persons, that displease more by their vain talk, than they delight with their company' (p. 54). By likening books to interlocutors, Cavendish's protagonist recalls the reiterated argument in conduct books that reading is useful to improve one's conversational skills, an asset in educated women that is widely valued.[28] Still in conduct-book style, she proceeds to give reasons for her preferences, some of which correspond to common assumptions, whereas others challenge received ideas. Thus, in accordance with conduct-book tradition, she claims that 'romances' 'in youth . . . beget wanton desires, and amorous affections' (p. 54) and rejects Philip Sidney's famous claim that even a questionable text like the romance of *Amadis* may inspire readers to more virtuous behaviour.[29] Her subsequent justification, however, is diametrically opposed to du Bosc's image of the insidious poisonous influence of romance's wicked aspects, as she states instead that romances 'extoll virtue so much as begets an envy, in those that have it not, and know, they cannot attain unto that perfection' (p. 54).[30] Cavendish's heroine, who initially seems to intone conduct-book discourse, turns out to show equal irreverence to other standard affirmations of the genre, condemning for example histories, which du Bosc propagates as a preferable choice to romances.[31] Indeed, the protagonist rejects all genres but two, as the following overview of her arguments in form of a table shows (pp. 54–5).

Genre	'Good' books?	Reasons
'romances'	no	'extoll virtue so much as begets an envy'
		'beat infirmities so cruelly, as it begets pity, and by that a kind of love'
		'impossibilities makes them ridiculous to reason'
		'in youth they beget wanton desires, and amorous affections'
'natural philosophy'	no	'mere opinions'
		'if there be any truths . . . they are so buried under falsehood, as they cannot be found out'

Genre	'Good' books?	Reasons
'moral philosophy'	no	'divide the passions so nicely, and command with such severity as it is against nature, to follow them, and impossible to perform them'
'logic'	no	'are nothing but sophistry, making factious disputes, but conclude of nothing'
'history'	no	'seldom writ in the time of action, but a long time after, when truth is forgotten'
		'if they be writ at present, yet partiality or ambition, or fear bears too much sway'
'divine books'	no	'raise up such controversies, as they cannot be allayed again'
		'tormenting the mind about that they cannot know whilst they live'
		'frights their consciences so as makes man afraid to die'
'play-books'	yes	'discovers and expresses the humours and manners of men, by which I shall know myself and others the better, and in shorter time than experience can teach me'
'mathematical' books	yes	'I shall learn'
		'to demonstrate truth by reason'
		'to measure out my life by the rule of good actions'
		'to set ciphers and figures on those persons to whom I ought to be grateful'
		'to number my days by pious devotions, that I may be found weighty, when I am put in the scales of God's justice'
		'all arts useful and pleasant for the life of man, as music, architecture, navigation, fortification, water-works, fire-works, all engines, instruments, wheels and many such like, which are useful'
		'to measure the earth, to reach the heavens, to number the stars, to know the motions of the planets, to divide time and to compass the whole world'
		'mathematics is a candle of truth, whereby I may peep into the works of Nature to imitate her in little therein, it comprises all that truth can challenge, all other books disturb the life of man, this only settles it and composes it in sweet delight'

Cavendish's heroine justifies her evaluation of genres with the same motivations conduct books put forward, namely piety and usefulness, but instead of Codrington's 'Books of Piety' and the practical household books like herbals, pattern or conduct books, she singles out 'play-books' and 'mathematical' ones as the only acceptable genres to help her lead a 'pious' life and understand other 'useful and pleasant' arts, and even 'the works of Nature' (p. 55).

This stance is clearly informed by the lived experience of the Civil War and contemporary developments in the sciences, and it is also not entirely disinterested. Cavendish implies that in the wake of Civil War propaganda and conflicting accounts of the war and the roles played by statesmen like, for example, Cavendish's husband, histories can no longer be read as truthful and straightforward educational works because they are inherently skewed, due either to having been written after the events or to being informed by party politics.[32] Cavendish was not alone in her critical stance towards histories, as ironically shown by the mocking remarks of Samuel Pepys on Cavendish's account of her husband's deeds in the Civil War.[33] Cavendish's heroine also seems to pick up on, or perhaps foretell, the development of contemporary opinions with her positive characterisation of plays as educational source material for the study of human nature.[34] As mentioned above, Codrington's 1664 conduct book condones moderate play-going, a judgement that is reiterated in Hannah Woolley's widely read *Gentlewomans Companion* (1673).[35] Yet, considering that Cavendish published her own plays in 1662, six years after 'Assaulted and Pursued Chastity', the protagonist's praise of plays is perhaps not innocent, and it also seems intriguing that in his section 'Of Learned Ladies and Gentlewomen' Codrington singles out 'that great Mirrour of her Sex, and of our Age, the *Marchioness* of *Newcastle*' as the example of present 'Ladies' who 'do so excell in Knowledge, as it is much to be lamented, that the tyranny of Custome hath hindered many of them from publishing their Works', adding that, by contrast, Cavendish 'is only happy, by leaving the benefit of her Writings to Posterity'.[36] Whether or not Cavendish's and Codrington's propagation of plays' usefulness is a concerted effort rather than a coincidence, it is taken up in later conduct discourse as evidenced by an *Essay in Defence of the Female Sex* from the end of the century, which describes 'Theaters' as 'the best Schools in the World of Wit, Humanity, and Manners'.[37]

Finally, the focus on scientific study in the heroine's reading programme can be read in relation to Cavendish's real-life aspiration to enter the exclusive male domain of the natural sciences.[38] It could, however, also respond to a minority strand in the discourse on female education, advocating that (elite) women should also be taught subjects usually reserved for men. In her treatise published originally in Latin (1638, revised 1641) and later in French (1646) and English (1659), the Dutch Anna von Schurman argues 'all honest Discipline, ... the Circle and Crown of liberal Arts and Sciences (as the proper and universal Good and Ornament of Mankind) to be convenient for the *Head* of our *Christian Maid*'.[39] Schurman thereby privileges 'All which may advance to the more facile and full understanding of *Holy Scripture*', as opposed to sciences like '*Mathematicks*', which she classifies as 'pretty Ornaments and ingenious Recreations'.[40] Schurman's ideas were taken up by Bathsua Makin, who in her defence of women's education insisted that: 'The whole *Encyclopedeia* of Learning may be useful some way or other to' women, including 'Mathematicks'.[41] Cavendish's protagonist employs similar arguments, portraying mathematical works as conducive to leading a pious life, but in contrast to Schurman's encompassing view of education, she is decidedly radical in her rejection of all theoretical speculation, be it based on philosophy, logic or religious faith. Thus, as with mainstream conduct-book discourse, Cavendish's heroine endorses some of Schurman's ideas while at the same time introducing far more subversive ones.[42]

The usefulness of the protagonist's reading programme, in line with Makin's justification of female education, is borne out by her further adventures in the text. As she in turn takes on the roles of a shipmaster's adopted son, a godly emissary and an army general, she needs knowledge of 'navigation, fortification, water-works, fire-works, all engines, instruments, wheels and many such like' (p. 55); in other words, knowledge of applied 'arts' based on mathematics. Furthermore, she constantly needs to turn dangerous situations to her favour by manipulating, convincing and encouraging other people, which presupposes the kind of knowledge of human nature and different characters that can be gained from plays, according to the heroine. The heroine's success legitimates not only her choice of reading, but indirectly also her potentially problematic self-determination.

However, whereas the plot of Cavendish's narrative vindicates the heroine's generic preferences, matters become less clear-cut if one considers the genre of the text in which she herself is emplotted. The narrative, with its adventures, travel and focus on virtue, clearly partakes of the romance genre; that is, the very first genre the protagonist rejects – and also the very first genre she is offered by her guardian, who would like to make her amenable to the Prince's advances.[43] Moreover, the heroine's character corresponds perfectly to the romance protagonist of exaggerated virtue, and her experiences are full of potentially 'ridiculous' 'impossibilities', in addition to the text's repeated representation of 'wanton desires, and amorous affections' in the figure of the Prince pursuing the heroine. The heroine's arguments against romance and for mathematics thus take themselves the form of romance, begging the question of how we should interpret this circumstance. Why does Cavendish have recourse to romance conventions although she famously (and not quite truthfully, one assumes) declines reading romance?[44] Did she choose the romance genre on purpose because of its continued popularity despite conduct-book condemnations, the better to smuggle in her own ideas concerning reading and to make them more palatable through the very genre she seeks to overcome?[45] Or does her choice of genre slyly undercut the heroine's self-determined education and contingent aspirations, exposing her reading programme as an idealised fantasy or signifying that even with all this acquired knowledge upper-class women cannot escape the romance world and its traditional conclusion, matrimony? The text gives no indication of how to resolve the contradiction of subscribing to traditional ideas about young women's reading by denigrating romance as an inappropriate genre while at the same time proposing a radical alternative reading programme in the form of a romance-like text. Cavendish's narrative is thus simultaneously daring in its proposals for women's reading and potentially undermining its claims on a meta-poetic level through its very form, making it difficult to ascertain to what extent the proposed reading programme expresses Cavendish's views on what women should or should not read.

'[T]he gay part of reading'

Manley's treatment of women's reading is likewise conflicted, appearing to uphold traditional ideas concerning reading, while undercutting them within the narrative. As already seen, the first reading programme for young women proposed by the narrative is traditional, and it meets with success as Charlot turns into a virtuous and innocent young woman. Her guardian the Duke then falls in love with her and, in order to possess her, decides to corrupt and seduce her. He therefore 'presented her with the key' to his library, containing 'a collection of the most valuable authors, with a mixture of the most amorous', and initiates her new reading programme by handing her 'an Ovid, and opening it just at the love of Myrra for her father' (p. 35). The success of the Duke's stratagem is immediate, affecting Charlot emotionally and making her receptive to his kisses (pp. 35–6). The Duke then 'recommended to her reading the most dangerous books of love – Ovid, Petrarch, Tibullus' and 'left her such [books] as explained the nature, manners and raptures of enjoyment' (p. 37). The allegorical figure Intelligence is emphatic in her condemnation of such reading matter for young women, insisting that: 'There are books dangerous to the community of mankind, abominable for virgins, and destructive to youth; such as explain the mysteries of nature, the congregated pleasures of Venus, the full delight of mutual lovers and which rather ought to pass the fire than the press' (p. 37).

The statement seems an obvious echo of du Bosc's condemnation of books that 'verily deserve not to be put to light, unles [sic] that of the fire, and whose impression rather then [sic] the reading were to be hindred'.[46] This idea, which is repeated by Codrington,[47] appears in conjunction with the equally reiterated notion that women should not aspire to read a great number of works, but should restrict themselves to a few 'pleasing and profitable' ones, since 'one sole booke when it is good, may serve for a great Library'.[48] Manley's narrative seems to refer to this notion as well, as it repeatedly stresses the problematic lack of control over Charlot's 'indefatigable' reading once she is granted access to the Duke's library and 'Whole nights were wasted by her in that gallery' (p. 37). Hence Charlot's second reading programme is just as traditional as her first, in that it constitutes the specifically inappropriate reading programme for young women. Moreover, unlike Cavendish's heroine, Charlot corresponds to the typical young and 'curious' reader, as she eagerly pursues her new studies and gives herself over to 'the gay part of reading' (p. 35).

However, Charlot's story does not stop there. Despite her improper reading, she does not turn into a loose woman, and the Duke, though succeeding in making her fall for him, does not immediately gain his ends. When Charlot first allows his kisses, the Duke decides to 'steal himself into her soul' rather than to 'rush upon the possession of the fair' (p. 37), only to find himself caught at his own game. When they meet again:

> Charlot by this time had informed her self [sic] that there were such terrible things as perfidy and inconstancy in mankind, that even the very favours they received often disgusted, and that to be entirely happy one ought never to think of the faithless sex. . . .
>
> She had learnt to manage the Duke and to distrust herself. She would no more permit of kisses, that sweet and dangerous commerce. The Duke had made her wise at his own cost and vainly languished for a repetition of delight. (p. 38)

In contrast to her explicit condemnation of 'dangerous reading', the narrating voice of Intelligence does not emphasise the connection between Charlot's inappropriate reading and her valuable gain of knowledge, but instead merely states it matter-of-factly: 'The Duke had made her wise at his own cost' (p. 38). Yet considering the foregoing insight readers are given into the Duke's selfish motivations and desires, it seems clear that this wisdom, however inappropriately acquired, is far more useful and necessary to Charlot than her original reading education, which leaves her a vulnerable object of desire. Unfortunately for Charlot, her 'distrust' still does not go far enough, so that the Duke eventually manages to rape her and thus to deprive her of her temporary agency and bargaining power.

As part of her scandalous *roman à clef*, Manley's sordid tale of Charlot's depravation by her guardian of course aims to slur the reputation of the Duke's real-life counterpart, the Dutch Hans Willem Bentinck, first Earl of Portland (cf. p. 273, n. 74). Beyond this party-political attack, however, the episode reflects critically on the education of women through reading programmes which, for better or for worse, are imposed on women by men to turn them into objects of their liking rather than truly to educate them. Only when it is already too late does a court lady attempt to equip

Charlot with an alternative historical 'conduct book' for dealing with the Duke by making 'her read the history of Roxelana who, by her wise address brought an imperious sultan, . . . to divide with her the royal throne' (p. 41). Like Cavendish, Manley does not question the affective power of reading, but the episode's meta-poetic reflection on *The New Atalantis* as a whole is less conflicted – if perhaps more subversive – than in Cavendish's case. *The New Atalantis* with its liberal and at times detailed graphic depiction of sexual affairs certainly falls into the category of 'dangerous' rather than 'pious' reading material. Yet the episode implies that in an age of general depravity, such doubtful reading may be more useful and empowering than the aspiration to innocence and virtue.[49] Manley's narrative thus offers an extreme illustration of Pierre Daniel Huet's affirmation in his influential *Traité de l'origine des romans* (1670), translated into English in 1672, 'that it is even in some sort necessary, that the young persons of the World should be acquainted with this passion [i.e., love], that they may stop their ears to that which is criminal, and be better enabled to deal with its artifices' because 'such as are least acquainted with Love, are most obnoxious to it; and the most ignorant are the soonest Duped'.[50]

Conclusion

Both of the fictional episodes on women's reading programmes discussed above occur early on in the respective narratives. In the case of Manley this means near the beginning of her *roman à clef*. In Cavendish's volume of poems and tales *Ntures Pictures*, the narrative 'Assaulted and Pursued Chastity' occupies a central position in the work (pages 218 to 272 out of a total 404), but resonates with the illustration on the frontispiece that shows a social gathering presided by Cavendish and her husband above the inscription:

> Thus in this Semy-Circle, wher they Sitt,
> Telling of Tales of pleasure & of witt,
> Heer you may read without a Sinn or Crime,
> And how more innocently pass your tyme.[51]

Moreover, the question of what constitutes good educational reading material is also taken up at the end of the volume, where the eponymous 'She Anchoret' discusses the worth of poetical and historical writing and the Greek Pantheon proceeds to purge 'Heavens Library' before the volume concludes with Cavendish's 'true Relation of my Birth, Breeding, and Life'.[52]

'THE GAY PART OF READING': CORRUPTION THROUGH READING? 53

The prominent positioning of the episodes in the respective works underlines their similarity to prefatory comments, functioning as meta-poetic reflections on the texts and as instructions to readers on how to read the narratives. In contrast to prefatory material, however, which is often directly associated with the voice of the author, the negotiation of fictional characters' reading programmes arguably provides authors with more freedom to voice unconventional or subversive ideas, especially if, as in Cavendish's text, the ideas are put forward by the character. Cavendish and Manley certainly make use of this licence, criticising the power exerted over women through their reading education. Furthermore, their depiction of reading shows a keen awareness of contemporary conduct-book discourse on women's reading and its normative categorisation of genres. Cavendish and Manley's narratives seem, at least on the surface, to endorse central tenets maintained by conduct books while at the same time deviating from traditional conduct-book assertions. They reflect critically on the prestige accorded to literary genres and suggest alternative evaluations, with Cavendish's protagonist discarding the usually positively connoted histories and 'divine books' in favour of plays and mathematical works, and Manley's text suggesting that genres like romance, deemed 'dangerous' for depicting amorous passions, may have unexpectedly positive educational effects. Cavendish and Manley thus simultaneously put forward alternative reading programmes and attempt to counteract the problem that they are voicing their criticism of female education through the less prestigious genres condemned by conduct books. Hence, both texts are daring interventions in the discussion of women's reading education through their fictional depiction of female readers, but they remain conflicted: Cavendish's text because its reading programme criticises the very genre in which it is presented, and Manley's because, in contrast to its superficial endorsement of normative ideas on women's reading, it can only imply but not explicitly affirm the worth of reading works like *The New Atalantis*.

Notes

1. Jacques du Bosc, *The Compleat Woman* (London: T. Harper and R. Hodgkinson, 1639), p. 12.

2. *Conduct Literature for Women, 1640–1710*, ed. by William St Clair and Irmgard Maassen, [Facs. reprints], 6 vols (London: Pickering & Chatto, 2002), I, pp. 2–4.

3. St Clair and Maassen, *Conduct Literature for Women*, I, pp. xxvii, 3–4, 5.

4. Assumptions concerning the affective impact of orations and reading derive from classical rhetoric and poetics and the ideology of humanist pedagogy. See, for instance, Peter Mack on the importance of moral reading in the classroom: Peter

Mack, *Elizabethan Rhetoric: Theory and Practice* (Cambridge: Cambridge University Press, 2002), pp. 12, 15, 17, 34.

5. François de Salignac de La Mothe-Fénelon, *Instructions for the Education of a Daughter. To Which Is Added, a Small Tract of Instructions for the Conduct of Young Ladies of the Highest Rank. With Suitable Devotions Annexed*, trans. and ed. by George Hickes (London: J. Bowyer, 1707), p. 34.

6. Delarivier Manley, *The New Atalantis*, ed. by Ros Ballaster (London: Pickering and Chatto, 1991), p. 30. Further references are in the text.

7. Margaret Cavendish, *The Description of a New World Called the Blazing World and Other Writings*, ed. by Kate Lilley (London: Pickering, 1992), p. 47. Further references are in the text.

8. Jacques du Bosc, *L'Honneste femme, divisée en trois parties*, 4th edn (Paris: H. Le Gras and M. Bobin, 1658), p. 10.

9. du Bosc, *The Compleat Woman*, p. 9; St Clair and Maassen, *Conduct Literature for Women*, I, p. 48.

10. For an early discussion of Manley's endorsement of conduct-book ideas on the effects of reading, see Paul Bunyan Anderson, 'Delariviere Manley's Prose Fiction.', *Philological Quarterly*, 13 (1934), 168–88 (pp. 179–80).

11. Robert Codrington, *The Second Part of Youths Behavior* (London: W. Lee, 1664), p. 5.

12. Fénelon, *Instructions*, pp. 292–9.

13. Fénelon, *Instructions*, p. 294.

14. Fénelon, *Instructions*, p. 237.

15. Fénelon, *Instructions*, pp. 238, 242, 246.

16. Fénelon, *Instructions*, pp. 248–9.

17. See, for instance, *Women's Bookscapes in Early Modern Britain: Reading, Ownership, Circulation*, ed. by Leah Knight, Micheline White and Elizabeth Sauer (Ann Arbor: University of Michigan Press, 2018).

18. Codrington, *The Second Part*, p. 163.

19. Codrington, *The Second Part*, p. 169.

20. Codrington, *The Second Part*, pp. 6–7.

21. Codrington, *The Second Part*, pp, 28–30. For continued criticism of play-going, see, for example, George Savile Halifax, *The Lady's New-Year's Gift, or, Advice to a Daughter* . . . (London: M. Gilliflower and J. Partridge, 1692), pp. 157–8.

22. Joseph L. Black, 'Women's Libraries in the Private Libraries in Renaissance England Project', in Knight, White and Sauer, *Women's Bookscapes*, pp. 214–30 (p. 224); Marie-Louise Coolahan and Mark Empey, 'Women's Book Ownership and the Reception of Early Modern Women's Texts, 1545–1700', in Knight, White and Sauer, *Women's Bookscapes*, pp. 231–52 (p. 240); David Pearson, *Book Ownership in Stuart England: The Lyell Lectures 2018* (Oxford: Oxford University Press, 2021), ch. 3 (pp. 35–67); Georgianna Ziegler, 'Patterns in Women's Book Ownership, 1500–1700', in *Women's Labour and the History of the Book in Early Modern England*, ed. by Valerie Wayne (London: The Arden Shakespeare, 2020), pp. 207–23 (pp. 209–10).

23. Ziegler, 'Patterns', pp. 211–12; Coolahan and Empey, 'Women's Book Ownership', p. 236; Black, 'Women's Libraries', pp. 227–9.

24. Coolahan and Empey, 'Women's Book Ownership', pp. 247, 240.

25. Sarah Lindenbaum, 'Hiding in Plain Sight: How Electronic Records Can Lead Us to Early Modern Women Readers', in Knight, White and Sauer, *Women's Bookscapes*, pp. 193–213 (p. 197).

'THE GAY PART OF READING': CORRUPTION THROUGH READING? 55

26. Kate Loveman, *Samuel Pepys and His Books: Reading, Newsgathering, and Sociability, 1660–1703* (Oxford: Oxford University Press, 2015), pp. 151–152, 260–1.

27. du Bosc, *The Compleat Woman*, p. 5.

28. See, for instance, du Bosc, *The Compleat Woman*, p. 1.

29. Philip Sidney, *Defence of Poesie, Astrophil and Stella and Other Writings*, ed. by Elizabeth Porges Watson (London: Everyman, 1997), p. 101.

30. See also Cavendish's similar criticism of romance exaggeration in Margaret Cavendish, *The Worlds Olio* (London: J. Martin and J. Allestrye, 1655), p. 9.

31. du Bosc, *The Compleat Woman*, pp. 10–11.

32. See also the criticism of writing history in the narrative, 'The She Anchoret', in Margaret Cavendish, *Natures Pictures Drawn by Fancies Pencil to the Life* (London: J. Martin and J. Allestrye, 1656), pp. 354–5. Similarly, 'the Virgins' in Cavendish's play *The Unnatural Tragedy* criticise histories that pretend to record extempore speeches and private thoughts and exchanges verbatim when compiled after the facts; see Margaret Cavendish, *Playes* (London: John Martyn, James Allestry and Tho. Dicas, 1662), pp. 335–6. By contrast, in *The Worlds Olio* Cavendish presents history in more traditionally positive terms as aspiring to portray historical events truthfully (Cavendish, *The Worlds Olio*, pp. 6–10). For further discussions of Cavendish's engagement with Roman history, see Julie Crawford, 'Margaret Cavendish's Books', in Knight, White and Sauer, *Women's Bookscapes*, pp. 94–114; Lara Dodds, 'Reading and Writing in *Sociable Letters*; Or, How Margaret Cavendish Read Her Plutarch', *English Literary Renaissance*, 41.1 (2011), 189–218.

33. See Loveman's chapter on Restoration scepticism towards reading history (Loveman, *Samuel Pepys and His Books*, pp. 109–34), esp. pp. 122–3).

34. See also Cavendish's similar praise of Shakespeare's plays for truthfully depicting 'all Sorts of Persons, of what Quality, Profession, Degree, Breeding, or Birth soever' and 'the Divers, and Different Humours, or Natures, or Several Passions', Margaret Cavendish, *CCXI Sociable Letters* (London: W. Wilson, 1664), p. 245.

35. Codrington, *The Second Part*, pp. 28–30; Hannah Woolley, *The Gentlewomans Companion; or, A Guide to the Female Sex Containing Directions of Behaviour, in All Places, Companies, Relations, and Conditions, from their Childhood down to Old Age* (London: D. Norman, 1673), p. 78.

36. Codrington, *The Second Part*, p. 62.

37. Anonymous, *An Essay in Defence of the Female Sex in Which Are Inserted the Characters of a Pedant, a Squire, a Beau, a Vertuoso, a Poetaster, a City-Critick, &c. in a Letter to a Lady* (London: A. Roper and R. Clavel, 1697), p. 49.

38. Gary Waller, 'From Baroque to Enlightenment: Margaret Cavendish and Aphra Behn', in *The Female Baroque in Early Modern English Literary Culture: From Mary Sidney to Aphra Behn* (Amsterdam: Amsterdam University Press, 2020), pp. 235–76 (pp. 253–6).

39. Anna Maria van Schurman, *The Learned Maid; or, Whether a Maid May Be a Scholar? A Logick Exercise* (London: J. Redmayne, 1659), p. 4.

40. Schurman, *The Learned Maid*, p. 5.

41. Bathusa Makin, *An Essay to Revive the Antient Education of Gentlewomen in Religion, Manners, Arts & Tongues with an Answer to the Objections against This Way of Education* (London: J. Darby, 1673), p. 24.

42. For alternative discussions of Cavendish's views on reading and her reading practices, see Deborah Boyle, 'Fame, Virtue, and Government: Margaret Cavendish on Ethics and Politics', *Journal of the History of Ideas*, 67 (2006), 251–90; Deborah

Boyle, 'Margaret Cavendish on Gender, Nature, and Freedom', *Hypatia*, 28 (2013), 516–32; Crawford, 'Margaret Cavendish's Books'; Dodds, 'Reading and Writing in *Sociable Letters*'.

43. Helen Hackett also discusses Cavendish's 'ambivalent' 'attitude to romance', cf. *Women and Romance Fiction in the English Renaissance* (Cambridge: Cambridge University Press, 2000), esp. pp. 184–6.

44. See Hackett, *Women and Romance Fiction*, p. 184. See also Lara Dodds, *The Literary Invention of Margaret Cavendish*, Medieval & Renaissance Literary Studies (Pittsburgh: Duquesne University Press, 2013), pp. 11, 229.

45. Kate Lilley assumes that Cavendish was fascinated 'with the possibilities of romance as the scene of a woman's heroic agency and successful negotiation of the theatres of power' (Cavendish, *The Blazing World*, p. xx).

46. du Bosc, *The Compleat Woman*, p. 4.

47. Codrington, *The Second Part*, p. 158.

48. du Bosc, *The Compleat Woman*, p. 6. See also Codrington, *The Second Part*, pp. 160–1; Woolley, *The Gentlewoman's Companion*, p. 87.

49. See also Barbara Benedict's similar assertion that Manley presents 'her own novel as a vehicle of female information', Barbara M. Benedict, 'The Curious Genre: Female Inquiry in Amatory Fiction', *Studies in the Novel*, 30 (1998), 194–210 (p. 198).

50. Pierre-Daniel Huet, *A Treatise of Romances and their Original* (London: S. Heyrick, 1672), p. 108.

51. Cavendish, *Natures Pictures*.

52. Cavendish, *Natures Pictures*, pp. 287–357, 357–62, 368–91. Similarly to the protagonist's reading programme in 'Assaulted and Pursued Chastity', the Greek gods decide to throw all works out of 'Heavens Library' that are 'destructive to Truth', including 'Records that were of Usurpers' and 'Fabulous and Profitless Records' (presumably histories), as well as 'wanton and Amorous Records', 'Records of useless Laws, and Inhumane Sacrifices', 'Tedious speeches' and 'obstructive controversy', p. 358; on Cavendish's autobiographical representation of her reading, see Dodds, *Literary Invention*, pp. 11, 15.

Bibliography of secondary literature

Anderson, Paul Bunyan, 'Delariviere Manley's Prose Fiction', *Philological Quarterly*, 13 (1934), 168–88

Benedict, Barbara M., 'The Curious Genre: Female Inquiry in Amatory Fiction', *Studies in the Novel*, 30 (1998), 194–210

Black, Joseph L., 'Women's Libraries in the Private Libraries in Renaissance England Project', in *Women's Bookscapes in Early Modern Britain: Reading, Ownership, Circulation*, ed. by Leah Knight, Micheline White and Elizabeth Sauer (Ann Arbor: University of Michigan Press, 2018), pp. 214–30

Boyle, Deborah, 'Fame, Virtue, and Government: Margaret Cavendish on Ethics and Politics', *Journal of the History of Ideas*, 67 (2006), 251–90

Boyle, Deborah, 'Margaret Cavendish on Gender, Nature, and Freedom', *Hypatia*, 28 (2013), 516–32

Coolahan, Marie-Louise and Mark Empey, 'Women's Book Ownership and the Reception of Early Modern Women's Texts, 1545–1700', in *Women's Bookscapes in Early Modern Britain: Reading, Ownership, Circulation*, ed. by Leah Knight, Micheline White and Elizabeth Sauer (Ann Arbor: University of Michigan Press, 2018), pp. 231–52

Crawford, Julie, 'Margaret Cavendish's Books', in *Women's Bookscapes in Early Modern Britain: Reading, Ownership, Circulation*, ed. by Leah Knight, Micheline White and Elizabeth Sauer (Ann Arbor: University of Michigan Press, 2018), pp. 94–114

Dodds, Lara, *The Literary Invention of Margaret Cavendish*, Medieval & Renaissance Literary Studies (Pittsburgh: Duquesne University Press, 2013)

Dodds, Lara, 'Reading and Writing in *Sociable Letters*; Or, How Margaret Cavendish Read Her Plutarch', *English Literary Renaissance*, 41.1 (2011), 189–218

Hackett, Helen, *Women and Romance Fiction in the English Renaissance* (Cambridge: Cambridge University Press, 2000)

Knight, Leah, Micheline White and Elizabeth Sauer (eds), *Women's Bookscapes in Early Modern Britain: Reading, Ownership, Circulation* (Ann Arbor: University of Michigan Press, 2018)

Lilley, Kate, [Introduction and Notes], in Margaret Cavendish, *The Description of a New World Called the Blazing World and Other Writings*, ed. by Kate Lilley (London: Pickering & Chatto, 1992), Introduction pp. ix–xxxii; Notes pp. 226–30

Lindenbaum, Sarah, 'Hiding in Plain Sight: How Electronic Records Can Lead Us to Early Modern Women Readers', in *Women's Bookscapes in Early Modern Britain: Reading, Ownership, Circulation*, ed. by Leah

Knight, Micheline White and Elizabeth Sauer (Ann Arbor: University of Michigan Press, 2018), pp. 193–213

Loveman, Kate, *Samuel Pepys and His Books: Reading, Newsgathering, and Sociability, 1660–1703* (Oxford: Oxford University Press, 2015)

Mack, Peter, *Elizabethan Rhetoric: Theory and Practice* (Cambridge: Cambridge University Press, 2002)

Pearson, David, *Book Ownership in Stuart England: The Lyell Lectures 2018* (Oxford: Oxford University Press, 2021)

St Clair, William and Irmgard Maassen, 'General Introduction', in St Clair and Maassen (eds), *Conduct Literature for Women, 1640–1710*, 6 vols (London: Pickering & Chatto, 2002), I, pp. ix–xxxviii

Waller, Gary, 'From Baroque to Enlightenment: Margaret Cavendish and Aphra Behn', in *The Female Baroque in Early Modern English Literary Culture: From Mary Sidney to Aphra Behn* (Amsterdam: Amsterdam University Press, 2020), pp. 235–76

Ziegler, Georgianna, 'Patterns in Women's Book Ownership, 1500–1700', in *Women's Labour and the History of the Book in Early Modern England*, ed. by Valerie Wayne (London: The Arden Shakespeare, 2020), pp. 207–23

Chapter 3

'Fling *Peregrine Pickle* under the toilet': reading fiction together in the eighteenth century

Abigail Williams

Do fictional representations of reading show us how we *do* read – or how we *should* read? Or even how we should *not* read? Within many eighteenth-century novels, the answer is probably a bit of all three. In an era in which the consumption of fiction was in itself highly controversial, imagined scenes of bookish engagement can help us to better understand historical anxieties about what was read and how. We might see them alongside non-fictional sources, such as diaries and commonplace books and inventories and elocution manuals, as rich resources for understanding the history of reading. But fictional reading also presents a particularly complex form of evidence, as a source which can be both mimetic and didactic, descriptive and performative. The rise of the novel over the course of the eighteenth century saw profound debates about what to read and how to relate to the fictional world. These debates centred on the value and danger of novels, and types of readers. This chapter explores the way in which fiction refracted these debates, and refracted concerns about fiction and interiority, performance and gender. As we shall see, fictional accounts of reading could operate not merely as a straightforward reflection of historical practice, but also as shorthand for a web of wider arguments and issues.

Reading right

> Here, my dear Lucy, hide these books. – Quick, quick. – Fling *Peregrine Pickle* under the toilet – throw *Roderick Random* into the closet – put *the Innocent Adultery* into *The Whole Duty of Man* – thrust *Lord Aimworth* under the sofa . . . leave *Fordyce's Sermons* open upon the table.[1]

This passage comes from Richard Sheridan's 1775 comedy of manners, *The Rivals*. Lydia Languish, a young woman hopelessly addicted to popular fiction, and intent on leading her life like a romantic heroine, is surprised in her room by her family, and has to disguise quickly what she is doing: it is a furtive attempt to ensure that Lydia is *seen* to be doing the right kind of reading. Novels are quickly shoved out of sight, and what remains on show is what is respectable: the conduct book *The Whole Duty of Man* and James Fordyce's sermons. As Lydia hurries to arrange the right kind of reading matter for her family, we are reminded of the use of books as indicators of the moral propriety of their owners, a shorthand for the kind of person that they really are. It is a little vignette that speaks to habits of reading people through their bookshelves, habits which can be seen in prints and novels throughout the eighteenth century, which often use the titles of books visible in the home as a sign of moral rectitude, or otherwise.

This is not just a fictional trope. As I have argued in *The Social Life of Books*, the history of reading in the eighteenth-century home reveals that, in the context of domestic sociability, what you read and what you said were often seen as a show to present to the world, rather than as a fundamental aspect of intellectual or personal identity.[2] The writer and journalist Harriet Martineau looked back scornfully at this practice, within which the female reader was:

> expected to sit down in the parlour with her sewing, listen to a book read aloud, and hold herself ready for [female] callers. When the callers came, conversation often turned naturally on the book just laid down, which must therefore be very carefully chosen lest the shocked visitor should carry to the house where she paid her next call an account of the deplorable laxity shown by the family she had left.[3]

The spectacle of the reading woman, and the conversation that her book furnished her with, were typically ways in which visitors were to evaluate a person and a home. For Martineau, this window-dressing is explicitly gendered. Reading was both a performance and a showcase for social and moral status. But the *Rivals* passage is also concerned with the vexed moral status of the novel as a genre in the eighteenth century.

By the late eighteenth century there was a well-developed opposition to novels and novel reading which was as much about who read, and how, as it was about the books themselves.[4] Anxious commentators pointed to a nation of women addicted to the seductions of fiction.

One of the most prominent of these was the cultural critic and educationalist Vicesimus Knox, who lamented the way in which modern fictions:

> Not only tend to give the mind a degree of weakness, which renders it unable to resist the slightest impulse of libidinous passion, but also indirectly insinuate, that the attempt is unnatural . . . Every corner of the kingdom is abundantly supplied with them. In vain is youth secluded from the corruptions of the living world. Books are commonly allowed them with little restriction, as innocent amusements: yet these often pollute the heart in the recesses of the closet, inflame the passions at a distance from temptation, and teach all the malignity of vice in solitude.[5]

Knox here presents a series of powerful claims about the novel which are reflected widely in the period: he alludes to the erotic temptations of the fictional text; to the danger of readerly overidentification; a fashion for solitary reading; and the widespread availability of prose fiction.

The furore around narrative fiction was almost certainly a gross distortion of the realities of reading by women and men of the time, but it nonetheless came to shape the way novels were presented in relation to domestic spaces.[6] Opponents of novel-reading focused on the excessive consumption of fiction by young people, especially women, whose solitary, compulsive reading of fiction in their closets was apt to encourage lascivious thoughts and false expectations. Novels were addictive, serving only to increase the appetite, and critics drew on a vocabulary of gorging, devouring and digestion. The conduct writer Thomas Gisborne described with some alarm the steady corruption of a girl's virtue:

> The appetite becomes too keen to be denied; and in proportion as it is more urgent, grows less nice and select in its fare. What would formerly have given offence, now gives none. The palate is vitiated or made dull. The produce of the book-club, and the contents of the circulating library, are devoured with indiscriminate and insatiable avidity.[7]

The Edinburgh novelist and editor Henry Mackenzie, writing in the *Lounger*, further developed the dietary metaphor: 'when the sweetened poison is removed, plain and wholesome food will always be relished. The growing mind will crave nourishment.'[8]

Visual representations of women's reading reflect this emphasis on the solitary female reader.[9] Although books had long been depicted in western painting as emblems of moral virtue or self-improvement, during the eighteenth century they began to reflect the perceived sexualisation of novel reading.[10] In images such as the French painter Jean-Baptiste Greuze's *Lady Reading the Letters of Heloise and Abelard* (circa 1780) (Figure 3.1), the book in hand is associated with sexual license and solipsistic dreaming. Within Greuze's painting we see a solitary reader overwhelmed with passion, lips open, hands languorous, and on her table, next to a billet-doux, a book entitled *The Art of Love*. The lighting and the proximity of the book, the dress and the bosom invite us to see a link between all three: it is this book – which could be either a translation of Ovid's popular *Ars amatoria* or the poem attributed to Charles Hopkins – that has transported its reader into a state of distracted arousal. Many paintings and prints of solitary readers depict a degree of absorption in which the painted reader becomes a synecdoche, a shorthand, for the interiority depicted within the fiction itself, and the intimacy of the reading experience.[11]

Communal reading

It is in the context of these kinds of concerns, this element of moral panic, that we should understand the role of communal reading. Shared domestic reading was presented as a kind of cultural prophylactic. It protected women against the dangers hidden within novels, whilst simultaneously reinforcing the values and the discipline of wholesome family life. To consider a novel within the context of the family circle was a very different thing to envisaging it in the hands of the idle and unguided young. In reading together, the reciter could take guidance from those around: ideally a young woman would read in the domestic circle, and she would discuss what she read with her parents or preceptor, so that any misapprehensions into which she slipped could be corrected.[12] She could use the notion of family reading as a benchmark for what to read on her own: if a book was not fit to be read in company, it was not fit to be read at all. Communal reading offered the chance to gloss what had been read, and many descriptions of family reading frequently imply that the readings were interrupted for commentary, either by the reader or by his or her audience.[13] The feminist and political radical Mary Wollstonecraft argued that a pointed delivery could shape reception:

> If a judicious person, with some turn for humour, would read several [novels] to a young girl, and point out both by tones, and apt

Figure 3.1. Auguste Bernard d'Agesci, *Lady Reading the Letters of Heloise and Abelard*, circa 1780, oil on canvas. The Art Institute of Chicago. CC0 designation.

comparisons with pathetic incidents and heroic characters in history, how foolishly and ridiculously they caricatured human nature, just opinions might be substituted instead of romantic sentiments.[14]

One of the reasons why young women, in particular, were seen to be so susceptible to the 'giddy and fantastical notions of love and gallantry' imbibed from novels was that they were perceived to read differently from men. The female reading experience was not ballasted by intellectual engagement but was apt to lapse into affective identification with the characters described.[15] Unable to apply rational judgement to distance themselves from the worlds evoked in the pages before them, women, it was claimed, responded instead with their hearts and imaginations.[16]

Reading together had the potential to replace the subjective identification of silent absorption with the socialized framework of the group. And so we find that eighteenth-century novels are peppered with positive instances of communal reading. Rather than seeing those instances as straightforward examples of historical practice, we might also recognise how such passages model correct forms of sociable reading in the context of the moral argument about the dangers of solitary novel reading. Sometimes this practice is shown to enable those involved to establish the correct interpretation of a text. In Fanny Burney's *Evelina* (1778), Evelina describes the way in which she reads with her suitor, Lord Orville: 'When we read, he marks the passages most worthy to be noticed, draws out my sentiments, and favours me with his own.'[17] Similarly, shared reading is modelled in Richardson's sequel to *Pamela*, *Pamela in Her Exalted Condition* (1742), in which Lady Davers describes the way in which she and her rather frivolous friends have been educated by their communal reading of Pamela's story: 'We have been exceedingly diverted with your Papers. You have given us, by their Means, many a delightful Hour, that otherwise would have hung heavy upon us; and we are all charm'd with you . . . Lady Betty says, it is the best Story she has heard, and the most instructive.'[18] Lady Davers and her friends are the kind to read novels badly. In both cases, the experience of reading together enables those present to step back from the text in hand and to establish a critical distance through sociable discussion. Other novels emphasised the way in which reading together enabled characters to communicate with one another, or to acquire critical judgement. In the Gothic novel *The Mysteries of Udolpho* (1794), Emily recalls the way in which her suitor Valancourt had read to her:

> she had often sat and worked, while he conversed, or read; and she now well remembered with what discriminating judgement, with what tempered energy, he used to repeat some of the sublimest passages of their favourite authors; how often he would pause to admire with her their excellence, and with what tender delight he would listen to her remarks, and correct her taste.[19]

In Charlotte Smith's early novels, reading is shown to be a way of establishing social bonds and strengthening friendship – in *Emmeline: or The Orphan of the Castle* (1788) the heroine takes much comfort from

READING FICTION TOGETHER IN THE EIGHTEENTH CENTURY 65

reading with a sympathetic friend.[20] In Austen's *Mansfield Park* (1814) there are – as we shall see – prominent examples of the negative aspects of reading as performance, but also examples of reading together as a form of moral and aesthetic guidance. We hear that Fanny is guided by Edmund: 'he recommended the books which charmed her leisure hours, he encouraged her taste, and corrected her judgment; he made reading useful by talking to her of what she read, and heightened its attraction by judicious praise'.[21]

These fictional examples all illustrate the notion of reading aloud as a corrective to the solipsism of reading silently. Other works addressed the damaging effects of fiction within their prefatory material. The championing of the novel in company is manifest in the publication of Samuel Richardson's *Pamela* (1740). *Pamela* is a work which in some ways embodied controversy about the value of prose fiction. As a story of a servant-girl who resisted the approaches of her master, only to be rewarded by marriage to him (once he had reformed), Pamela polarised contemporary opinion. Was it a morally uplifting fable about the triumph of virtue over vice? Or a voyeuristic encomium to a young jilt? Richardson was concerned that his readers might enjoy his book for the wrong reasons. *Pamela* was a work designed 'to inculcate Religion and Morality', not a titillating romance. And part of Richardson's strategy in securing the 'right' kind of reading of his novel was to present it as a book that was and should be read in a group.[22]

In his letters, Richardson emphasised the way the novel had evolved as a communal exercise. When he revised *Pamela* for its second edition, he did so by surrounding it with documents that illustrated its use in the family circle. The dramatist Aaron Hill, along with many of Richardson's friends, had written to the author in praise of his novel. In the second edition, Richardson cited Hill's letters in response to the barrage of criticism of the novel's inflaming and 'low' scenes. In the first excerpt used, Hill declared that: 'I have done nothing but read it to others, and hear others again read it, to me, ever since it came into my Hands; and I find I am likely to do nothing else.'[23] Hill's comments identify *Pamela* as the kind of book to be shared, not read furtively alone in closets or languorously on sofas. His emphasis is on the novel within the family:

> 'Tis sure, that no Family is without Sisters, or Brothers, or Daughters, or Sons, who can *read*; or wants Fathers, or Mothers, or Friends, who can *think*; so equally certain it is, that the Train to a Parcel of Powder does not run on with more natural Tendency, till it set the whole Heap in a Blaze, than that *Pamela*, inchanting from Family to Family, will overspread all the Hearts of the Kingdom.[24]

Hill seems to be taking the metaphors of contagion used by contemporary critics of the novel and reusing them to suggest that Pamela's virtue was infectious. He effectively repositions the novel in the parlour, where it was relished as the topic of polite discussion amongst wholesome families. He finishes the letter with an anecdote about one particular collective reading of the novel, involving a young child. The little boy stole into an assembled family group while Hill was reading an affecting passage in which Pamela momentarily contemplated drowning herself after having tried to escape from the house of her pursuer. Hill says that the child had sat in front of him with his head hung low:

> He had sat for some time in this Posture, with a Stillness, that made us conclude him asleep: when, on a sudden, we heard a Succession of heart-heaving Sobs; which while he strove to conceal from our Notice, his little Sides swell'd, as if they wou'd burst, with the throbbling restraint of his Sorrow . . . All the Ladies in Company were ready to devour him with Kisses: and he has, since, become doubly a Favourite— and is perhaps the youngest of *Pamela's Converts*.[25]

Hill's anecdote reversed the expectations around novel reading. Novels were thought to be bad for unformed minds, yet here we have a story of a child who is a 'convert' to Pamela, who is visibly moved not by her sexuality, but by her moral sentiments. The group reading provided him with controlled access to the book, and his response was applauded by the other adults, who affirmed his 'right' reading of the novel. Here, the little boy's physical response to the text becomes a testament to the novel's ability to refine the feelings of everyone who hears it.

There were paradoxes at the heart of novel reading. On the one hand, young people were warned against the tendency of novels to 'pollute the heart in the recesses of the closet, inflame the passions at a distance from temptation', as Vicesimus Knox put it. Readers became too involved in fictional worlds and were thus unable to distinguish between life and fantasy. On the other hand, a child's ability to manifest an emotional response in a social setting was lauded as evidence of precocious sensibility. The anecdote we are given here of the little boy illustrates the way in which the *concept* of reading together could be used to shape the idealised presentation of a novel.

Fiction and performance

As this discussion suggests, perceived anxieties about the moral dangers of fiction were framed within novels themselves. Fictional reading

READING FICTION TOGETHER IN THE EIGHTEENTH CENTURY   67

reflected external reality, but it was also used to address concerns about habits of reading and their impact on readers. In referencing, and performing acts of reading, fiction stages its own metafictional debates. If part of the suspicion of the novel was its fomenting of interiorised imaginative excess, another key element was the idea of performance, which was also acted out at the level of fictional representation.

Here is one of the most famous – and for many readers, surprising – instances of domestic performance in Jane Austen's fiction:

> To the Theater he went, and reached it just in time to witness the first meeting of his father and his friend. Sir Thomas had been a good deal surprized to find candles burning in his room; and on casting his eye round it, to see other symptoms of recent habitation and a general air of confusion in the furniture. The removal of the bookcase from before the billiard-room door struck him especially, but he had scarcely more than time to feel astonished at all this, before there were sounds from the billiard-room to astonish him still farther. Some one was talking there in a very loud accent; he did not know the voice – *more* than talking – almost hallooing. He stept to the door, rejoicing at that moment in having the means of immediate communication, and opening it, found himself on the stage of a theater, and opposed to a ranting young man, who appeared likely to knock him down backwards.[26]

The Bertrams' amateur performance of *Lovers' Vows* in Jane Austen's *Mansfield Park* is probably one of the most celebrated fictional examples of the performance of drama at home in this period. The passage above describes Sir Thomas Bertram's surprised disapproval on returning home to find rehearsals in full flow. It is a puzzling moment in Austen's novel for many modern readers, an instance of historical disconnect. Generations of readers have wondered over exactly what was so wrong with staging a play at home. They have interpreted the incident as an indicator of Sir Thomas's tyrannical tendencies, or as Austen's way of signalling the theme of dissimulation.[27] Yet placing this scene within the context of eighteenth-century domestic culture, we can see that it also neatly frames its era's moral concerns with how to read at home, and how it makes distinctions between recitation and performance.

The context of the passage within Austen's novel is that the Bertrams are preparing an amateur performance of an English adaptation of a German romantic play, *Lovers' Vows*. The virtuous Edmund Bertram is not keen on this plan, and makes his discomfort clear, urging the group of young people that the absent father of the family, Sir Thomas Bertram, would have been deeply disapproving of such an enterprise. In an attempt to overcome this opposition to the *Lovers' Vows* performance, Tom Bertram,

68 ABIGAIL WILLIAMS

leading the play, had earlier reminded the would-be actors that his father had in fact always encouraged domestic recitation:

> and for any thing of the acting, spouting, reciting kind, I think he has always a decided taste. I am sure he encouraged it in us as boys. How many a time have we mourned over the dead body of Julius Caesar, and *to be'd* and not *to be'd*, in this very room, for his amusement! And I am sure, *my name was Norval*, every evening of my life through one Christmas holidays.[28]

Tom reminisces affectionately about the way in which their family had read aloud bits of famous plays, mentioning here lines from *Hamlet*, and with 'Norval, Norval' from John Home's hugely popular blank verse tragedy, *Douglas* (1756). But in his linking of 'acting, spouting, reciting', Tom conflates disingenuously the planned private theatricals, of which his father would not have approved, with the social recitation that was widely acceptable.[29] And they were putting on not just any kind of amateur theatrical: the play which the Bertrams had chosen was a high-water mark of Romantic sensibility, a story of illicit love, dubious morality and high passion. *Lovers' Vows*, first performed in October 1798, was a play freely adapted by Elizabeth Inchbald from August F. F. von Kotzebue's sentimental melodrama *Das Kind der Liebe* (1790). While it was commercially successful, and a popular subject for amateur performance, from its first public performance onwards it also attracted robust moral criticism for its representation of lower-class characters and scenes of seduction. Although Inchbald claimed that she had tamed the excesses of the original to suit English tastes, it remained unpalatable to some audiences on moral and political grounds.[30]

The late eighteenth century saw a vogue for amateur dramatic performance, largely associated with a social elite, which generated significant moral debate. But for many middling sorts of eighteenth-century readers, it was seen as perfectly fine, even morally improving, to *read* plays, or parts of plays, aloud at home. They were seen as totally different kinds of activity. The quotations to which Tom alludes were probably taken from one of the most popular recital miscellanies of the late eighteenth century, William Enfield's *The Speaker* (1774).[31] Enfield was a Unitarian minister and tutor in *belles lettres* at Warrington Academy, and his book, like many other compilations of the time, yoked together moral and social improvement.[32] Enfield prefaced the book with a substantial essay on elocution, in which he argued that oratorical skill was not to be used by readers merely for social show, but for speaking in public life.[33] Yet as Tom's reminiscence suggests, the collection was also much used for domestic entertainment, in this case, during the Christmas holidays, a period long associated with 'gambols'.

What has happened in this situation at Mansfield Park is that the Bertrams have confused wholesome recitation with amateur theatricals. The fictional event described here is used to frame contemporary debate about what kind of play-reading is acceptable, and what is not. Where did honest family fun end and narcissistic and dangerous self-display begin? Private theatricals were a huge vogue towards the end of the eighteenth and in the early nineteenth centuries: we have collections of some of the printed ephemera from these events and can see a rich history of amateur performance often enacted in country houses.[34] This practice aroused a furore of virtuous disapproval in contemporary onlookers. Recitation was pleasurable and improving – but the kinds of lavish theatrical spectacles that became fashionable in the later decades of the eighteenth century were widely perceived as corrupting. Critical attacks highlighted the dangers of confusing stage and domestic practice. Vicesimus Knox, who was the compiler of the popular recitation anthology *Elegant Extracts*, was severe in his condemnation. In an essay criticising the current fashion for acting plays at home, he began by noting the positive social attractions: 'Nothing can enliven a rural residence more effectually than the prevailing practice of representing plays in a neighbourly way by friends and relations. Music, poetry, painting, fine dresses, personal beauty, and polished eloquence, combine to please all who are admitted to partake of the entertainment.'[35] Yet warming to his theme, Knox warned of hidden dangers: the ruinous cost of such productions, and worse still, the erotic temptations that followed the acting out of romantic scenes (to which stage actors were apparently immune by virtue of their professionalism). 'Paint and gaudy dress' encouraged vanity and folly, while amateur actresses immersed in the sentimental displays of the emotion were, he thought, likely to neglect their families: this is his caution to women considering acting out plays at home: 'Let us see no more your black velvet train, your disheveled hair, and your white handkerchief. Be no longer desirous of personating the afflicted parent on the stage, but go home and be the good mother in your nursery and at your family fire-side.'[36]

Knox's arguments defined the home as a place of responsible parenting and household duty rather than as a venue for show and entertainment.[37] He suggested that those who truly loved drama should either see it in a public theatre, or:

> If, indeed, they are lovers of dramatic poetry, and possess taste and
> sense enough to be delighted with fine composition, independently of

dress, stage-trick, and scenery, why will they not acquiesce in reading the best plays in their closet, or in the family circle?[38]

His advice makes explicit the responsible reader's choice – between the superficial temptations of dramatic performance and the improving benefits of recital in the family circle or closet.

Other critics also focused on the unseemliness of certain kinds of dramatic performance in the home, worrying that would-be actors were likely to confuse their roles in life and art, to the degree that: 'the open embraces of the Actor are exchanged without difficulty for the private of the Seducer'.[39] All these critics articulate a concern that in acting out scenes of passion and illicit love, ordinary men and women might begin to muddle up their stage roles and their domestic ones, and accidentally begin to live out the imagined lives they read about.

What we see here, as in the earlier passage from *The Rivals*, is the way in which eighteenth-century debates about what and how to read focussed on the dynamic between real-world reading and the fictional world. Both in the case of the novel debate, and the furore over amateur theatricals, there is a concern over the reader's over-identification with the invented worlds of books, whether they might be unable to distinguish between on-page and off-page reality, and how best to manage the confusion between the two. And what we also see in both these cases is the way fiction provides a space for talking about those issues. One of the questions at the heart of this volume is 'how far does fiction mirror reality?' But what we have seen in the examples above is a more complex relationship between fiction and reality, one in which fiction created a unique space for a self-conscious reflection on its own form. Fiction offers far more than a mimetic representation of historical reading – it offers a way of exploring what the very nature of reading is and means.

Notes

1. Richard Brinsley Sheridan, *The Rivals, a Comedy*, in *The Dramatic Works of Richard Brinsley Sheridan*, ed. by Cecil Price, 2 vols (Oxford: Clarendon, 1973), vol. 1, p. 25 (Act I, Scene ii).

2. Abigail Williams, *The Social Life of Books: Reading Together in the Eighteenth-Century Home* (New Haven and London: Yale University Press, 2017).

3. Amy Cruse, *The Englishman and His Books in the Early Nineteenth Century* (London: Harrap, 1930), quoted in Steven Roger Fischer, *A History of Reading* (London: Reaktion, 2003), p. 273.

4. For a sense of the range of debate about the novel over the century, see *Novel and Romance 1700–1800: A Documentary Record*, ed. by Ioan Williams (London: Routledge & Kegan Paul, 1970).

READING FICTION TOGETHER IN THE EIGHTEENTH CENTURY   71

5. Vicesimus Knox, '"On Novel Reading", No. XIV, Essays Moral and Literary, 1778', in Williams, *Novel and Romance 1700–1800*, pp. 304–7.

6. Jan Fergus's work on the sales and circulation of books in provincial libraries around Daventry and Rugby shows substantial evidence of men's interest in fiction by women, and in their borrowing of novels in general. Jan Fergus, *Provincial Readers in Eighteenth-Century England* (Oxford: Oxford University Press, 2006), pp. 40–7.

7. Thomas Gisborne, *An Enquiry into the Duties of the Female Sex*, 3rd edn, corr. (London: T. Cadell and W. Davies, 1798), pp. 228–9.

8. Knox, 'On Novel Reading', in Williams, *Novel and Romance 1700–1800*, p. 306.

9. See William Beatty Warner, 'Staging Readers Reading', *Eighteenth-Century Fiction*, 12 (2000), 391–416.

10. Warner, 'Staging Readers', p. 393.

11. Robert Folkenflik, 'Reading Richardson/Richardson Reading', in *Representation, Heterodoxy, and Aesthetics: Essays in Honor of Ronald Paulson*, ed. by Ashley Marshall (London: University of Delaware Press, 2015), pp. 41–59 (p. 43); see also Roger Chartier discussing Chardin's painting of a woman with a book in *The Amusements of Private Life* (1745): 'a pictorial synecdoche: the part (reading) stands for the whole (private life). A single practice, that of reading, stands for the whole range of private pleasures in the time left free after family chores and obligations.' Roger Chartier, 'The Practical Impact of Writing', in *A History of Private Life: Passions of the Renaissance*, ed. by Philippe Aries and Georges Duby (Cambridge, MA: Belknap Press of Harvard University Press, 2003), pp. 111–60 (p. 144).

12. On the importance of communal domestic reading in contemporary novels, see Jacqueline Pearson, *Women's Reading in Britain, 1750–1835: A Dangerous Recreation* (Cambridge: Cambridge University Press, 1999), pp. 17–175.

13. See accounts of the Burney family reading practices described by Patricia Michaelson in *Speaking Volumes: Women, Reading and Speech in the Age of Austen* (Stanford, CA: Stanford University Press, 2002), p. 165.

14. Mary Wollstonecraft, *Vindication of the Rights of Woman* (London: J. Johnson, 1782) p. 431.

15. 'Mr Urban', *The Gentleman's Magazine* (Dec. 1767), p. 580.

16. See Cynthia Richards, '"The Pleasures of Complicity": Sympathetic Identification and the Female Reader in early Eighteenth-Century Women's Amatory Fiction', *The Eighteenth Century*, 36 (1995), 220–33.

17. Frances Burney, *Evelina or the History of a Young Lady's Entrance into the World*, ed. by Edward A. Bloom (London: Oxford University Press, 1968), p. 296 (letter LXV).

18. 'Letter VI. From Lady Davers to Mrs. B', Samuel Richardson, *Pamela in her Exalted Condition*, ed. by Albert J. Rivero (Cambridge: Cambridge University Press, 2012), p. 24.

19. Ann Radcliffe, *The Mysteries of Udolpho*, ed. by Bonamy Dobree with commentary by Terry Castle (Oxford: Oxford University Press, 2020), p. 585 (ch. 10).

20. See Joe Bray, *The Female Reader in the English Novel: From Burney to Austen* (London: Routledge, 2009), pp. 35–8. For a modern edition of Emmeline, see Charlotte Smith, *Emmeline: The Orphan of the Castle*, ed. by Anne Henry Ehrenpreis (London: Oxford University Press, 1971).

21. Jane Austen, *Mansfield Park*, ed. by John Wiltshire (Cambridge: Cambridge University Press, 2005), p. 25 (ch. 2).

22. For fuller discussion, see Folkenflik, 'Reading Richardson/Richardson Reading', pp. 41–59.

23. Introduction to the second edition of *Pamela: Or, Virtue Rewarded* (London: C. Rivington and J. Osborn, 1741), in Samuel Richardson, *Pamela: Or Virtue Rewarded*, ed. by Albert J. Rivero (Cambridge: Cambridge University Press, 2011), p. 464.

24. Richardson, *Pamela*, p. 471.

25. Richardson, *Pamela*, p. 473.

26. Austen, *Mansfield Park*, p. 213.

27. For discussion of the episode, and the wider depiction of reading in the novel, see Michaelson, *Speaking Volumes*, pp. 127–34.

28. Austen, *Mansfield Park*, p. 149.

29. The disapproval might additionally be related to the presence of Mr Yates, who is not a member of the family, but who is performing in the play. A similar instance involving a private theatrical occurs in Fanny Burney, *The Wanderer* (1814).

30. For fuller discussion of the play and its contemporary reception, see Laura Carroll, 'Introductory Note on *Lovers Vows*', in *Mansfield Park*, ed. by Wiltshire, pp. 549–53.

31. See Margaret Weedon, 'Jane Austen and William Enfield's *The Speaker*', *Journal for Eighteenth-Century Studies*, 11 (1988), 159–62.

32. William Enfield, *The Speaker: Or, Miscellaneous Pieces, Selected from the Best English Writers, And Disposed Under Proper Heads* (London: L. Davis et al., 1774), p. iii.

33. William Enfield, 'An Essay on Elocution', prefixed to *The Speaker: Or, Miscellaneous Pieces*, pp. iii–xxviii (p. xxviii).

34. The fullest collection of documents relating to private theatre in this period is the scrapbook of playbills, printed programmes, newspaper cuttings and tickets assembled by Charles Burney and Sarah Sophia Banks. British Library, *A Collection of Playbills, Notices, and Press Cuttings Dealing with Private Theatricals, 1750–1808*. See Gillian Russell, 'Sarah Sophia Banks's Private Theatricals: Ephemera, Sociability, and the Archiving of Fashionable Life', *Eighteenth-Century Fiction*, 27(3–4) (2015), 535–55. A full account of elite theatrical domestic performance can be found in Sybil Rosenfeld, *Temples of Thespis: Some Private Theatres and Theatricals in England and Wales, 1700–1820* (London: Society for Theatre Research, 1978).

35. Vicesimus Knox, 'Of the Prevailing Practice of acting Plays by private Gentlemen and Ladies', in *Winter Evenings: or Lucubrations on Life and Letters*, 3 vols (London, 1788), III:33.

36. Knox, 'Of the Prevailing Practice', pp. 35, 37.

37. For a discussion of the gendering of the debate about amateur theatricals, see Michaelson, *Speaking Volumes*, pp. 127–34.

38. Knox, 'Of the Prevailing Practice', p. 38.

39. *The Oracle*, 9 March 1798; see also Rosenfeld, *Temples of Thespis*, pp. 12–15.

Bibliography of secondary literature

Bray, Joe, *The Female Reader in the English Novel: From Burney to Austen* (London: Routledge, 2009)

Carroll, Laura, 'Introductory Note on *Lovers Vows*', in Jane Austen, *Mansfield Park*, ed. by John Wiltshire (Cambridge: Cambridge University Press, 2005), pp. 549–53

Chartier, Roger, 'The Practical Impact of Writing', in *A History of Private Life: Passions of the Renaissance*, ed. by Philippe Aries and Georges Duby (Cambridge, MA: Belknap Press of Harvard University Press, 2003), pp. 111–60

Fergus, Jan, *Provincial Readers in Eighteenth-Century England* (Oxford: Oxford University Press, 2006)

Fischer, Steven Roger, *A History of Reading* (London: Reaktion, 2003)

Folkenflik, Robert, 'Reading Richardson/Richardson Reading', in *Representation, Heterodoxy, and Aesthetics: Essays in Honor of Ronald Paulson*, ed. by Ashley Marshall (London: University of Delaware Press, 2015), pp. 41–59

Michaelson, Patricia, *Speaking Volumes: Women, Reading and Speech in the Age of Austen* (Stanford, CA: Stanford University Press, 2002)

Pearson, Jacqueline, *Women's Reading in Britain, 1750–1835: A Dangerous Recreation* (Cambridge: Cambridge University Press, 1999)

Richards, Cynthia, '"The Pleasures of Complicity": Sympathetic Identification and the Female Reader in early Eighteenth-Century Women's Amatory Fiction', *The Eighteenth Century*, 36 (1995), 220–33

Rosenfeld, Sybil, *Temples of Thespis: Some Private Theatres and Theatricals in England and Wales, 1700–1820* (London: Society for Theatre Research, 1978)

Russell, Gillian, 'Sarah Sophia Banks's Private Theatricals: Ephemera, Sociability, and the Archiving of Fashionable Life', *Eighteenth-Century Fiction*, 27(3–4) (2015), 535–55

Warner, William Beatty, 'Staging Readers Reading', *Eighteenth-Century Fiction*, 12 (2000), 391–416

Weedon, Margaret, 'Jane Austen and William Enfield's *The Speaker*', *Journal for Eighteenth-Century Studies*, 11 (1988), 159–62

Williams, Abigail, *The Social Life of Books: Reading Together in the Eighteenth-Century Home* (New Haven and London: Yale University Press, 2017)

Williams Ioan (ed.), *Novel and Romance 1700–1800: A Documentary Record* (London: Routledge & Kegan Paul, 1970)

Chapter 4

Jane Austen's refinement of the intradiegetic novel reader in *Northanger Abbey*: a study in Ricoeurian hermeneutics of recuperation

Monika Class

Jane Austen's *Northanger Abbey* (1818) marks a crucial intervention in the literary history of the novel reader inside the novel. I will use the term 'intradiegetic novel reader' for this trope, since 'intradiegetic' signifies that the novel reader is a fictional character inside the narrated world (diegesis) who distinguishes herself through her relation to novels. Austen composed the narrative in *Northanger Abbey* to register text–reader interactions constantly in a manner that exemplifies the metafictional demands that the heterodiegetic narrator, whose disembodied voice resides neither in the narrated world nor in the real world, makes in Chapter 5 in the central passage on novels and novel readers:

> Yes, novels; – for – I will not adopt that ungenerous and impolitic custom so common with novel writers, of degrading by their contemptuous censure the very performances, to the number of which they are themselves adding – joining with their greatest enemies in bestowing the harshest epithets on such works, and scarcely ever permitting them to be read by their own heroine, who, if she accidentally take up a novel, is sure to turn over its insipid pages with disgust. Alas! if the heroine of one novel be not patronized by the heroine of another, from whom can she expect protection and regard? I cannot approve of it. Let us not desert one another; we are an injured body.[1]

This passage contains Austen's most ambitious defence of the novel. Novelists, the narrator claims, should endorse novel reading in their works by constructing a positive image of intradiegetic novel readers rather than degrading them. The narratorial intervention disapproves of the typical eighteenth-century trope according to which the heroine of a novel encounters novels only by accident and loathes them. Conversely, this genre convention tends to relegate intradiegetic novel readers to the margins of the plot. In the exceptional case that the main protagonist enjoys novel reading, her taste is shown to need reform or, even worse, her addiction to need cure. Austen's extradiegetic comment, then, contains an important piece of novel theory, since it identifies that eighteenth-century novels paradoxically deprecate themselves as a literary genre inside the diegesis.

On the one hand, the passage suggests that the intradiegetic novel reader is a major trope through which Austen's forbears cultivate the generic self-deprecation of the novel in English. Austen criticises novelists for conjuring up the negative side-effects of novel reading as part of their rhetorical strategy to enhance the social acceptability of this young, ostensibly inferior genre.[2] On the other hand, the interjection anticipates postmodern developments according to which successive generations of novelists and readers have erased the boundary between novel-driven fantasy and real life.[3] The assertive phrase 'Yes, novels' mutes the otherwise common apostrophe to 'the reader' found in traditional eighteenth-century novels, leaving instead 'the dialogic trace of a tacit interlocution between author and reader'.[4] The breathless exclamations followed by questions and an appeal written in the first-person plural mark the climax of the metafictional interruption of the narrated sociability revolving around Catherine Morland and her friend Isabella Thorpe, who on rainy days 'shut themselves up, to read novels together'.[5] Austen's impatience with the lack of respectability for the novel shines through the narratorial voice and contrasts sharply with the otherwise characteristic restraint of her disembodied narratorial voice.[6] The last two sentences defiantly collapse novelists, narrators, fictional characters and novel readers into an ailing body that their unnamed 'greatest enemies' has harmed.

Novel readers inside the narrated world are, this chapter argues, a foundational trope in the diachronic development of the realist novel in English.[7] Jane Austen's *Northanger Abbey* can be seen as a game-changer for the intradiegetic novel reader, since Austen achieved a composition that ambivalently elevates the genre both on the level of the story, in which the two novel readers – Catherine Morland and Henry Tilney – feature as the heroic love match, and on the level of narrative discourse, which cues readers to mock and empathise with Catherine. In so doing, *Northanger Abbey* remodels the quixotic inflection of the early realist novel in English.[8] To gain literary acceptance, eighteenth-century novelists honed 'the mimetic powers' of the genre to render representations life-like.[9] Influential advocates like James Beattie and Clara Reeve defended the novel as an instrument of moral edification, plausibility and modernisation, opposing it to the old romance.[10] For Beattie, ancient romance of chivalry is just a container for extravagant excess, wild fabulation and unfounded invention. I should note that the eponymous knight of Miguel de Cervantes Saavedra's *Don Quijote de la Mancha* (1605–15) is a, if not *the*, prototypical intradiegetic novel reader. According to Beattie, however, Cervantes's novel is an attempt to end the 'frantick demeanour [sic]' of the 'Old Romance'.[11] Beattie describes Don Quixote's story as the romance-induced descent into madness and thus as a warning that reading romances leads to the corruption of moral and mental health. This one-sided interpretation plays an influential role in the variations of the intradiegetic novel reader in the long eighteenth century, as it associates the trope with the ridicule, naivety, inexperience, gullibility and feminised inferiority of both novel and romance readers.

This claim raises the question of how Austen refined the signification of intradiegetic novel readers and what the effect of this refinement was and still is, apart from the well-known endorsement of the young, disregarded genre called 'the novel'.[12] To answer, the present chapter compares the novel readers inside *Sense and Sensibility*, *Pride and Prejudice* and above all *Northanger Abbey* (1818) with those in Tobias Smollett's *The Adventures of Roderick Random* (1748) and in Charlotte Lennox's *The Female Quixote* (1752) within the framework of hermeneutical phenomenology. Scholarly interest in hermeneutical phenomenology has been on the rise. Ricoeur's monumental *Time and Narrative* (1984–8) is regarded as one of the foundational theories within the burgeoning field of postclassical narratology.[13] Besides that, his name has gained traction in Anglo-American literary studies as part of the debate on postcritique.[14] The present chapter contributes to the debate on the uses of literature as well as affect in literary criticism. It is informed by the premise of reparative reading proposed by Eve Kosofsky Sedgwick and especially her contention that Austen scholarship should not focus on the girl (reader) being taught a lesson.[15] However, contrary to postcritique, I propose that Ricoeur's theory is not part of the problem, but rather part of the solution. The field of postcritique associates his name exclusively with the 'hermeneutics of suspicion' – a term which loosely refers to Ricoeur's analysis of Freud, Marx and Nietzsche in *Freud and Philosophy*.[16] The proponents of postcritique have disregarded the other side of Ricoeur's hermeneutics, which I call the hermeneutics of recuperation.[17] Put simply, the goal of the hermeneutics of suspicion is to expose fiction's servility to ideologies and hidden epistemic violence. The suspicious hermeneut is said to unmask novels as cheap entertainment and novel readers as a gullible mass. Conversely, the goal of the hermeneutics of recuperation is the study of the evocation of reading experiences in general and, more specifically, the transformation of self through the narrative mediation of the other.[18] In other words, the hermeneutics of suspicion disenchants, exposing readerly delusion, while the hermeneutics of recuperation studies the visceral effects of reading experiences that precede or underpin acts of interpretation.

Northanger Abbey's Catherine Morland illustrates an important aspect of the hermeneutics of recuperation: she embodies the visceral novel reader who attaches to fictional characters, thereby transgressing the boundaries of fiction and reality by applying the fiction to herself as she inhabits the world outside the book. The fictional character is prefigured by certain progressive aspects of Austen's upbringing: the family's reading habits. Contrary to the dominant taste of the time, the Austen family endorsed novel reading. Jane Austen's letter of 18–19 December 1798 to her sister Cassandra asserts the virtues of the new literary genre by mocking the customary hypocrisy surrounding secular lending collections, which tended to disguise the fact that novels were one of their main attractions:[19]

> I have received a very civil note from Mrs Martin requesting my name as a Subscriber to her Library ... – As an inducement to subscribe Mrs Martin tells us that her Collection is not to consist only of Novels, but of every kind of Literature &c &c—She might have spared this pretension to *our* family, who are great Novel-readers & not ashamed of being so; – but it was necessary I suppose to the self-consequence of half her Subscribers.[20]

The letter mocks the acquaintance, Mrs Martin, because of her misplaced need to validate her circulating library by distancing it from novels. Austen's sarcasm targets the dominant societal norm of the period that downgraded novels to a guilty pleasure. The Austen family, by contrast, considered themselves 'great Novel-readers & not ashamed of being so'. The excerpt gives us a glimpse of the literary underpinnings of Austen's complex novel-reading character in *Northanger Abbey*, Catherine Morland. This chapter contends that the protagonist can be seen as the author's most sustained effort at fictionalising the enthusiasm for novels that the Austen family nurtured.

To unfold the subtleties of Austen's intradiegetic novel readers, I will draw on the work of the French philosopher Paul Ricoeur. Emphasising the coproduction of meaning by the reader and the text, Ricoeur conceives of mimesis as a dynamic process that is divided into three interconnected parts. The first stage, mimesis$_1$, captures how novels are prefigured by dominant norms in the real world. This stage is called prefiguration.[21] The second stage, mimesis$_2$, encompasses how narrative configures texts through devices such as plot, tropes and narrative perspective. This stage is called configuration. Mimesis$_3$ connotes the transformative process of reading, since it pertains to the ways in which real-life readers enact their reading in the real world. Ricoeur's triple mimesis has the conceptual advantage of comprising the narrated world inside the book and the lived world outside it. Triple mimesis thus offers a versatile model to gauge the relation of intradiegetic and real-life novel readers. Moreover, it does much to rehabilitate certain modes that blur the boundary between fiction and reality during and after the act of reading.

Focusing on the transition from mimesis$_2$ to mimesis$_3$, from narrative composition to reception, my contention is that the intradiegetic novel reader operates as a cue for novelistic self-evaluation in terms of genre as well as an implicit instruction in terms of reading behaviour. In the case of *Northanger Abbey*, the expressive devices point real-life readers to the positive re-evaluation of visceral engagement with novels and, concomitantly, the elevation of the novel to the category of high literature.

Austen's foil: the novel-induced corruption inside *Roderick Random* and *The Female Quixote*

The variable figurations of the intradiegetic novel reader provided and still provide real-life readers with clues about how to monitor their reading behaviour, depending on the intradiegetic novel reader's fate. Historically speaking, *Northanger Abbey* marks a highly influential departure from the typical mid-eighteenth-century intradiegetic novel reader, who is exemplified in *The Adventures of Roderick Random* and *The Female Quixote*. In their respective books, Smollett and Lennox present characters who show that novels cause moral and physical harm, and that engagement with the novel requires above all reform, distance and renunciation. Smollett's picaresque novel first appeared in two volumes in 1748. This first-person narrative relates the adventures of Rory, an impoverished young nobleman from the Scottish Highlands. Notably, the intradiegetic novel reader is a feature on the margins of the story.

The main plot tells us how it comes about that Rory relocates to London, first working as a navy surgeon and then living as a fortune hunter, until he is reunited with his father and marries his beloved Narcissa, an English aristocrat. It is significant that neither Rory nor his love object is interested in novels, since this implies a more sophisticated taste. Rather, Smollett casts Narcissa's maid Nancy Williams in the role of the reformed romance reader. Miss Williams, who personifies the impressionable woman novel reader, serves as a warning against the moral contamination brought on by devouring too many romances, which the novel, through the maid's story, ranks as titillating trash.

Smollett interweaves this subplot of the reformed fallen woman with the trope of the intradiegetic novel reader. Chapter 22 contains an analepsis, which narrates Miss Williams's (first-person) confession, entitled 'The History of Miss Williams': the once-beloved daughter of a wealthy merchant degrades into a woman of the town.[22] Miss Williams's confession suggests that the projection of the world of the novel into her actual world is the primary reason for which she fell prey to the false promises of a noble suitor, eloping with him, becoming pregnant and eventually suffering a miscarriage. This figuration suggests that reading novels is dangerous because it arouses female sexual desire, increases credulity and weakens women's health to such an extent that it affects their fertility. Smollett's intradiegetic novel reader relegates novels to inferior print productions and warns readers, particularly women, against modelling their own behaviour on the form. Additionally, the figure of Miss Williams incorporates the proto-hysteric views that we find in the medical self-help texts written by the Swiss physician Samuel Auguste Tissot and the English physician Thomas Beddoes.[23] Both physicians condemned novel reading above all other forms of reading, pointing to the act as the cause of female nervous disease and the root of women's incapacity to engage in wholesome pursuits. Mirroring the medical discourse, Smollett integrated Miss Williams's story as an implicit moralist disclaimer and a means to increase the respectability of his novelistic production.[24]

Charlotte Lennox's *The Female Quixote, or The Adventures of Arabella* was published in 1752. The novel focuses on a young heiress, Arabella, whose sheltered life in a remote country estate is shaped by her singular interest in romance novels. Indeed, Arabella's most prominent character trait is her absorption into the world of badly translated seventeenth-century French romances. Unlike Miss Williams in Smollett's publication, Arabella is the novel's heroine. The value of novels is more ambivalent than in *Roderick Random*, where Miss Williams's experience with novels is unequivocally negative. For Lennox's heroine, the romances she reads actually help her to protect her virtue throughout the story. Arabella's romance-induced eloquence, for instance, astonishes and demands the respect of other fictional characters in the narrated world.[25] Nevertheless, early in the novel, the heterodiegetic narrator pathologises Arabella's novel-induced imagination. He describes the young woman, for instance, as someone who is 'always prepossessed with the same fantastic Ideas'.[26]

Like Cervantes's Don Quixote, Arabella interprets the world through the lens of the romances she has read, modelling her ideas and behaviours on the heroines she encounters therein. This leads to a series of unfortunate incidents. For example, Arabella mistakes a young gardener for a disguised nobleman with designs upon her, when his real objective is to steal fish from the estate. She also suspects her uncle, the father of her devout suitor Glanville, of harbouring an incestuous passion for her. What is more, she rushes to rescue a cross-dressed prostitute from her rowdy companions in Vauxhall Gardens, imagining her to be a disguised noblewoman about to be raped. This sequence of events culminates in her near-fatal illness, which she contracts as the consequence of an ill-judged jump into the river to escape imaginary ravishers. The narrative concludes with the heroine's consent to marry the long-suffering Glanville after Arabella renounces her passion for novels. Despite the ambiguity associated with the perusal of novels, the final chapters thus tip the weight towards the condemnation of romance novels. In the penultimate chapter, headed 'Being in the Author's Opinion, the best Chapter in this History',[27] the doctor heals Arabella from her addiction through the application of rigorous logic. Proceeding in a manner resembling a philosophical dialogue in the Platonic tradition, he debunks the reputation of novels by inferring: 'First, That these Histories . . . are Fictions. / Next, That they are absurd. / And Lastly, That they are Criminal.'[28] Reinforced by the chapter heading, this judgement is an indicator to real-life readers that they should reconsider the literary genre at hand and carefully avoid any application of prose fiction to the real world. If Lennox's configuration of her eponymous archetype, the female Quixote, validates novel reading to some degree, it does so *ex negativo*: only the implicit discouragement from immersion justifies the perusal of romance.

Austen's early intradiegetic novels readers: *Sense and Sensibility* and *Pride and Prejudice*

Like Smollett and Lennox, Austen portrayed the dangers of romance in her first two published novels. However, her composition does not suggest that romantic fiction is to be blamed for elopements and feminine disgrace. Both *Sense and Sensibility* and *Pride and Prejudice* feature female characters who are too easily impressed by rakish charms. In *Sense and Sensibility,* Miss Williams bears Willoughby an illegitimate child, and, in *Pride and Prejudice,* Lydia Bennet and Miss Darcy (nearly) elope with Wickham. Conversely, neither heroine, Elinor Dashwood nor Elizabeth Bennet, distinguishes herself as a novel reader or a literary connoisseur. When called a 'great reader, [who] has no pleasure in anything else', Elizabeth objects 'I am not a great reader.'[29] She apparently prefers country walks and balls to sedentary perusals. Reading only absorbs her when the letter comes from Mr Darcy which reveals Wickham's dishonesty. Like Elizabeth, Elinor attributes little importance to her love object's literary qualifications, nor does she particularly value novels. Elinor regards 'simple and elegant prose',[30] such as novels, merely as a more suitable choice for a poor performer like Edward, for whom William Cowper's impassioned verse proves too demanding to be read aloud adequately. Elinor's sister, Marianne, makes a tragic mistake by considering literature a litmus test for potential husbands. Wickham passes all reading tests from Shakespeare's *Hamlet* to Sir Walter Scott with flying colours, and yet he turns out to be a spineless fortune hunter and a rake.

Even so, the intolerance for novels serves as the target for the narrator's satire in *Pride and Prejudice.* Austen sets up Mr Collins as the most undesirable suitor and humourless hypocrite of the novel by showcasing his protest against novels. The clergyman declines the invitation to read a chapter from a novel belonging to a 'circulating library' and offers instead 'Fordyce's Sermons' for entertainment to the Bennet household.[31] The ironic passage pokes fun at Mr Collins, lampooning him as the dull, 'monotonous' voice of conduct literature exemplified by James Fordyce's *Sermons for Young Women* (1765).[32] Fordyce's well-known *Sermons* warned against the moral danger posed by novels and circulating libraries for girls and young women.[33] Collins's outright rejection of novels, then, serves as a cue for the character's undesirability. However, a lively interest in novels alone remains an ambivalent character trait in *Sense and Sensibility* and *Pride and Prejudice.*[34] By comparison, novel-reading features more prominently in *Northanger Abbey* and is associated more closely with character development.

Austen's playful endorsement of the visceral novel reader in *Northanger Abbey*

In *Northanger Abbey,* Austen unapologetically placed Catherine Morland, the inexperienced novel reader, at the centre of her plot. Combining Gothic romance with feminine *Bildungsroman, Northanger Abbey* interweaves the visceral reception modes of the former with the disciplining elements of the latter. In so doing, the novel opposes the convention of the corrupted intradiegetic novel reader. In *Northanger Abbey*, novels do not lead to moral and physical damage. On the contrary, they might even help prepare you for adult life and help you find your love match. At the time of its first publication in 1818, the novel thus counteracted anxieties about the corruption of human consciousness through novel-reading by showing how the heroine benefits from reading novels and is united with her love object, Henry Tilney, despite her conflation of the fictional and real worlds. Crucially, Catherine's indulgence in Gothic novels induces in her a warranted suspicion of General Tilney, the personification of hegemonic masculinity. Such insight can be seen as an endorsement of visceral novel-reading experiences, including the application of fiction to real life.[35]

Austen's novel delineates how it comes about that a perfectly ordinary seventeen-year-old country girl, Catherine, ends up happily married and thus socially accepted despite unwittingly eschewing the strict eighteenth-century novel-reading protocol by stubbornly perceiving the world around her through the lens of such Gothic novels as Ann Radcliffe's *The Romance of the Forest* (1791).[36] Scholars disagree about whether Catherine renounces her passion for novels eventually, perhaps in part because of the novel's conclusion, in which the narrator poses a rhetorical question: Does the story advocate parental tyranny or reward filial disobedience? It is the latter that brings about their marriage, not filial obedience. Crucially, Catherine learns this distrust of the tyrannical father, General Tilney, from Ann Radcliffe's novels. In Radcliffe's *The Romance of the Forest*, for instance, the heroine Adeline is threatened by the corrupt uncle, Montalt, who, she also discovers, has murdered her father, and whom she helps to bring to justice. Real-life readers of *Northanger Abbey* are cued to see through Catherine's eyes as she sees through those of Adeline. While the narrator of Austen's novel remains covert through much of the narrative, the interspersed overt narration blends experienced, distant, disembodied observation with the inexperienced, involved and embodied life of the heroic novel reader. By virtue of this narrative technique, Catherine Morland becomes the main focalising instance of the novel. It is her perspective, her perceptions and her feelings through which the narrated world sometimes discloses itself to real-life readers. The narrative, then, invites real-life readers to empathise with an inexperienced heroine as she draws on Gothic novels to navigate the patriarchal codes of courtship to somewhat disobedient effect.

From the novel's outset, the heterodiegetic narrator clarifies Catherine's position as an intradiegetic novel reader who applies fiction to life.

The narrator describes Catherine's novel-reading habits in detail: '[F]rom fifteen to seventeen she was in training for a heroine; she read all such works as heroines must read to supply their memories with those quotations which are so serviceable and so soothing in the vicissitudes of their eventful lives'.[37] Chapter 5 focuses on Catherine's singular interest in novels written by women, but the first two chapters describe her practice of memorising quotations taken from poetry written by men. Lines of verse supply Catherine with a stock of elegant phrases that she has taken from Alexander Pope's 'Elegy to the Memory of an Unfortunate Lady' (1717), Thomas Gray's *Elegy Written in a Country Churchyard* (1751), James Thomson's *The Seasons* (1730) and William Shakespeare's *Measure for Measure* and *Twelfth Night*. These memorised excerpts indicate Catherine's early application of literature to life and point to her progressive upbringing as a middle-class girl from the country. In the absence of girls' formal education in the long eighteenth century, the representation of Catherine's stock of verse tapped into then-emergent practices of equipping girls with memorised phrases to apply to their social life on the level of mimesis.[38] These representations subverted the dominant norms of womanhood and thus the prefiguration of *Northanger Abbey*.[39] After all, as Benedict and Le Faye assert, 'until well into the nineteenth century . . . any form of intellect in girls' was regarded with 'deep-rooted' prejudice.[40] This prejudice is the target of the narrator's cynical commentary: 'A Woman especially, if she have the misfortune of knowing any thing, should conceal it as well as she can.'[41] Tellingly, however, none of the memorised phrases informs Catherine's action over the course of the novel. Instead, novels are the primary reading material that shape her character and induce her actions. Catherine frankly confesses that she is a novice reader while on a walk with Henry Tilney. She casually remarks that she does 'not much like any other' sort of reading than novels, that Gothic romances such as *The Mysteries of Udolpho* are her favourite; she also declares that 'poetry and plays, and things of that sort' are tolerable and that she does 'not dislike travels'.[42] Catherine does not memorise any of the novels, but she immerses herself so fully in them that they become part of an embodied repertoire, which she in turn enacts in the world around her. Her behaviour, then, instantiates 'the operation of refiguration' insofar as she incorporates into her selfhood the novel she has read in the hope of increasing 'the prior readability' of the world outside of books.[43]

Henry Tilney is often cast as the lover-mentor who reforms, educates and ultimately disciplines the girl reader.[44] However, this interpretation overlooks that he is as enthralled by *The Mysteries of Udolpho* as Catherine is. He asserts his visceral reading experience of Radcliffe's Gothic romance in a flirtatious conversation with the heroine. So transported was he into the world of Gothic castles while reading the novel aloud to his sister that he could not wait for her return when she was called away, rather proceeding without her, reading silently, and pacing up and down the 'Hermitage-walk' at his family abbey:

> Here was I, in my eagerness to get on, refusing to wait only five min-utes for my sister; breaking the promise I had made of reading it aloud, and keeping her in suspense at a most interesting part, by running away with the volume, which, you are to observe, was her own, par-ticularly her own. I am proud when I reflect on it, and I think it must establish me in your good opinion.[45]

Catherine and Henry bond over their mutual pleasure in novel-reading, which extends to their full absorption into the narrated world. The dia-logue does much to establish them as the heroic love match of this feminine *Bildungsroman*. Yet Austen cued real-life readers to filter the narrated events through Catherine's novel-inflected consciousness.

Indeed, it is Catherine's consciousness that *Northanger Abbey* renders 'more completely than other characters'.[46] Austen deploys free indirect speech to encourage real-life readers to imagine Catherine's novel-induced imaginings. A prime example of Catherine's enactment of Gothic novels in her ordinary surroundings occurs when, immersed in Radcliffe's *The Romance of the Forest*, she wrongly suspects General Tilney of mur-dering Mrs Tilney. We, as first-time readers of *Northanger Abbey*, are kept in suspense because the episode is focalised through Catherine's limited consciousness. This episode lampoons Catherine's novel-induced behav-iour since it recounts how the girl cannot resist opening the ebony cabinet in her bedroom; upon unlocking it, she finds, much to her delightful ter-ror, 'the precious manuscript' that she has expected to find based on her perusal of *The Romance of the Forest*.[47] Catherine's body displays typi-cally visceral effects: her 'heart beat quick', her 'cheek flushed', 'her heart fluttered, her knees trembled, and her cheeks grew pale'.[48] The configura-tion of Catherine's immediate embodied response to the manuscript left, and leaves, room for interpretation. Upon first perusal, it cues real-life readers to believe in the impending revelation of murder. Like Radcliffe, Austen postponed the disenchanting cue intentionally to keep readers in suspense. Only in the following chapter does Catherine realise that she has mistaken a laundry bill for a written testimony of murder.[49] The mun-dane bill pokes fun at Catherine's gullibility.

As mentioned, Austen hinges the narrative composition of this epi-sode primarily on Catherine's consciousness, with the result that all the events at *Northanger Abbey* are interpreted through Catherine's experi-ence of reading Radcliffe's Gothic romances. Yet Austen refrains from further cues of mockery and deploys instead a high degree of refined ambiguity. It is free indirect discourse that discloses Catherine's embarrassment to real-life readers: 'Could it be possible, or did not her senses play her false? . . . Could not the adventure of the chest have taught her wisdom? . . . How could she have so imposed on herself?' If readers were or are in any doubt as to whether these reported questions represent Catherine's self-accusation or the narrator's judgement, the subsequent exclamation did and still does much to indicate Catherine's interiority: 'Heaven forbid that Henry Tilney should ever know her folly!'[50] In this episode, then, Austen ridicules Catherine's misplaced imitation of novels, but reinforces the connection of her heroine's reading and actions irrespectively. The ambiguity cues readers simultaneously to maintain their distance from and share their feelings with the heroine. According to Ricoeur, such free indirect speech 'constitutes the most complete integration within the narrative fabric of others' thoughts and words'.[51] Expressive devices such as free indirect speech cue real-life readers to see through Catherine's novel-induced perspective even if the narrative still pokes fun at the heroine's visceral reading habits in this instance.

Another episode suggests Catherine's novel-induced recognition of General Tilney's tyrannical behaviour while she resides at *Northanger Abbey*. Driven by her distrust of cruel patriarchs, she continually looks for traces of murder. Similarly, Austen continues her use of free indirect speech to invite real-life readers to see playfully through the heroine's novel-inflected eyes. That said, free indirect speech generally oscillates between the narratorial voice and the character's thought:[52]

> She [Catherine] came to a resolution of making her next attempt on the forbidden door alone. It would be much better in every respect that Eleanor should know nothing of the matter. To involve her in the danger of a second detection . . . could not be the office of a friend. The General's utmost anger could not be to herself what it might be to a daughter; and, besides, she thought the examination itself would be more satisfactory if made without any companion. It would be impossible to explain to Eleanor the suspicions . . . nor could she therefore, in her presence, search for those proofs of the General's cruelty.[53]

Real-life readers are invited both to empathise with and to judge Catherine's state of mind. First, she considers her options for how best to enter the room of the late Mrs Tilney so as to avoid detection; second, she anticipates General Tilney's anger; and third, she resolves to act alone and to conceal her suspicions of murder from her friend, Eleanor Tilney. While the passage leaves room for satire, the subsequent events redeem Catherine's distrust because the General banishes the young woman from his home without justification. In doing so, he commits an act of cruelty in several ways: his young guest has not offended him; she is far away from home; and she needs assistance to return to her parents' home, which he refuses to provide. The banishment, then, corroborates Catherine's novel-induced suspicions retrospectively. The interplay of free indirect speech and this peripeteia, which is a crucial part of the emplotment, signals a positive evaluation of the heroine's transformation of self through the novels she has read.[54]

To offset this playful endorsement of the intradiegetic novel reader, Austen pairs Catherine with Isabella Thorpe. The latter closely resembles that of the fallen-woman novel reader. She only devours fashionable Gothic romances and disregards other novels, such as those written by Samuel Richardson, which she dismisses as 'amazing [sic] horrid'.[55] Not only does the wily Isabella have a list of the latest 'pocket-books' of imitations of Radcliffe's Gothic work, but she also titillates her friend Catherine with such questions as: 'Are not you wild to know [what is behind the black veil in *The Mysteries of Udolpho*]?'[56] The fashionable, socially ambitious Isabella does much to convey her contagious passion of Gothic novels to Catherine, the new arrival on the Bath ballroom scene. The narrative echoes the misogynistic norms of the Georgian era, insofar as it suggests Isabella's voracious reading to be a reflection of her sexual appetite and insatiable hunger for wealth and social status. Once Isabella becomes aware of Catherine's brother's low income, she loses interest in him despite their engagement. The narrative further insinuates her affair with the libertine Frederick Tilney during James's absence from Bath. Both James and Frederick eventually abandon Isabella, leaving her with the reputation of a fallen woman. Austen thus uses the stereotype of the promiscuous woman romance reader in the mould of Smollett's Nancy Williams to mark Isabella proleptically as the 'vain coquette'.[57]

As an intradiegetic novel reader, Isabella reinforces the common stigmatisation of the woman novel reader. On the one hand, she stands in for the dominant pathologisation of novel reading during the Georgian period.[58] On the other, Austen's figuration deviates fundamentally from the model of novel-induced corruption of femininity, since *Northanger Abbey* does not support the misogynist stereotype that Gothic novels irrevocably stirred up Isabella's seemingly monstrous desires. On the contrary, Isabella instrumentalises the imitations of Radcliffe's novels to be part of the latest fashion at Bath. She is resourceful and socially ambitious irrespective of novels; what is more, novels neither harm nor corrupt her moral or physical health. Yet at no stage in the narrative does Isabella resemble such a picture of guileless innocence as does Catherine. Revolving around frivolity, Isabella's character conveys the reading lesson, if any, that literary fashions rarely ever last and that true novel readers should read extensively and know the traditions of the entire genre.[59] By setting a negative example, even such an ambivalent intradiegetic novel reader as Isabella operates as an implicit reinforcement of the novel as a literary genre. By way of contrast, her superficial appropriation of Gothic romance sheds a positive light on Catherine's inexperienced yet formative engagement with novels.

Conclusion

An interpretation of *Northanger Abbey* based on the hermeneutics of recuperation highlights how Austen's publication belongs to the kind of 'classic novel – from *La Princesse de Clèves* or the eighteenth-century English novel to Dostoyevsky and Tolstoy [that] can be said to have explored the intermediary space of variations, where, through transformations of the character, the identification of the same decreases without disappearing entirely'.[60] In *Northanger Abbey*, Austen decisively focussed on and re-evaluated the quixotic trope of the intradiegetic novel reader. One of Catherine's invariant character traits is her passion for novels. Paradoxically, this invariance opens her character up to constant transformation. This creative decision allows Austen to harness the paradoxical dynamic of the invariant change and unchanging variation. In so doing, the novelist dares to deviate from the dominant pathologisation of quixotism by integrating novels into a respectable part of character formation. This configuration marks a distinct departure from the denigration of intradiegetic novel readers in early realist novels exemplified by *Roderick Random* and *The Female Quixote*.

Based on *Time and Narrative*, the hermeneutics of recuperation further enhances our understanding of the initial and lasting effects of the intradiegetic novel reader as a cue for any real-life reader, past and present alike. Since the nineteenth century, the view that novels (and modern romances) have the potential to transform personal and communal identities has gradually gained social acceptance and is no longer seen as a threat,[61] as the dominant eighteenth-century tastemaker Samuel Johnson believed.[62] To historicise the significance of the principal intradiegetic novel reader in *Northanger Abbey*, we can detect a gendered model of novel-induced self-transformation that is part of the protagonist's coming-of-age. Catherine's modest independence while en route from Northanger Abbey in Gloucestershire to her parents' home in Wiltshire instantiates the way Austen's narrative composition opposes the then-dominant norms of female stasis through Catherine's presence as a figure of feminine character growth. This plot dynamic thus exemplifies intradiegetic refiguration, and in so doing signifies the transformative power of novels. Implicitly theorising the generic virtues of the novel, Austen innovated the intradiegetic novel reader in *Northanger Abbey* to counteract long-eighteenth-century anxieties about the damaging effect of reading novels. In so doing, the novelist composes stylistic cues that continue to guide our reading today towards visceral reading experiences. In this way, *Northanger Abbey* represents a milestone in the development of the early realist novel and a distinct refinement of the intradiegetic novel reader that paves the way for further endorsements of visceral modes of novel reception.[63]

Notes

1. Jane Austen, *Northanger Abbey*, ed. by Barbara M. Benedict and Deirdre Le Faye (Cambridge: Cambridge University Press, 2006), vol. 1, ch. 5, p. 30. Although general editorial practice in this volume is to place references to frequently quoted books within the text, we have deviated from that practice here because Benedict and Le Faye use Jane Austen's volume and chapter numbers in their one-volume edition, and the length of reference necessitated by the inclusion of the volume number impedes clarity.

2. See William Beatty Warner, *Licensing Entertainment: The Elevation of Novel Reading in Britain, 1684–1750* (Berkeley: University of California Press, 1998), p. 224.

3. This refers to Jorge Luis Borges's 'Parable of Cervantes and the Quixote'. See Peter Boxall, *The Prosthetic Imagination: A History of the Novel as Artificial Life* (Cambridge: Cambridge University Press, 2020), p. 60.

4. Garrett Stewart, *Dear Reader: The Conscripted Audience in Nineteenth-Century British Fiction* (Baltimore, MD: Johns Hopkins University Press, 1999), p. 93.

5. *Northanger Abbey*, vol. 1, ch. 5, p. 30.

6. D. A. Miller, *Jane Austen, or, The Secret of Style* (Princeton, NJ: Princeton University Press, 2003), p. 34.

7. One conceptualisation of this development is 'the rise of the novel' established by Ian Watt in *The Rise of the Novel: Studies in Defoe, Richardson and Fielding* (London: Chatto & Windus, 1957).

8. For an overview on eighteenth-century Quixote studies see Amelia Dale, *The Printed Reader: Gender, Quixotism, and Textual Bodies in Eighteenth-Century Britain* (Lewisburg, PA: Bucknell University Press, 2019), pp. i–iv.

9. Deidre Lynch, 'Early Gothic Novels and the Belief in Fiction', in *The Oxford History of the Novel in English, vol. 2: English and British Fiction, 1750–1820*, ed. by Peter Garside and Karen O'Brien (Oxford: Oxford University Press, 2015), pp. 182–98 (p. 183).

10. Ioan M. Williams, *Novel and Romance 1700–1800: A Documentary Record* (London: Routledge & Paul Kegan, 1970), pp. 319–20. See also Clara Reeve, *The Progress of Romance and the History of Charoba, Queen of AEgypt* (Colchester: W. Keymer, 1785; repr. New York: Facsimile Text Society, 1930).

11. Beattie quoted by Williams, *Novel and Romance*, p. 320.

12. I use the term 'intradiegetic novel reader' synonymously with 'the novel reader inside the novel'.

13. Monika Fludernik, *Towards a 'Natural' Narratology* (London: Routledge, 1996), p. 16; see also *Postclassical Narratology: Approaches and Analyses*, ed. by Jan Alber and Monika Fludernik (Columbus: Ohio State University Press, 2010).

14. Rita Felski, *Uses of Literature* (Oxford: Blackwell, 2008); Rita Felski, *The Limits of Critique* (Chicago, IL: University of Chicago Press, 2015); *Critique and Postcritique*, ed. by Elizabeth S. Anker and Rita Felski (Durham, NC: Duke University Press, 2017). Jonathan Culler, 'Hermeneutics and Literature', in *The Cambridge Companion to Hermeneutics*, ed. by Kristin Gjesdal and Michael N. Forster (Cambridge: Cambridge University Press, 2019), pp. 304–25 (p. 319).

15. Eve Kosofsky Sedgwick, 'Jane Austen and the Masturbating Girl', *Critical Inquiry*, 17(4) (1991), 818–37 (p. 833). See also Eve Kosofsky Sedgwick, 'Paranoid Reading and Reparative Reading; or, You're so Paranoid, You Probably Think This Essay Is About You', in *Touching Feeling: Affect, Pedagogy, Performativity*, ed. by Eve Kosofsky Sedgwick et al. (Durham, NC: Duke University Press, 2002), pp. 123–51.

16. Paul Ricoeur, *Freud and Philosophy: An Essay on Interpretation*, trans. by Denis Savage (New Haven, CT: Yale University Press, 1970), pp. 25–7, 33–5, 53–5, 59–64; Sebastian Gardner, 'Hermeneutics and Psychoanalysis', in *The Cambridge Companion to Hermeneutics*, ed. by Kristin Gjesdal and Michael N. Forster (Cambridge: Cambridge University Press, 2019), pp. 184–210 (pp. 208–9).

17. My term refers broadly to Ricoeur's theory in, among others, the following works: Paul Ricoeur, *Time and Narrative*, trans. by Kathleen Blamey and David Pellauer, 3 vols (Chicago, IL: University of Chicago Press, 1984–1988); Paul Ricoeur, 'Intellectual Autobiography', in *The Philosophy of Paul Ricoeur*, ed. by Lewis Edwin Hahn (Chicago, IL: Open Court, 1995), pp. 3–53; Paul Ricoeur, *Memory, History, Forgetting* (Chicago, IL: University of Chicago Press, 2004).

18. Paul Ricoeur, *Oneself as Another* (Chicago, IL: University of Chicago Press, 1992), p. 140; Ricoeur, *Time and Narrative*, vol. 3 (1988), p. 247.

19. See David Allan, 'Circulation', *The Oxford History of the Novel in English, vol. 2*, pp. 53–72.

20. *Jane Austen's Letters*, 4th edn, ed. by Deirdre Le Faye (Oxford: Oxford University Press, 2011), letter 14 (pp. 26–9), p. 27.

21. Ricoeur, *Time and Narrative*, vol. 1 (1984), pp. 52–86.

22. Tobias Smollett, *The Adventures of Roderick Random* (Cambridge: Penguin, 1996), p. 188.

23. S. A. Tissot, *The Lady's Physician. A Practical Treatise on the Various Disorders Incident to the Fair Sex* (London: J. Pridden, 1766), p. 17; Thomas Beddoes, *Hygeia: or, Essays Moral and Medical on the Causes Affecting the Personal State of Our Middling and Affluent Classes*, 3 vols (Bristol: R. Phillips, 1802), II, p. 77.

24. For a detailed explanation, see Monika Class, 'The Visceral Novel Reader and Novelized Medicine in Georgian Britain', *Literature and Medicine*, 34 (2016), 341–69 (p. 359).

25. For the ambivalent evaluation of novels in *The Female Quixote* see Deborah Ross, 'Mirror, Mirror: The Didactic Dilemma of *The Female Quixote*', *Studies in English Literature 1500–1900*, 27 (1987), 455–73 (p. 466).

26. Charlotte Lennox, *The Female Quixote*, ed. by Margaret Dalziel (Oxford: Oxford University Press, 1998), p. 21.

27. Lennox, *Female Quixote*, p. 368.

28. Lennox, *Female Quixote*, p. 374.

29. Jane Austen, *Pride and Prejudice*, ed. by Pat Rogers (Cambridge: Cambridge University Press, 2006), ch. 8, pp. 40–1.

30. Jane Austen, *Sense and Sensibility*, ed. by Edward Copeland (Cambridge: Cambridge University Press, 2006), ch. 3, p. 20.

31. *Pride and Prejudice*, ch. 14, p. 76.

32. *Pride and Prejudice*, ch. 14, p. 76.

33. For a detailed analysis of the role of Fordyce's *Sermons* in Austen's defence of novels, see Katie Halsey, *Jane Austen and her Readers, 1786–1945* (Cambridge: Cambridge University Press, 2012), pp. 40–1.

34. For a discussion of the reading heroine in Austen's later novels, *Mansfield Park* (1814) and *Persuasion* (1818), see Joe Bray, *The Female Reader in the English Novel* (New York & London: Routledge, 2009), pp. 162–74. See also Alan Richardson, 'Reading Practices', in *Jane Austen in Context*, ed. by Janet Todd (Cambridge: Cambridge University Press, 2005), pp. 397–405.

35. This interpretation builds on reading *Northanger Abbey* as an endorsement of Gothic novels rather than a spoof; see Claudia L. Johnson and Clara Tuite, *30 Great Myths About Jane Austen* (Hoboken, NJ: Wiley-Blackwell, 2020), pp. 43–9. See also Bray, who deploys models from cognitive psychology and cognitive poetics to argue that 'Catherine is able to keep one foot in the "real" world of her immediate surroundings, even as she is most immersed in the fictional worlds of her reading' (*Female Reader*, pp. 144–50; quotation, p. 144).

36. For a detailed analysis of this novel see Monika Class, 'Ann Radcliffe, *The Romance of the Forest* (1791)', in *Handbook of the British Novel in the Long Eighteenth Century*, ed. by Berndt Katrin and Johns Alessa (Berlin: De Gruyter, 2022), pp. 417–34.

37. *Northanger Abbey*, vol. 1, ch. 1, p. 7.

38. Merve Emre, *Paraliterary: The Making of Bad Readers in Postwar America* (Chicago, IL: University of Chicago Press, 2017), p. 25.

39. Ricoeur, *Time and Narrative*, vol. 1, pp. 54–64.

40. *Northanger Abbey*, notes, p. 332.

41. *Northanger Abbey*, vol. 1, ch. 14, p. 112.

42. *Northanger Abbey*, vol. 1, ch. 14, p. 109.

43. Ricoeur, *Time and Narrative*, vol. 3, p. 179.

44. For a literature review on Henry Tilney, see Dorothee Birke, *Writing the Reader: Configurations of a Cultural Practice in the English Novel* (Berlin: De Gruyter, 2016), pp. 101–5.

45. *Northanger Abbey*, vol. 1, ch. 14, p. 108.

46. Watt, *The Rise of the Novel*, p. 297.

47. In Radcliffe's 1791 novel, Adeline discovers a manuscript in the vaults of the ruined Abbey that she eventually recognises to be her biological father's last words before he was killed by his tyrannical brother.

48. *Northanger Abbey*, vol. 2, ch. 6, pp. 173–4.

49. *Northanger Abbey*, vol. 2, ch. 7, p. 176.

50. *Northanger Abbey*, vol. 2, ch. 7, pp. 176–7.

51. Ricoeur, *Time and Narrative*, vol. 2, p. 90.

52. For Ricoeur, such oscillation imitates 'the crowning touch of the "magic" of internal transparency' (Ricoeur, *Time and Narrative*, vol. 2, p. 91).

53. *Northanger Abbey*, vol. 2, ch. 9, p. 198.

54. For an explanation of the notion of emplotment see Ricoeur, *Time and Narrative*, vol. 1, pp. 64–70.

55. *Northanger Abbey*, vol. 1, ch. 6, p. 35.

56. *Northanger Abbey*, vol. 1, ch. 6, p. 33. Isabella's list contains nine 'Horrid Mysteries', the titles of which refers to actual novels published by Minerva Press. See James Raven, 'Production', in *The Oxford History of the Novel in English, vol. 2*, pp. 3–28 (p. 19).

57. *Northanger Abbey*, vol. 2, ch. 12, p. 224.

58. The gendered pathologisation of novel reading has been studied by, for instance, James Kennaway, 'Two Kinds of "Literary Poison": Diseases of the Learned and Overstimulating Novels in Georgian Britain', *Literature and Medicine*, 34 (2016), 252–77; Class, 'Visceral Novel Reader', pp. 353–60.

59. As the paratextual commentary explains, this is a salient point in the history of *Northanger Abbey*, since the publication was delayed until the craze for Gothic novels dwindled in the late 1810s and early 1820s.

60. Ricoeur, *Oneself*, p. 148. The argument is compatible with Boxall's claim that Austen created a prototype for the novelistic conversion of 'the disintegration caused by rapid technological transformation into a newly integrated subjecthood, a kind of being that thrives on ontological instability' (*Prosthetic Imagination*, p. 164). Ontological instability does not amount to the full disintegration of character. Conversely, Ricoeur's notion of narrative identity revolves around the instability and opacity of self.

61. Michiko Kakutani, *Ex Libris: 100 Books for Everyone's Bookshelf* (New York: Random House, 2020), p. 14.

62. See *Samuel Johnson: The Yale Edition of Works; the Rambler*, ed. by W. J. Bate and Albrecht B. Strauss, 22 vols (New Haven, CT & London: Yale University Press, 1969), III, p. 21.

63. This work was supported by the German Research Foundation (DFG) under the project 'The Visceral Novel Reader: A Cultural History of Embodied Novel Reading in Britain, 1688–1927' (P422574378).

Bibliography of secondary literature

Alber, Jan and Monika Fludernik (eds), *Postclassical Narratology: Approaches and Analyses* (Columbus: Ohio State University Press, 2010)

Anker, Elizabeth S. and Rita Felski (eds), *Critique and Postcritique* (Durham, NC: Duke University Press, 2017)

Austen, Jane, *Jane Austen's Letters*, 4th edn, ed. by Deirdre Le Faye (Oxford: Oxford University Press, 2011)

Birke, Dorothee, *Writing the Reader: Configurations of a Cultural Practice in the English Novel* (Berlin: De Gruyter, 2016)

Boxall, Peter, *The Prosthetic Imagination: A History of the Novel as Artificial Life* (Cambridge: Cambridge University Press, 2020)

Bray, Joe, *The Female Reader in the English Novel* (New York & London: Routledge, 2009)

Class, Monika, 'Ann Radcliffe, *The Romance of the Forest* (1791)', in *Handbook of the British Novel in the Long Eighteenth Century*, ed. by Berndt Katrin and Johns Alessa (Berlin: De Gruyter, 2022), pp. 417–34.

Class, Monika, 'The Visceral Novel Reader and Novelized Medicine in Georgian Britain', *Literature and Medicine*, 34 (2016), 341–69

Culler, Jonathan, 'Hermeneutics and Literature', in *The Cambridge Companion to Hermeneutics*, ed. by Kristin Gjesdal and Michael N. Forster (Cambridge: Cambridge University Press, 2019), pp. 304–25

Dale, Amelia, *The Printed Reader: Gender, Quixotism, and Textual Bodies in Eighteenth-Century Britain* (Lewisburg, PA: Bucknell University Press, 2019)

Emre, Merve, *Paraliterary: The Making of Bad Readers in Postwar America* (Chicago, IL: University of Chicago Press, 2017)

Felski, Rita, *The Limits of Critique* (Chicago, IL: University of Chicago Press, 2015)

Felski, Rita, *Uses of Literature* (Oxford: Blackwell, 2008)

Fludernik, Monika, *Towards a 'Natural' Narratology* (London: Routledge, 1996)

Gardner, Sebastian, 'Hermeneutics and Psychoanalysis', in *The Cambridge Companion to Hermeneutics*, ed. by Kristin Gjesdal and Michael N. Forster (Cambridge: Cambridge University Press, 2019), pp. 184–210

Garside, Peter and Karen O'Brien (eds), *The Oxford History of the Novel in English, vol. 2: English and British Fiction, 1750–1820* (Oxford: Oxford University Press, 2015)

Halsey, Katie, *Jane Austen and her Readers, 1786–1945* (Cambridge: Cambridge University Press, 2012)

Johnson, Claudia L. and Clara Tuite, *30 Great Myths About Jane Austen* (Hoboken, NJ: Wiley-Blackwell, 2020)

Kakutani, Michiko, *Ex Libris: 100 Books for Everyone's Bookshelf* (New York: Random House, 2020)

Kennaway, James, 'Two Kinds of "Literary Poison": Diseases of the Learned and Overstimulating Novels in Georgian Britain', *Literature and Medicine*, 34 (2016), 252–77

Miller, D. A., *Jane Austen, or, The Secret of Style* (Princeton, NJ: Princeton University Press, 2003)

Richardson, Alan, 'Reading Practices', in *Jane Austen in Context*, ed. by Janet Todd (Cambridge: Cambridge University Press, 2005), pp. 397–405

Ricoeur, Paul, *Freud and Philosophy: An Essay on Interpretation*, trans. by Denis Savage (New Haven, CT: Yale University Press, 1970)

Ricoeur, Paul, 'Intellectual Autobiography', in *The Philosophy of Paul Ricoeur*, ed. by Lewis Edwin Hahn (Chicago, IL: Open Court, 1995), pp. 3–53

Ricoeur, Paul, *Memory, History, Forgetting* (Chicago, IL: University of Chicago Press, 2004)

Ricoeur, Paul, *Oneself as Another* (Chicago, IL: University of Chicago Press, 1992)

Ricoeur, Paul, *Time and Narrative*, trans. by Kathleen Blamey and David Pellauer, 3 vols (Chicago, IL: University of Chicago Press, 1984–8)

Ross, Deborah, 'Mirror, Mirror: The Didactic Dilemma of *The Female Quixote*', *Studies in English Literature 1500–1900*, 27 (1987), 455–73

Sedgwick, Eve Kosofsky, 'Jane Austen and the Masturbating Girl', *Critical Inquiry*, 17(4) (1991), 818–37

Sedgwick, Eve Kosofsky, 'Paranoid Reading and Reparative Reading; or, You're so Paranoid, You Probably Think This Essay Is About You', in *Touching Feeling: Affect, Pedagogy, Performativity*, ed. by Eve Kosofsky Sedgwick et al. (Durham, NC: Duke University Press, 2002), pp. 123–51

Stewart, Garrett, *Dear Reader: The Conscripted Audience in Nineteenth-Century British Fiction* (Baltimore, MD: Johns Hopkins University Press, 1999)

Warner, William Beatty, *Licensing Entertainment: The Elevation of Novel Reading in Britain, 1684–1750* (Berkeley: University of California Press, 1998)

Watt, Ian, *The Rise of the Novel: Studies in Defoe, Richardson and Fielding* (London: Chatto & Windus, 1957)

Williams, Ioan M., *Novel and Romance 1700–1800: A Documentary Record* (London: Routledge & Paul Kegan, 1970)

Chapter 5

Evaluating negative representations of reading: Ivan Turgenev's *Faust* (1855)

Shafquat Towheed

We all love to talk about a good book, but what about the books we hate, or refuse to read? How do we register and interpret negative responses to books? How do we avoid confirmation bias in research gathering readers' responses to their reading? The same questions arise when we consider the representation of negative responses to reading, or indeed to non-reading. As several of the chapters in this volume demonstrate, writers have often included representations of negative responses to reading and to the refusal to read within their works of fiction; often these serve a clearly didactic or moralistic purpose. From W. M. Thackeray's *Vanity Fair* (1848) to Oscar Wilde's *The Picture of Dorian Gray* (1890–1), there are many representations of books, poems and plays in works of literary fiction, which either should not have been read by their fictional protagonists or are read with hugely damaging outcomes, or where the refusal to read certain types of fiction is endorsed by the narrative. Although the perceived moral danger of taking fiction as literally true has been with us for centuries, negative representations of reading fiction within fictional narratives have often been seen simply as a truism: is there such a thing as a bad book, or only a bad (insufficiently skilled) reader? From books which are perceived as being morally harmful and should not be read (such as Dorian Gray's 'Yellow Book') to books whose reading within the narrative precipitate an existential crisis (such as Goethe's *Faust* in Turgenev's *Faust*), many novelists have played with the idea of an act of reading a fictional work that has serious negative consequences. In a similar vein, some novelists have examined through their fiction whether refusing to read a literary work, the very act of non-reading, can also be consequentially damaging. Ideological arguments about the value of 'correct' reading as opposed to the moral dangers of incorrect, incomplete or incoherent reading have been played out through the pages of fiction, with writers, editors, reviewers, translators and readers all complicit in the fashioning of value judgements about how a literary work should be interpreted, and what a negative representation of reading actually means.

In this chapter, I look at some of these negative representations of reading in Turgenev's novella *Faust*, and interrogate a central paradox: can a work of literature in all honesty represent the act of reading (or refusal to read) a 'bad' book in a positive light? Can literary fiction ever endorse an individual's refusal to read another work of imaginative literature on moral, ethical or philosophical grounds? I do this through three complementary approaches. First, by outlining the extent to which Goethe's *Faust, Part I* (1828) serves as intertext and metanarrative in Turgenev's *Faust*, a novella which reinterprets several of the key themes of the earlier work. Second, I offer a detailed close reading of the representations of negative responses to reading – and resistances to reading – in Turgenev's *Faust*, teasing out the complex ways in which different types of readerly interpretation are modelled and critiqued in the novella. Finally, I place Turgenev's discussion of the potentially disastrous impact of inadequate critical reading in the context of the wider discussions and moral panics about the rise of literacy and popular reading in the 1850s. Turgenev's *Faust* offers us a compelling insight into the representations of negative responses to reading and serves as a warning about the limitations of reading as always being a beneficial activity. At the same time, I would argue that it is a focalising literary work during a period of intense debate about the purpose and function of literary fiction. Despite considerable contemporary ideological and moral pressure to demonstrate the benefits of good reading and condemn the reading of bad and allegedly morally corrupting books, Turgenev refuses to endorse any kind of totalising position about how negative responses might be interpreted. Instead, as I will demonstrate, Turgenev explores through the complex readerly engagements represented in *Faust* how we might interpret and negotiate the seemingly contradictory position of a text that is pleasurable to read, but where the act of reading itself leads to a disastrous outcome.

Goethe's *Faust, Part I* (1828) and Turgenev's *Faust* (1855)

As documented in his correspondence and corroborated by his biographers, Turgenev had an intimate and lifelong relationship with the works of Johann Wolfgang von Goethe (1749–1832), and in particular with *Faust, Part I*. It is likely that Turgenev first read Goethe's *Faust, Part I* as a student in Berlin in the late 1830s, at a time when he was romantically attracted to Bettina von Arnim (1785–1859), the German aristocrat, Romantic writer and close friend of Goethe; von Arnim had just published a fictionalised correspondence between herself and Goethe in *Goethes Briefwechsel mit einem Kinde* ('Goethe's Correspondence with a Child', 1835). One of Turgenev's friends and fellow students in Berlin at this time was G. H. Lewes (1817–78), who would later become a famous literary critic, essayist and the first English biographer of Goethe; Lewes's biography of Goethe was published in 1855, the same year as Turgenev's *Faust*. Indeed, reading Faust would lead directly to Turgenev's first serious literary publication, which, as Turgenev's biographer Leonard Schapiro points out, was 'a critical essay inspired by a Russian translation of *Faust*' which appeared as a review in the journal *Annals of the Fatherland* (No. 2, February 1845).[1]

Turgenev's correspondence is peppered with allusions to Goethe's *Faust, Part I*, and interestingly, he often draws direct comparisons (both positive and negative) between his own tastes and preferences and those of the fictional characters in *Faust*. Writing to the music and art critic V. V. Stasov (1824–1906) about the relative paucity of Russian artistic production, Turgenev compared himself to Faust's student Wagner: 'I'll be the first to rejoice over Russian art; but I don't want to be like Wagner, of whom Goethe says that: *"with greedy hands he digs for treasures – And is happy if he finds worms"*'.[2] Turgenev's overwhelming preference for *Faust, Part I* over *Part II* is also extensively glossed in his correspondence, with any preference by other readers for *Part II* seen as a defect on their part. Writing to his friend the famous Russian literary critic P. V. Annenkov (1813–87) in 1853, at the time when he was working on his own version of *Faust*, Turgenev criticises a recent acquaintance for being 'a systematician, and not very bright – that is why he holds the second part of Goethe's *Faust* in such reverence'.[3] As Leonard Schapiro notes, the works of Goethe were well represented in Turgenev's library at Spasskoe, which is now rehoused in the museum in Orel, and his library 'reflects the various stages in the development of his intellectual interests'.[4]

Turgenev was actively engaged in rereading Goethe's writing, especially his correspondence, at the time of writing his own *Faust*; as Leonard

Schapiro observes, Turgenev 're-read the classics such as Homer, Molière, and above all, *Don Quixote*, which in the summer he intended to translate into Russian, if he should eventually decide not to go on writing his novel . . . in the spring of 1853 he was much absorbed with the correspondence of Goethe's friend H. J. Merck'.[5] The fact that Goethe's letters were reread at the same time as Cervantes's *Don Quixote* strongly indicates Turgenev's interest in the potentially negative impact of reading as represented in some literary classics he already knew well. As Schapiro observes about Turgenev's novella, 'the story, which is told in a series of letters, is remarkable . . . for the evidence which it provides of Turgenev's continuing preoccupation with Goethe, and particularly with Part I of *Faust*'.[6] Turgenev read out the manuscript version of his *Faust* in preparation for publication just before another trip to England in 1855, but, as Patrick Waddington notes, he was particularly selective about which version of the Faust legend he drew upon. While he had read and knew Marlowe's version of the Faust story, 'Turgenev did not borrow anything from Marlowe, even though . . . he was already well acquainted with *Doctor Faustus*.'[7] Indeed, as far as Turgenev was concerned in terms of his own retelling of the Faust myth, it was Goethe's *Faust, Part I* alone that stood as the central intertextual reference. The plot of Turgenev's novella draws heavily on the premise of Goethe's play, but even more impressive are the very specific references to editions of the work in the story, editions of the text which Turgenev himself had read and owned.

Turgenev's 1855 novella *Faust* has at its centre multiple readings and critical interpretations of Goethe's *Faust, Part I*. Turgenev's *Faust*, subtitled 'A Story in Nine Letters', is an epistolary novella which takes place between June 1850 and March 1853. The letters are written by Pavel Alexandrovich B (PB) to his university friend in St Petersburg, Semyon Nikolayevich V (SV). Pavel spends three months of the summer (June–September 1850) in his ancestral village; his family is a member of the landowning elite. Here he meets again his neighbour and childhood sweetheart, Vera Nikolayevna, who is now a married woman and a mother. Nearly a decade earlier, Pavel had proposed marriage to Vera, a proposal that was rejected by Vera's formidable (and now deceased) mother, Mrs Yeltsova. Vera is the product of a peculiar and experimental educational upbringing, for Mrs Yeltsova, had banned her daughter from reading imaginative literature of any kind. Vera's reading is entirely of factual material and she reaches adulthood without ever having read a single work of fiction, poetry or drama. This makes her uniquely vulnerable as a potentially over-affective and over-identifying reader, one who will struggle to disentangle fact from fiction, real human emotions from their literary representations. Over the course of the summer, and mediated through repeated shared reading experiences, an illicit love affair develops between Pavel and Vera, and this ends disastrously, with Vera's death. In Turgenev's *Faust*, both love and death are staged and structured through multiple acts of reading.

Goethe's *Faust Part I* serves as both a metanarrative and an essential intertext throughout the novella. There is a complex interplay between the Faust legend, Goethe's *Faust Part I*, and Turgenev's novella, and the influence of Goethe's text plays itself out in Turgenev's novella with anatomical precision. Turgenev's frame of reference is precise, his bibliographic credibility formidable. As Pavel tells us when he unpacks his portable library for his summer in his family dacha, he is carrying with him his German student edition of *Faust Part I*; we know it is only Part I because of the date. His description of it as a 'poor edition' disguises the fact that the 1828–9 revised edition was the final publication of *Faust Part I* edited and approved by Goethe in his lifetime. *Faust Part II* appeared posthumously in 1832, and in keeping with Turgenev's disdain for it, is not in the frame of reference anywhere in the novella. Pavel describes his student edition with a combination of affection and bibliographical precision: 'with what an inexpressible feeling did I catch sight of the little book I knew all too well (a poor edition from 1828!) I carried it off with me, lay down on the bed, and began to read'.[8] Pavel's comment about his 'poor edition' of 1828 shows his awareness of the specific translations and editions of the work. The 1828 French translation of *Faust* had seventeen beautiful lithographic illustrations by Eugene Delacroix; Pavel's comment about his own 'poor edition' in German stands in contrast to the lavishly illustrated Charles Motte 1828 Paris edition. It is in fact this student edition – just like the one Turgenev himself read as a student in Berlin in the 1830s – that becomes central to the unfolding disaster told in the narrative.

Negative representations of reading in Turgenev's *Faust*

Turgenev explores different models of (and competences for) reading in this novella, one where the act of reading Goethe's *Faust* has a disastrous outcome only for the heroine, Vera Nikolayevna. Through the novella, Turgenev challenges us to consider the moral responsibilities of both readers and recommenders, without making any direct judgement; the seemingly innocent activity of recommending a favourite literary work is charged with ethical implications.

It is not just the bibliographical references in Turgenev's novella, mentioned earlier, that are precise: so are the details about reading. It is clear from early on in the novella that Vera has been the subject of a particular pedagogical experiment, inflicted upon her by her mother, Mrs Yeltsova. This is Pavel's account of Mrs Yeltsova's reading regime:

> Mrs Yeltsova was a very strange woman with a strong character, insistent and intense. She had a powerful influence on me: I was both respectful and a little afraid of her. She had everything done according to a system, and she had brought her daughter up according to a system too, but had not restricted her freedom. Her daughter loved her and had blind faith in her. Mrs Yeltsova only had to give her a book and say: 'don't read this page', and she would miss out the preceding page rather than catch a glimpse of the forbidden one. Yet Mrs Yeltsova had her *idées fixes* as well, her hobby horses. For example, she feared like fire anything that might affect the imagination; and so her daughter, right up the age of seventeen, had not read a single story, nor a single poem, whereas in geography, history and even natural history she would quite often have me stumped – me, a graduate, and not a bad one either, as you perhaps recall. I once tried to have a talk with Mrs Yeltsova about her hobby horse, although it was difficult to draw her into conversation: she was very taciturn. She only shook her head.
>
> 'You say,' she said finally, 'reading works of poetry is *both* beneficial *and* pleasant . . . I think in life one has to choose in advance: *either* the beneficial *or* the pleasant, and so come to a decision once and for all. I too once wanted to combine both the one and the other . . . It is not possible, and it leads either to ruin or vulgarity.' (p. 19)

Vera's calm and passive demeanour is attributed to the influence of her late mother's utilitarian education system, one that has banished imaginative literature – poetry, drama and fiction – from her mental and emotional development. Turgenev's depiction of Mrs Yeltsova's reading regime bears more than a passing resemblance to Dickens's satire on utilitarianism in the figure of Gradgrind in the contemporaneously published *Hard Times* (1854). Indeed, Turgenev and Dickens shared cultural space for English readers, for Turgenev's first stories in English translation, from the collection *A Sportsman's Sketches* rather than *Faust*, would appear in the pages of *Household Words* not long after the serialisation of *Hard Times*. Vera's name glosses both the Russian word for faith (*Bepa*), and the Latin word for truth (*Verus*), and she remains entirely faithful to Mrs Yeltsova's regime, even after the latter's death. Pavel decides to take it upon himself to rectify this, as he writes to Semyon in his third letter:

> I kept on involuntarily glancing at the gloomy portrait of Yeltsova. Vera Nikolayevna sat directly beneath it: that's her favourite place. Imagine

EVALUATING NEGATIVE REPRESENTATIONS OF READING   101

my surprise: Vera Nikolayevna has still not read a single novel, or a single poem, in short, not a single – as she expresses it – invented work! This incomprehensible indifference to the most elevated pleasures of the mind made me angry. In a woman who is intelligent and, so far as I can judge, highly sensitive, it is simply unforgivable.

'Why is it,' I asked, 'that you've made a point of never reading such books?'

'I've not had occasion,' she replied, 'there's been no time.' (p. 23)

Pavel engages Vera in a discussion about her lack of reading fiction, poetry or drama; she responds by confirming her allegiance to her mother's system: 'I've been accustomed from childhood not to read these invented works; that was the way Mother wanted it, and the longer I live, the more convinced I become that everything that Mother did, everything she said, was the truth, the holy truth' (p. 23). Pavel's actions in recommending Goethe's *Faust, Part I* is in direct opposition to an established reading regime and a household ideology built upon uncritical obedience, a system that values facts as 'truth' and derides imaginative literature as lies.

Vera insists that while her mother's prohibition on reading imaginative literature was withdrawn as soon as she married, she herself has never felt any inclination to read for pleasure: 'as soon as I was married, my mother withdrew any sort of prohibition from me', she tells Pavel, stressing that this was a matter of habit, rather than compulsion: 'it didn't occur to me myself to read . . . how do you put it? . . . well, in short, to read novels' (p. 24). Pavel's response is immediate: Vera must be introduced to imaginative literature at the first opportunity:

'I'll bring you a book!' I exclaimed. (The *Faust* that I had recently read came suddenly to mind.)

Vera Nikolayevna sighed quietly.

'It . . . it won't be George Sand?' she asked, not without timidity.

'Ah, so you've heard of her? Well, perhaps even her, what's the harm? . . . No, I'll bring you another author. You haven't forgotten your German, have you?'

'No, I haven't.'

'She speaks it like a German,' Priyimkov joined in.

'That's fine then! I'll bring you . . . well, you'll see what an amazing thing I'll bring you.' (p. 24)

Pavel wastes no time and springs into action by proposing a shared reading of Goethe's *Faust, Part I* in the Chinese pavilion the following evening. Writing to Semyon, he confesses immediately that he has misgivings about his choice of first literary work for Vera, a virgin reader of imaginative literature:

> When I got home from the Priyimkovs' I repented of having specified *Faust*; Schiller would have suited much better for the first occasion, if we were to be dealing with the Germans. I was particularly worried about the first scenes before the meeting with Gretchen; I wasn't happy as regards Mephistopheles either. But I was under the influence of *Faust* and could not willingly have read anything else. When it was already grown completely dark, we set off for the Chinese summer house; it had been put in order the day before. (p. 28)

'Under the influence of Faust', Pavel offers to read out aloud from Goethe's play, but this ostensibly public performance soon becomes a private reading, with Pavel focussed entirely on Vera's response:

> Vera Nikolayevna did not stir; I stole a couple of glances at her: her eyes were fixed directly and attentively upon me; her face seemed to me pale. After Faust's first meeting with Gretchen she moved forward from the back of her armchair, folded her arms and remained motionless in that position until the end. I sensed that Priyimkov was having a wretched time of it, and this at first turned me cold, but little by little I forgot about him, became excited and read with fervour, with passion . . . I was reading for Vera Nikolayevna alone: an inner voice told me that *Faust* was having an effect on her. (p. 29)

Possessed by the voice of Faust, Pavel continues to read, only too aware of the effect he is having on his first-time listener. Vera Nikolayenva's first response to hearing *Faust* read aloud is physical and results in action, rather than a verbalised opinion, whether favourable or not:

> I wanted to hear what she would say. She got up, took some indecisive steps towards the door, stood for a while on the threshold and went quietly out into the garden. I rushed after her. She had already managed to move several steps away; the whiteness of her dress could just be seen in the dense shadow.
>
> 'Well, then,' I cried, 'didn't you enjoy it?'
>
> She stopped.
>
> 'Can you leave that book with me?' her voice rang out.

EVALUATING NEGATIVE REPRESENTATIONS OF READING 103

'I'll give it to you as a gift, Vera Nikolayevna, if you wish to have it.'
(pp. 29–30)

Public shared reading leads to private reading: Vera takes Pavel's copy of *Faust* and immediately continues to read it alone, in her bedroom. What is particularly apposite here, given the way the plot develops, is Vera's total lack of any evaluative commentary on her first ever encounter with imaginative literature in general and Goethe's *Faust* in particular. Whether this is or is not a negative response to reading is at this point in the narrative impossible to surmise, except perhaps through some of Vera's gestures and bodily reactions. Pavel is reading the signs of Vera's body language meticulously, and even that is simply his subjective interpretation from an external point of view. Should we as readers even trust Pavel's reading of Vera's responses, given his own emotional investment in her? Vera herself says nothing, but her physical response suggests intense emotional affect, and is confirmed by her husband, Priyimkov, in the conversation over dinner that follows:

'Just imagine, I've gone upstairs to her room, and I find her crying. It's a long time since she's been like this. I can tell you when the last time she cried was: when our Sasha passed away. There's what you've done with your *Faust*!', he added, with a smile.

'So now, Vera Nikolayevna,' I began, 'you can see that I was right when . . .'

'I didn't expect this,' she interrupted me, 'but still, God knows whether you're right. Perhaps Mother forbade me to read such books for the very reason that she knew . . .' (p. 31)

Emotional affect leads to compulsive, monomaniacal behaviour, and Vera's relentlessly immersive intensive reading of Goethe's play means she cannot sleep, as Pavel learns the next morning:

'I've been awake all night,' she told me, 'I've got a headache; I came out into the air – perhaps it will pass.'

'Surely it's not because of yesterday's reading?' I asked.

'Of course: I'm not used to it. In that book of yours there are things I simply can't escape from; I think they're what is burning my head so,' she added, putting her hand to her forehead.

'That's splendid,' I said, 'but this is the bad part: I'm afraid this insomnia and headache might dispel your desire to read such things.' (p. 32)

Vera is trapped by her reading, her brain seared by what she has encountered. Far from the headache-ridden sleepless night discouraging her, over the coming weeks she becomes a compulsive reader, one increasingly obsessed with *Faust*, seeing her own emotional life through the filter of Goethe's play, making life mirror art. Inevitably, she realises that she has fallen in love with Pavel, with disastrous consequences:

> When I went in to Vera she looked at me intently and did not reply to my bow. She was sitting by the window; on her lap lay a book which I recognised at once: it was my *Faust*. Her face expressed fatigue. I sat down opposite her. She asked me to read out loud the scene between Faust and Gretchen where she asks him whether he believes in God. I took the book and began reading. When I had finished, I glanced at her. With her head leaning against the back of the armchair and her arms crossed on her breast, she was still looking at me just as intently.
>
> I don't know why, but my heart suddenly began pounding.
>
> 'What have you done to me!' she said in a slow voice.
>
> 'What?' I asked in confusion.
>
> 'Yes, what have you done to me!' she repeated.
>
> 'Do you mean,' I began, 'why did I persuade you to read such books?'
>
> She stood up in silence and went to leave the room. I gazed after her.
>
> On the threshold she stopped and turned back to me.
>
> 'I love you,' she said, 'that's what you've done to me.'
>
> The blood rushed to my head . . .
>
> 'I love you, I'm in love with you,' repeated Vera. (pp. 49–50)

Far from generating empathy, understanding or wellbeing, the reading of *Faust* provokes a disastrous explosion of uncontrollable passion. After finally declaring their love for one another over that shared, gifted student copy of *Faust, Part I*, Pavel and Vera agree a secret tryst by the Chinese summer house the following day. They share a first and only kiss, but their secret moment of bliss is shattered when Vera sees the ghost of her dead mother, Mrs Yeltsova, staring at them. Vera flees in terror, immediately falls ill, and never recovers. Pavel's account of Vera's sudden illness and rapid demise links her fate directly to the emotional arousal caused by Goethe's text:

The illness, to use the words of the doctor, took shape, and Vera died of that illness. She did not live even two weeks after the fateful day of our fleeting tryst. I saw her once more before her death. I have no memory more cruel . . . almost throughout her illness she raved about *Faust* and her mother, whom she sometimes called Martha, sometimes Gretchen's mother. (p. 56)

Earlier in this chapter, I suggested three categories of representations of negative responses to reading in fiction, which I summarised in the following way: (1) where a character in a novel has reacted negatively to a work that they have read, evidenced either through their own words, comments from others, or via omniscient narration; (2) where an act of reading influences a character negatively and results directly in a disastrous outcome; (3) where a conspicuous act of non-reading (or refusing to read) is articulated (either endorsed or criticised) in the text. Turgenev's novella demonstrates both the latter two, but not as far as I can tell, the first: none of the readers of Goethe's *Faust* express a negative opinion of it as a literary work, not even in passing – and pointedly, Vera never offers a negative response to it, even while her obsession with *Faust* drives her to mental instability and eventually to death. A negative outcome as a result of a naïve, insufficient or inept reading of a fictional work has been an absolute staple of literary fiction from Cervantes's *Don Quixote* (1605–15) to the present day. In this category definition, it is the lack of critical distance and over-identification with a character in a fictional work that is sometimes humorous and often fatal, and this serves again as a reminder for us to be sufficiently sceptical, not to over-identify too much, to keep our affective response in check. But who is the 'bad' reader in this novella? Is it Vera, whose total lack of expertise as a critical reader, caused by her peculiarly constrained and impoverished education, means that she literally expects her own life to mirror that of Gretchen in *Faust*? Or is it Pavel, who should know better, as a repeated reader of *Faust* and someone who himself claims to be 'under the influence of *Faust*', and therefore, should not be recommending it to a naïve, emotionally susceptible reader?

The phrase 'I wish I had never read . . .' is a common expression of regret in a negative response to reading, either actual or fictionally represented. And yet such an expression of regret is not found anywhere in Turgenev's novella, even after Vera's death. Turgenev's reluctance to explicitly voice negative responses to reading imaginative literature can partly be explained by the much wider cultural anxieties over mass reading taking place at the time, which often placed novelists in a precarious position: at once celebrated for providing quality literature for a fast expanding reading public, while at the same time heavily scrutinised and sometimes policed for the possibility that literature might corrupt a new generation of inexperienced, first-time readers of fiction.

Anxieties over fiction and the (mass) reading public

The 1850s were marked by widespread cultural anxieties over the reading of fiction by newly literate and variedly skilled mass reading publics.[9] This was the case in both Britain and Russia, despite the specific and substantial differences in terms of literacy rates and access to printed books and serials in the two empires, as well as wider issues around censorship and freedom or artistic expression specific to the Russian Empire. Debates about how, where and why writers of quality fiction could serve an expanding reading public, many of them hungry for entertainment but potentially inexpert in their reading skills, raged across the popular press, in literary journals and in the corridors of power. In Britain, the possibilities and challenges of the ever-expanding reading public were succinctly summarised by the novelist Wilkie Collins (1824–89) in his essay 'The Unknown Public' (1858), which appeared in the Dickens orchestrated pages of *Household Words*; for Collins, the challenge was one of literary taste, to turn a newly functionally literate population into avid readers of good quality fiction: 'An immense public has been discovered: the next thing to be done is, in a literary sense, to teach that public how to read.'[10] While anxieties in Britain about the mass reading public were primarily focussed on elevating the quality of what was read, in Russia there was a wider concern about harnessing literacy for self-improvement, in the face of both widespread scepticism about the value of reading for ordinary people, and state-sanctioned censorship of political or morally subversive content. Jeffrey Brooks notes that the greatest expansion of the mass reading public in Russia took place in the decades immediately after the emancipation of the serfs in 1861, and that top-down attempts to encourage literacy were sometimes met with bewilderment and resistance from the peasantry. 'Educated Russians', Brooks observed, 'thought of literacy as a gift the peasants would be eager to receive' but often in reality, 'most peasants were indifferent to literacy at the time of the emancipation'; the greatest diffusion in literacy happened only once the peasantry discovered the day-to-day utility of literacy skills.[11] The expansion of literacy and the rise of a new class of readers of literary fiction took place in a policed cultural space, one where all publications had to be registered for approval via the state censorship committee in Saint Petersburg. The committee was staffed primarily by professors of literature and published writers, such as Ivan Goncharov (1812–91), who wrote his masterpiece *Oblomov* (1859) while serving as a censor in the 1850s; Turgenev's *Faust* was approved for publication by this very committee. Censorship visibly demonstrated the Tsarist state's anxieties of the potential negative impact of literary works which might be politically or morally subversive, but it also indicates the primacy of paternalistic ideas about what people should read to what end.

More than a decade earlier, Nikolai Gogol (1809–52) had wrestled with many of the same issues in relation to the reception and potential misreading of his masterpiece, *Dead Souls* (1842), a text which, like *Faust*, is centrally invested in the ways in which inexperienced readers of fiction might misread or misunderstand his intentions. These anxieties about the potential ineptitude of readers are ever-present in Gogol's novel. As Anne Lounsbery observes, '*Dead Souls* incorporates commentary on its own readers' incompetence into its narrative tactics . . . by making the denizens of N stand in for the novel's readers'. Gogol, Lounsbery argues, explicitly 'calls our attention to *Dead Souls*' parody of its own readership'.[12] Gogol's critique, as Lounsbery notes, focuses on the perceived lack of intellectual and aesthetic development of the newly literate mass readerships emerging in Russia: 'all of the text's direct representations of reading and readers serve to reinforce our sense of an audience so lacking in aesthetic sophistication that virtually any work of art is beyond its comprehension'.[13] Gogol's text decries the provincialism, lack of aesthetic awareness and deficiency of critical thinking of mass Russian readers, and in doing so, ironically echoes some of the same paternalistic concerns of the Tsarist authorities: readers who are incapable of thinking for themselves should be told what to think.

Unlike Gogol, Turgenev in *Faust* does not offer an implicit or explicit critique of how people should read or how they should derive meaning and satisfaction from their reading. While Gogol is conscious of the limited capacity for literary interpretation of a relatively unsophisticated readership in the 1840s, Turgenev does not criticise the perceived critical limitations of his fictional readers in *Faust*. In modelling the disastrous shortcomings of Vera's utilitarian, fact-based education – an education that has provided her with no real emotional intelligence or psychological resilience – Turgenev is certainly making a broader claim about the value of imaginative literature in human development, as well as encoding a wider critique about the disastrous repercussions of censorship from the Tsarist state and prohibitions on certain types of literature emanating from the Russian Orthodox Church. Mrs Yeltsova's prescriptive education is a metaphor for nineteenth-century Russia as a whole, a society which through restrictions on creative expression has created a

Conclusion

Negative evaluations of reading, negative feelings associated with reading, and indeed, the refusal to engage in reading as a worthwhile activity, are common enough in the historical record, despite readers' own expectations that they ought to gain something positive and productive from the act of reading. The *UK Reading Experience Database, 1450–1945* (UK-RED), for example, has dozens of examples of negative responses to reading, such as Jane Austen's famously withering comment in a letter to her sister Cassandra about the English translation of Madame de Genlis's *Alphonsine: or Maternal Affection* (1806): '"Alphonsine" did not do. We were disgusted in twenty pages, as, independent of a bad translation, it has indelicacies which disgrace a pen hitherto so pure.'[14] The sense that time wasted on an unproductive, unfulfilling, unengaging or unsatisfactory book is something to mark down, so that the mistake is not made again, is just as prevalent today as it was two centuries ago for Jane Austen, as the many Goodreads lists of 'Books I wish I had never read' demonstrate.[15] There are many such lists to be found on social media platforms and the blogosphere, but the chief motivating factor behind the sense of disgust is time wasted: that the investment in reading did not provide a commensurate return. Not everyone is as judicious a reader as Austen, who dispensed with reading *Alphonsine* after just twenty pages. However, while the book that is discarded with a sense of disgust, or boredom, or wasted time clearly fits the category of a negative evaluation of reading, Turgenev in *Faust* through the figure of Vera's reading of Goethe's *Faust* offers us something altogether more complex: a first-time reading that results in compulsive intensive reading; an initial shared experience of reading aloud that results in private, silent reading; a reading experience that moves from being emotionally neutral to being overwrought; a reading encounter that becomes increasingly aesthetically pleasurable, just as at the same time it results in increasing emotional turmoil and eventually to Vera's death. Turgenev offers a compelling critique of utilitarianism and demonstrates the total inadequacy of Vera's factual education, and in doing so he makes an urgent case for the need for imaginative literature in education. At the same time, the means by which the importance of literature is demonstrated in the novel is through two negatives: Vera's lack of literary reading, and the disastrous impact that reading literature for the first time has on her. Despite the clearly negative impact that reading *Faust* has on Vera, at no point does anyone in the novella offer a negative evaluation of Goethe's play, and at no point is the book wrestled away from Vera's hands. Vera expresses no remorse at having read it; indeed, only Pavel expresses regret at having chosen Goethe's play as Vera's first work of imaginative literature to read. Turgenev presents us with a paradox, and a challenge for historians of reading to interpret: can a reader's encounter with an imaginative work of literature be aesthetically pleasurable but emotionally damaging?

Notes

1. Leonard Schapiro, *Turgenev His Life and Times* (Oxford: Oxford University Press, 1978), p. 21.

2. Turgenev to V. V. Stasov, 26 June 1872, in *Turgenev Letters*, trans. by David Lowe, 2 vols (Ann Arbor, MI: Ardis, 1983), vol. 2, p. 107.

3. Turgenev to P. V. Annenkov, 11 June 1853, in *Turgenev Letters*, vol. 1, p. 75.

4. Schapiro, *Turgenev*, p. 99.

5. Schapiro, *Turgenev*, p. 98.

6. Schapiro, *Turgenev*, p. 111.

7. Patrick Waddington, *Turgenev and England* (London: Macmillan, 1980), p. 14.

8. Ivan Turgenev, *Faust*, trans. by Hugh Aplin (London: Alma Classics, 2012), p. 13. All further references are in the text. Translation © Hugh Aplin 2003, 2012, reproduced with permission by Alma Books Ltd.

9. See, for example, Margaret Beetham, 'Domestic Servants as Poachers of Print: Reading, Authority and Resistance in Late Victorian Britain', in *The Politics of Domestic Authority in Britain since 1800*, ed. by Lucy Delap, Ben Griffin and Abigail Wills (Basingstoke: Palgrave Macmillan, 2009), pp. 185–203; Patrick M. Brantlinger, *The Reading Lesson: The Threat of Mass Literacy in Nineteenth-Century British Fiction* (Bloomington: Indiana University Press, 1908); Deborah Wynne, 'Readers and Reading Practices', in *The Oxford History of the Novel in English, Vol. 3: The Nineteenth-Century Novel 1820–1880*, ed. by John Kucich and Jenny Bourne Taylor (Oxford: Oxford University Press, 2011), pp. 22–36.

10. Wilkie Collins, 'The Unknown Public', *Household Words*, 18 (21 Aug. 1858), p. 222.

11. Jeffrey Brooks, *When Russia Learned to Read: Literacy and Popular Culture, 1861–1917* (Evanston, IL: Northwestern University Press, 2003), p. 3.

12. Anne Lounsbery, '"Russia! What Do You Want of Me?" The Russian Reading public in *Dead Souls*', *Slavic Review* 60(2) (Summer 2001), 367–89 (p. 371).

13. Lounsbery, 'Russia! . . .', p. 372.

14. Letter from Jane Austen to Cassandra Austen, 7–8 January 1807, in *Jane Austen's Letters*, ed. by Deirdre Le Faye (Oxford: Oxford University Press, 1995), pp. 115–16, http://www.open.ac.uk/Arts/reading/UK/record_details.php?id=10371, accessed 7 October 2023

15. Goodreads, 'Books I wish I had never read', https://www.goodreads.com/list/show/2850.Books_I_wish_I_had_never_read, accessed 7 October 2023.

Bibliography of secondary literature

Austen, Jane, *Jane Austen's Letters*, ed. by Deirdre Le Faye (Oxford: Oxford University Press, 1995)

Beetham, Margaret, 'Domestic Servants as Poachers of Print: Reading, Authority and Resistance in Late Victorian Britain', in *The Politics of Domestic Authority in Britain since 1800*, ed. by Lucy Delap, Ben Griffin and Abigail Wills (Basingstoke: Palgrave Macmillan, 2009), pp. 185–203

Brantlinger, Patrick M., *The Reading Lesson: The Threat of Mass Literacy in Nineteenth-Century British Fiction* (Bloomington: Indiana University Press, 1908)

Brooks, Jeffrey, *When Russia Learned to Read: Literacy and Popular Culture, 1861–1917* (Evanston, IL: Northwestern University Press, 2003)

Collins, Wilkie, 'The Unknown Public', *Household Words*, 18 (21 Aug. 1858), p. 222

Goodreads, 'Books I wish I had never read', https://www.goodreads.com/list/show/2850.Books_I_wish_I_had_never_read

Lounsbery, Anne, 'Russia! What Do You Want of Me?' The Russian Reading Public in *Dead Souls*, *Slavic Review* 60(2) (Summer 2001), 367–89

Schapiro, Leonard, *Turgenev His Life and Times* (Oxford: Oxford University Press, 1978)

Turgenev, Ivan Sergeevich, *Turgenev Letters*, trans. by David Lowe, 2 vols (Ann Arbor, MI: Ardis, 1983)

Waddington, Patrick, *Turgenev and England* (London: Macmillan, 1980)

Wynne, Deborah, 'Readers and Reading Practices', in *The Oxford History of the Novel in English, Vol. 3: The Nineteenth-Century Novel 1820–1880*, ed. by John Kucich and Jenny Bourne Taylor (Oxford: Oxford University Press, 2011), pp. 22–36

Chapter 6

'I spent all yesterday trying to read': reading in the face of existential threat in Bram Stoker's *Dracula*

Hannah Callahan

Beyond the common interpretations surrounding Victorian-era moral panic in Bram Stoker's 1897 horror classic *Dracula*, a recent strain of criticism has focused on the act of reading within the story, revealing a subtle but profound idea about the novel. Simply put, *Dracula* is not a book about vampires, but a book about reading. Caryn Radick points out that *Dracula* is 'often subject to readings that reflect contemporary concerns'.[1] For readers in the information age, facing global existential threats (climate change, disease, food insecurity and so forth), how Stoker's characters read in their own fight for survival can serve as a source of both motivation and caution for becoming better learners, seekers and users of information. *Dracula* remains relevant today as a literary work about the ethics of seeking, creating and sharing sources of information, and of developing a community of literacy in a time of crisis. This chapter weaves threads from recent scholarship on *Dracula* through a close reading of each character's reading habits and beliefs, showing how Stoker's characters read and learn in order to survive, and how the novel speaks to modern concepts of information literacy. As such, it aims to build on the notion of '*Dracula* as a representation of reading practices' in the interest of inspiring and improving our own.[2]

The reading characters in *Dracula* include the cast of heroes, often referred to as the Crew of Light, as well as the titular vampire villain.[3] In exploring how *Dracula* demonstrates the indispensability of books and reading in the face of an existential threat, I examine the reading habits of four major characters in the novel: Jonathan Harker, Mina Harker, Abraham Van Helsing and Count Dracula. Ultimately, the chapter will argue that Stoker presents a model of community-oriented, socially conscious reading that leads the novel's heroes to be victorious in their fight: a compelling ethos about power and responsibility that is reflected in many modern rubrics of information literacy.[4] The American Library Association (ALA) defines information literacy as a set of skills and principles one may use to 'find, evaluate, and use information effectively to solve a particular problem or make a decision'. In addition to those fundamental steps, virtues of information literacy outlined by the ALA include 'interacting with . . . the community at large' as an ideal component of a learning community.[5] Almost a century before frameworks and rubrics such as the ALA's were developed to define competency in information literacy, Stoker exemplified these readerly virtues in the heroes of *Dracula*, as well as the destruction wrought from their malicious manipulation in the actions of the story's villain.

The characters as readers

The first reader we meet in *Dracula* is Jonathan Harker, a solicitor from London on a visit to the mysterious Count Dracula at his castle in Transylvania, whom he is to assist with the purchase of a London property. The Count has been meticulously planning his move to London – a more bountiful locale for preying on humans – while Harker, our somewhat naive hero of the first few chapters, is characterised nevertheless as a dutiful researcher from the beginning. In his very first journal entry of the epistolary novel, Harker writes that in preparation for his trip he 'visited the British Museum, and made search among the books and maps in the library regarding Transylvania', thinking that it would benefit his meeting with the Count.[6] Throughout the novel, Harker reads not only in order to find new information, but also to review what he has already learned, and sometimes as a distraction. As Harker begins to feel distressed about the behaviour of his host, he writes: 'I had spent the day wearily over books, and, simply to keep my mind occupied, went over some of the matters I had been examined in at Lincoln's Inn' (ch. 3, p. 35). Later, feeling trapped, afraid and restless, Harker writes that he 'came back to the library, and read there till I fell asleep' (ch. 4, p. 55). In his growing discomfort with his situation, he turns to books, and seeks solace by reviewing texts he has studied before, perhaps in search of new insights.

Ultimately, Harker expresses a core belief about books, a conviction that each reading protagonist in the novel expresses at some point, often

READING IN THE FACE OF EXISTENTIAL THREAT IN BRAM STOKER'S *DRACULA*   113

more than once: that information can (and should) be 'verified by books and figures', so that 'there can be no doubt' (ch. 3, p. 35). Moments later, in response to Dracula's inquiries, Harker says: 'I had verified all as well as I could by the books available' (ch. 3, p. 37). These and other examples throughout the text indicate Harker's reverence to the authority of books and written records as sources of ultimate veracity. This is both an inspiring and yet troublesome point of view towards the inherent authority of texts, to which we will return later, as one of our protagonists demonstrates the value of reading with scepticism.

As the novel is composed almost entirely of journal entries and letters by the principal characters, all of the readers are also writers, and all are keenly aware of their writing as contributions to a textual record. In keeping a journal, Harker writes his own book on his experiences, not only saving them for posterity but justifying them to himself and to other readers: 'I began to fear as I wrote in this book that I was getting too diffuse; but now I am glad that I went into detail from the first, for there is something so strange about this place and all in it that I cannot but feel uneasy' (ch. 2, p. 30). Thus Harker finds value in keeping a detailed journal as a way of lending authority to an otherwise unbelievable experience, a neat reflection of his behaviour as a reader. This attitude towards written 'detail' proves vital later in the novel, when Van Helsing asks Mina to 'look up the copy of the diaries and find him the part of Harker's journal at the Castle' (ch. 25, p. 359). Once there, Van Helsing is able to find his way through the castle 'by memory of [reading Jonathan's] diary' (ch. 27, p. 390).

The perfect foil to Jonathan Harker as a reader is Stoker's archetypal villain Count Dracula. At the outset of the novel, Stoker immediately draws a parallel between Harker and Dracula as two highly literate researchers and avid readers. But each character's purpose in reading – one for a greater good and the other for selfish gain – is an important factor, as Stoker presents it, in why one succeeds and the other fails. In an early scene, Harker discovers the impressive library in Dracula's castle, filled with 'a vast number of English books . . . all relating to England and English life and customs' (ch. 2, p. 24). Dracula enters the library a moment later to demonstrate his only moment of warmth in the novel, an otherwise cold and calculating predator. '"These friends" – and he laid his hand on some of the books – "have been good friends to me, and for some years past, ever since I had the idea of going to London, have given me many hours of pleasure"' (ch. 2, p. 25). We are thus introduced to Dracula as 'a devoted – one wants to say voracious – reader' and prolific book collector.[7] We come to understand that he has been amassing this library and studying its contents as 'the work of centuries' (ch. 24, p. 339) in order to naturalise himself to London life, and to navigate the logistics of his relocation smoothly. That he is so well-read impresses even his enemies, who often remark on his immense knowledge on matters about which he has only ever read, never experienced. Harker himself observes that: 'For a man who was never in the country, and who did not evidently do much in the way of business, his knowledge and acumen were wonderful' (ch. 3, p. 37). Van Helsing considers Dracula such a dangerous adversary in no small part because 'He had a mighty brain, a learning beyond compare, . . . and there was no branch of knowledge of his time that he did not essay' (ch. 23, p. 320).

As an isolated and solitary predator, Dracula finds reading an indispensable tool. Whereas Harker is sometimes a 'naive reader',[8] Dracula is cunning, and sees texts as a potential danger in the hands of his enemies, attempting several times to destroy written and printed information. In his captivity, Harker on one occasion returns to his room to find that 'every scrap of paper was gone, and with it all my notes, my memoranda relating to the railways and travel, . . . in fact all that might be useful to me were I once outside the castle' (ch. 4, p. 49). Later, with the Crew of Light in his pursuit, Dracula attempts to throw them off his trail by creating an erroneous shipping invoice, knowing they would track down and read any seemingly 'authoritative' documents they could find to locate him (ch. 26, p. 372).

Much like our heroes, Dracula is a prolific reader and a lover of books. Unlike the Crew of Light, however, he uses reading to advance a self-serving and destructive agenda and sees others' reliance on reading as an opportunity to harm and deceive them. His primary threat is as a vampiric predator, of course, but Stoker also makes it clear that part of the danger Dracula presents is in his destruction, misuse and forgery of documents, his attempts to prevent others from reading and learning, and his disinterest in sharing information for the benefit of others. The Count is a persistent producer of 'dis-information', and in his destruction of documents, a manipulator of the truth. His handling of texts is both false *and* harmful – the very intersection of the types of 'information disorder' that threaten the value of truth and factuality in society.[9] In today's highly networked world, the production and spread of false and misleading information is of increasing concern in its ability to reach and influence larger audiences. There is a current need to 'work together on solutions driven by research and experimentation to mitigate dis-information and significantly improve information literacy'.[10] Just as this threat and its need for a communal solution is recognised today, so too Stoker recognised it as a suitably harmful tactic for a cunning villain, and one which was well combatted by a community working together.

On the other end of the spectrum of integrity, the speaker of *Dracula*'s core thesis on the power of reading is Dr Abraham Van Helsing, who says simply: 'I have a great task to do, and at the beginning it is to know' (ch. 14, p. 203). In other words, ahead of a significant and complicated challenge (in this case, foiling the Count), the very first step is to study and learn. Van Helsing is an eccentric Dutch scholar called in to help treat Lucy, the Count's first English victim, and in turn to help fight Dracula. In response to this prompt for knowledge before all else, Harker fetches him 'the bundle of papers' (ch. 13, p. 204) comprising his evolving written record concerning the Count for Van Helsing to read on his train trip back to Amsterdam. Here, text is valued as the ideal medium for conveying information: portable, efficient, convenient and fixed.

As in that example, reading is almost always the preferred medium for communicating and disseminating information among the Crew of Light, and they remark throughout the novel on their expectation that reading will prepare them to 'better enter [their] inquisition' (ch. 27, p. 234). After Harker has spent a day gathering new information on the Count's whereabouts, he returns to the Crew with new knowledge to share. Rather than ad lib his findings, he refers to his own diary, and 'simply read it off to them as the best means of letting them get abreast of my own information' (ch. 20, p. 285), preferring the text record he created over his own ability to recollect from memory.

Van Helsing is a serious, analytical reader, and, like Mina, an educator by profession. Yet he often withholds information from others if he believes it too soon to share: 'Better he not know as yet; perhaps he shall never know' (ch. 10, p. 131). Perhaps because he so strongly believes in the power of reading and writing, Van Helsing fears the potential damage of challenging what a reader believes to be true, if it is impossible to act wisely upon the knowledge gained. Like Harker, he spends extensive time in the story reading and researching his subject. Dr Seward once relays in his diary that: 'Van Helsing sits in my study poring over the record prepared by the Harkers; he seems to think that by accurate knowledge of all details he will light upon some clue' (ch. 20, p. 287). He is, for much of his time in the narrative, reading, studying or relating to others what he has gathered from doing so.

Often acknowledged as 'a model reader' both by critics of *Dracula* and by characters within the novel is Jonathan's wife, Mina.[11] Mina Harker, a schoolteacher, is the acting secretary and archivist for the Crew of Light's written and typed documents. As a major recorder of the novel's events, and sole compiler of the other characters' accounts, in a meta-narrative sense, Mina Harker is essentially the author of *Dracula*. Her work to preserve and disseminate a text record of the Crew of Light's experiences is utterly indispensable, and positions her as not only a highly literate and dedicated reader, but also as the facilitator of others' reading. At one moment, in an effort to get Van Helsing up to speed, Mina writes that she is 'so glad I have type-written out my own journal, . . . I can hand it to him; it will save much questioning' (ch. 14, p. 195), thus recognising the efficiency and clarity of reading over recounting aloud. With Mina's written record, everyone receives the same information and account of events, all have the same set of resources to which to refer, and the information is stored in a stable, unchanging form.

Mina advocates for making text the standard medium among the Crew of Light when she offers to transcribe Dr Seward's diary (which he records on phonograph cylinders) to a more user-friendly format for reference and dissemination. Seward is hesitant at first, but later recognises the value of her work: 'What a good thing that Mrs. Harker put my cylinders into type! We never could have found the dates otherwise' (ch. 17, p. 241). As a facilitator of others' reading, Mina also encourages critical thought and analysis. 'I shall give you a paper to read', she tells Van Helsing, 'I dare not say anything of it; you will read for yourself and judge' (ch. 14, p. 200). Here, Mina sees it as her job simply to impart information, and values the reader's ability and indeed right as a reader to synthesise the information into knowledge that can inform actions.

Jo nicely summarises the significance of Mina's work to generate reading material for the others with two points: that 'Mina's production or typewriting is a means of facilitating the characters' collective reading', and that 'Dracula's disempowerment goes hand in hand with the increase in the number of texts that Mina reproduces.'[12] Radick exemplifies Mina's arc as a reader in speaking to the main principle of reading in *Dracula*: 'Mina reads through the record she has kept of their experiences with the vampire. Only after doing this and consulting other resources is she able to correctly hypothesize Dracula's strategy, leading to their ultimate success. . . . she can only synthesize the information once she has done her reading.'[13] In other words, Mina's work in synthesising this information through reading generates half the power she cultivates in the fight; the other half comes from distributing that information to her cohort, replicating and therefore multiplying the empowerment she gained from reading by facilitating that reading among others. In her dedication to this work, Mina exemplifies the fourth 'advanced' skillset of information literacy: ethically communicating synthesised knowledge, which includes both sharing findings with peers, and archiving work for future accessibility.[14] It is no surprise that the novel's most steadfast and capable reader, and disseminator of texts, demonstrates the highest goals of modern

READING IN THE FACE OF EXISTENTIAL THREAT IN BRAM STOKER'S *DRACULA* 117

information literacy skills. Stoker very consistently characterises Mina's expertise and consideration in this regard throughout the novel, and indeed, her contributions to her reading community play a very significant role in overcoming the threat they all face.

'Authoritative texts' and critical thinking

As the most literate of the group, Mina is the character Stoker employs to teach a vital skill of information literacy: critical thinking about what qualifies a text as authoritative.[15] Later in the novel, she also suffers the deleterious effects of suppressing access to information, which will be explored at the end of this section.

While taking a walk in the graveyard in Whitby, Mina and her companion Lucy meet an old sailor, Mr Swales. In a previous interaction with Mina, Swales had revealed himself as a deep sceptic of the written word, declaring newspapers 'full of fool-talk' (ch. 6, p. 72). In this unusual scene, he cautions Mina and Lucy not to trust everything they read, but to consider the motives of those behind the words. His outburst is an education in critical thinking for Mina, a lesson on scrutiny toward the authority of a source, bias in writing and the fallibility of written information. He rants about 'illsome beuk-bodies' (book people), religious authorities 'printin' lies on paper' and most importantly, the writing all around them, literally in stone: the headstones, falling over 'with the weight o' the lies wrote on them' (ch. 6, p. 73). Swales picks out examples around them, pointing to graves known to be empty despite the claim 'here lies' (ch. 6, p. 74), and falsified causes of death. One can 'read the small-print of the lies from here' he says (ch. 6, p. 75). Mina counters at first that tombstones are there to please the deceased's relatives, but Swales, averse to any justification for misrepresentation in writing, argues: 'How will it pleasure their relatives to know that lies is wrote over them, and that everybody in the place knows that they be lies?' (ch. 6, p. 75). As something like an oral historian of Whitby, Swales demonstrates scepticism of the half-truths and deceptions written in stone all around him, and disdain for the perceived authority of the written word. His perspective presents a counterbalance to the virtuous readership of the novel's heroes, who, before they learn better, rarely question the authenticity or veracity of what they read.

Mina records this lesson in critical thinking around texts in her journal entry of 1 August. It proves to have had an effect on her readership two days later, when she rereads without pause a letter she had received from Jonathan a few weeks prior, but one we know Dracula forced him to falsify. 'I look at that last letter of his, but somehow it does not satisfy me.

It does not read like him, and yet it is his writing' (ch. 6, p. 82). Even if she cannot put her finger on why the letter is suspicious, after this lesson with Swales, she has acquired a significant new lens for scrutinising what she reads. She returns to a text, and for the first time evaluates it for authority, accuracy and reliability.[16]

During the second half of the novel, the men comprising the Crew of Light, at Van Helsing's initiation, agree to begin withholding the information in their diaries and correspondence from Mina, believing that their 'growing knowledge would be torture to her' (ch. 20, p. 284). Despite the fact that until this point in the story, the men believed 'it is due to [Mina's] energy and brains and foresight that the whole story is put together' in writing (ch. 19, p. 265), they conclude that the work is 'too great a strain for a woman to bear' and thus 'henceforth our work is to be a sealed book to her' both literally and metaphorically (ch. 19, p. 271). The next day, Mina recounts her troubled sleep the night before, when it becomes evident to us that she has been attacked by Dracula, making her his latest unwitting victim (ch. 19, p. 274). Her vulnerability is immediate; as soon as she is barred from the community of readers, she becomes defenceless, falling prey to the vampire. The following day, Mina reports feeling 'terribly weak and spiritless. I spent all day yesterday trying to read, or lying down dozing' (ch. 19, p. 277). Her readerly spirit is indomitable: facing not only the life-draining predation of Dracula, but also the forced ignorance of censorship, she musters what little waking energy she has in attempting to read.

Within two days, the men discover that Mina has been attacked by the Count, and decide no longer to withhold information from her (ch. 22, p. 308). She is restored access to 'all the papers or diaries and phonographs' and permitted 'to keep the record as she had done before' (ch. 22, p. 309). Thus the group recognises that, despite their best intentions to protect a supposedly vulnerable member of their group, restricting access to information caused more harm than good, and while Mina is not yet out of harm's way, the community is safer and stronger with free and equal readership than it is when placing restrictions on knowledge.

Free and public access to information is understood as a foundation for an information-literate society. In its report on information literacy, the ALA establishes that 'all people should have the right to information which can enhance their lives'.[17] *Dracula* powerfully demonstrates the importance of such a right, with Dracula's easy ability to prey on Mina the moment she loses that right. As discussed earlier, an informed *community* is required to overcome malicious intent in an information society. Here, the opposite holds true as well. When the reading community of *Dracula* is fractured, so too does it lose power against Dracula.

Reading with virtue

As Jo succinctly states, 'the most important activity that brings about the destruction of Dracula is the act of reading'.[18] In a broader sense, one of Stoker's strongest themes in *Dracula* is that reading can arm us as a community with the intellectual tools necessary to face down an existential threat. In that sense, my argument takes a decidedly utopian view of *Dracula* as defined by Anne DeLong: 'Utopian readings emphasize the novel's exchange of information as a bonding between the characters, one that serves to cement not only their relationships but also their common purpose.'[19] DeLong quotes Leah Richards's summation that: 'To know everything about Dracula is to know how to destroy him. It is information, gathered into a collaborative and comprehensive account [i.e. the book itself], that enables the group to defeat Dracula.'[20] The Crew of Light are empowered in their community effort because of their shared pursuit of knowledge; they are stronger against their adversary because they have studied and learned all they could about him, together.

In *Dracula*, Bram Stoker presents both our villain and our heroes as equally skilled and diligent researchers; in fact, despite his loss, the Count may indeed be a shrewder reader than any one individual in the Crew of Light. Where Stoker differentiates the value of any of their information literacy skills is in the integrity of the agenda that their reading serves, and in social participation. When our heroes 'read together and form a communal identity – a reading community' they build 'a solidarity that will maintain their bond throughout the novel'.[21] This reading community stays on the same page, so to speak, and in so doing, they form a shared narrative that motivates them, validates what they have experienced and thought, elucidates their shared purpose and values, unifies them in a strategy to protect one another and, as fully informed as they can be, prepares them to face the danger that threatens them and humanity at large. We also see that when members of this community withhold information from one another, or restrict access to new knowledge, they become fractured and vulnerable.

When Van Helsing presents some of his research on vampires to his cohort, he explains that although Dracula is well-educated and well-read, he is 'without heart or conscience' (ch. 18, p. 254). In contrast, the Crew of Light are dedicated to their work 'for the safety of one we love [and] for the good of mankind' (ch. 24, p. 341). Van Helsing believes that, despite the Count's acumen and cunning, the Crew will succeed because Dracula's work is 'selfish and therefore small' (ch. 25, p. 360). Our heroes arm themselves with knowledge through reading in order to protect others and prevent harm to innocent people, and are ultimately victorious in their fight. Our villain, too, arms himself with knowledge through reading, but in order to cause harm and take innocent lives. In *Dracula*, the power of knowledge gained through reading is universally attainable, but information, as a tool, is stronger within a network of people, and stronger still amongst those who do not abuse that power but wield it for the benefit of their community.

Reading in the new information age is something of an equaliser: it is easier than ever to create and disseminate work to a public audience, and similarly, anyone can find and use resources that support an agenda or confirm a bias. The 'diminishing role of facts and analysis' in modern life appears symbiotic with the new, multitudinous platforms for information spread, the erosion of trust in social institutions, and the intensity of political division.[22] In *Dracula*, we are shown the virtue and power of reading with compassion, conscience, conversation, generosity and critical thinking in a world of overwhelmingly bountiful access to ideas and information. The character of Count Dracula represents an existential threat to the human population. To our heroes, he presents not only a mortal threat, but also a threat to their sense of order, morality, human dignity and fairness. From the first glimpse of unease to the height of danger, these characters are reading incessantly. They read to make sense of what they have experienced, to prepare for the future, and to inform one another. At the end of the day, they also read to ease their minds. For the Crew of Light, reading is crucial to every component of their activism, and an exercise in their ethics of building community knowledge.

For the extra-textual reader, emulation of the Crew of Light's dedication to seeking, scrutinising, sharing and understanding information may enable us to advocate better for our moral convictions, cite recorded information that empowers our choices and band together with a wealth of knowledge to foster an informed society that values reading as a part of learning, living and caring for our communities. Indeed, the ALA pronounces information literacy a 'survival skill' crucial to intelligent decision-making, 'effective citizenship' and the practice of democracy itself.[23] Bram Stoker's *Dracula* moves beyond lurid horror, although it excels at that, and continues to inspire the genre well over a century later. At its deepest level it is, in fact, a rich compendium of democratic reading behaviours, an information literacy cautionary tale and the success story of a healthy, aspirational knowledge society. As we aspire to be ethical, engaged citizens in an information age, facing complex uncertainties, we have, as Van Helsing says, a great task to do, and in the beginning, it is to know.

Notes

1. Caryn Radick, '"Complete and in Order": Bram Stoker's *Dracula* and the Archival Profession', *American Archivist*, 76 (2013), 502–20 (p. 503).

2. Sunggyung Jo, '"Vampiric Reading": *Dracula* and Readerly Desire', *Texas Studies in Literature and Language*, 61 (2019), 225–43 (p. 226).

3. Christopher Craft coined the name 'Crew of Light' to refer to the novel's male protagonists Jonathan Harker, Abraham Van Helsing, John Seward, Quincey Morris and Arthur Holmwood. In this chapter, the use of this name refers to these characters *plus* Mina Harker. See Christopher Craft, 'Kiss Me with Those Red Lips: Gender and Inversion in Bram Stoker's *Dracula*', *Representations*, 8 (1984), 107–33 (p. 130).

4. See for example: https://www.mtu.edu/library/instruction/information-literacy/ and https://www.gvsu.edu/library/ilcc, two rubrics from university libraries that include the ethical use of information, including sharing with peers, as part of the information literacy skill set.

5. American Library Association, *Presidential Committee on Information Literacy: Final Report* (2006), http://www.ala.org/acrl/publications/whitepapers/presidential, accessed 22 November 2022.

6. Bram Stoker, *Dracula*, ed. by Brooke Allen (New York: Barnes & Noble Classics, 2003), p. 5. Further references are in the text.

7. Garrett Stewart, '"Count Me In": *Dracula*, Hypnotic Participation, and the Late-Victorian Gothic of Reading', *Horror Issue*, special issue of *Literature, Interpretation, Theory*, 5 (1994), 1–18 (p. 12).

8. Harriet Hustis, 'Black and White and Read All Over: Performative Textuality in Bram Stoker's *Dracula*', *Studies in the Novel*, 33 (2001), 19–33 (p. 23).

9. Claire Wardle and Hossein Derakhshan, *Information Disorder: Toward an Interdisciplinary Framework for Research and Policymaking* (Strasbourg: Council of Europe, 2017), p. 20.

10. Wardle and Derakhshan, *Information Disorder*, p. 79.

11. Jo, 'Vampiric Reading', p. 232.

12. Jo, 'Vampiric Reading', p. 234.

13. Radick, 'Complete and in Order', p. 508.

14. Sarah Beaubien et al., *Information Literacy Core Competencies* (Allendale, MI: Grand Valley State University, 2009), section on core competency #4. See n. 4.

15. Beaubien, section on core competency #3.

16. Beaubien, section on core competency #3.1.B.

17. American Library Association, *Final Report*.

18. Jo, 'Vampiric Reading', p. 226.

19. Anne DeLong, 'Communication Technologies in Bram Stoker's *Dracula*: Utopian or Dystopian?', in *Bram Stoker and the Late Victorian World*, ed. by Matthew Gibson and Sabine Lenore Müller (Clemson, SC: Clemson University Press, 2018), pp. 101–19 (p. 116).

20. Leah Richards, 'Mass Production and the Spread of Information in *Dracula*: "Proofs of So Wild a Story"', *English Literature in Transition, 1880–1920*, 52 (2009), 440–57 (p. 440).

21. Jo, 'Vampiric Reading', p. 235.

22. Jennifer Kavanaugh and Michael D. Rich, *Truth Decay: An Initial Exploration of the Diminishing Role of Facts and Analysis in American Public Life* (Santa Monica, CA: RAND Corporation, 2018), see figure 5.1, p. xvii, and the section on 'confirmation bias', pp. 82–5.

23. American Library Association, *Final Report.*

Bibliography of secondary literature

American Library Association, *Presidential Committee on Information Literacy: Final Report* (2006), http://www.ala.org/acrl/publications/whitepapers/presidential

Beaubien, Sarah et al., *Information Literacy Core Competencies* (Allendale, MI: Grand Valley State University, 2009)

Craft, Christopher, 'Kiss Me with Those Red Lips: Gender and Inversion in Bram Stoker's *Dracula*', *Representations*, 8 (1984), 107–33

DeLong, Anne, 'Communication Technologies in Bram Stoker's *Dracula*: Utopian or Dystopian?', in *Bram Stoker and the Late Victorian World*, ed. by Matthew Gibson and Sabine Lenore Müller (Clemson, SC: Clemson University Press, 2018), pp. 101–19

Hustis, Harriet, 'Black and White and Read All Over: Performative Textuality in Bram Stoker's *Dracula*', *Studies in the Novel*, 33 (2001), 19–33

Jo, Sunggyung, '"Vampiric Reading": *Dracula* and Readerly Desire', *Texas Studies in Literature and Language*, 61 (2019), 225–43

Kavanaugh, Jennifer and Michael D. Rich, *Truth Decay: An Initial Exploration of the Diminishing Role of Facts and Analysis in American Public Life* (Santa Monica, CA: RAND Corporation, 2018)

Radick, Caryn, '"Complete and in Order": Bram Stoker's *Dracula* and the Archival Profession', *American Archivist*, 76 (2013), 502–20

Richards, Leah, 'Mass Production and the Spread of Information in *Dracula*: "Proofs of So Wild a Story"', *English Literature in Transition, 1880–1920*, 52 (2009), 440–57

Stewart, Garrett, '"Count Me In": *Dracula*, Hypnotic Participation, and the Late-Victorian Gothic of Reading', *Horror Issue*, special issue of *Literature, Interpretation, Theory*, 5 (1994), 1–18

Wardle, Claire and Hossein Derakhshan, *Information Disorder: Toward an Interdisciplinary Framework for Research and Policymaking* (Strasbourg: Council of Europe, 2017)

Chapter 7

'Into separate *brochures*': stitched work and a *new* New Testament in Thomas Hardy's *Jude the Obscure*

Lucy Sixsmith

'Man shall not live by bread alone.'[1] In 1901, a correspondent of *Notes and Queries* reported the story of a woman who had not taken the Bible literally, but taken the Bible, literally:

> I am told by a lady resident that in the Hampshire parish in which I am writing there is living at the present time a good woman who once ate a New Testament, day by day and leaf by leaf, between two slices of bread and butter, as a remedy for fits.[2]

The letter-writer's piling up of clauses and phrases implies that we should find it crude or absurd so to use a New Testament as a totem or talisman. His readers are expected to laugh, or grimace or raise their eyebrows a little. 'There is living at the present time' is especially amplified, as if, after feeding so long on the Word of God, there might perhaps not have been. The distinction between 'lady resident' and 'good woman', too, may reveal the assumed detachment of one social class observing another, 'good' making condescending excuses for eccentric piety.

Yet the story is also striking because it is uncannily familiar. Such an 'extraordinary superstition', regular, domestic, 'day by day and leaf by leaf', recalls those quotidian habits of Bible-reading and prayer to which many Victorians were accustomed: *Morning by Morning* and *Evening by Evening*, for example, were devotional guides by the popular preacher Charles Spurgeon.[3] Superstition or not, the Hampshire woman may have found her practice sustaining and helpful. After all, if she had felt no difference, she could have stopped halfway through the volume. When contrasted with more conventional devotion, however, eating a New Testament raises questions about the materiality of the text. Did this New Testament come with endpapers, a title page, or introductory helps, and did she eat these too? Did she have a second copy to read alongside the half-eaten one? And what did she do afterwards with the emptied covers – was she taken aback to discover that the Bible faithfully internalised was a finite resource, and had disappeared in the process?

'[T]he thesis of this volume is . . . that the Bible loomed uniquely large in Victorian culture in fascinating and underexplored ways', writes Timothy Larsen, introducing his *A People of One Book*.[4] My own thesis is that one of these underexplored stories is the story of Victorian Bibles as material objects. This particular prism is a way of seeing Larsen's 'One Book' refracted into a multiplicity of books: Bibles annotated with family events, miniature 'Thumb Bibles', calf-bound and gilt-edged Bibles, lectern Bibles, pocket Bibles, cheap Bibles for schools and the poor.[5] Victorian Bible use was not limited to devotional or any other kind of reading: as Leah Price has shown, there were many ways of 'doing things with books' in this period, some of them documented in it-narratives like *The History of an Old Pocket Bible* (1812) or *The Story of a Red Velvet Bible* (1862).[6] Victorian Bibles influenced changes in the printing and bookbinding industries, such as those examined by Leslie Howsam, and are connected with the histories of labour, empire, education and the status of women.[7]

For readers of Victorian literature, the Bible offers plenty to think about without invoking these material questions. The Bible was a source of ideas and language; it was the subject of new hermeneutic trends. This is, after all, the level at which Benjamin Jowett argues for interpreting Scripture 'like any other book': '[t]he book itself remains as at the first unchanged amid the changing interpretations of it'.[8] 'Change' is changeable: Charles LaPorte puts a 'changing Bible' in the title of his study of the higher criticism and its influence on poetic experiments, while for Norman Vance what changes in this period is the extent of the Bible's authority.[9] These different approaches all take the Bible as text rather than book, The Bible rather than Bibles, words and concepts rather than ink and paper. Yet the ink-and-papery Bibles are near enough to reach in one quick Henry-Tilney-ish sidestep: when Catherine Morland asks, 'But now really, do not you think Udolpho the nicest book in the world?', Henry Tilney replies, 'The nicest; – by which I suppose you mean the neatest. That must depend upon the binding.'[10] Flipping from text to book is a bracingly down-to-earth move; the joke would do for any book, but has a special purpose here, bursting the bubble of Catherine Morland's sensationalism. Bibles, too, are printed and bound 'like any other book', while the Bible also has its own peculiarities, being unusually long, idiosyncratically subdivided, widely venerated and extensively disagreed about. Yet when materiality is the starting point, we have a grounded way of thinking into people's devotional and reading habits and imaginative lives. It is complicated to find out what people believe, but we can ask what they do with their books. The materiality of the Bible is like G. K. Chesterton's postman: so familiar that nobody even saw him, and yet he proved to be the murderer, the Invisible Man.[11]

In this chapter, I would like to think about how readers react to unexpected ways of handling books, and what readers of fiction might make of readers in fiction whose book-handling habits take them by surprise. What counts as damage and what counts as honourable wear and tear? Which marks in books are proof of faith, or at least of good reading, and what feels like sacrilege? These questions are particularly loaded when the book in question is deemed to be holy. Copies of the Bible attract special treatment, even when they are not handled in a deliberately reverent way. From the early nineteenth century, the British and Foreign Bible Society (BFBS) distributed Bibles bound with extra strong covers – as Leslie Howsam says, 'to withstand the intensive use that evangelicals made of their Bibles'.[12] In turn, the signs of wear and tear to the volume became a spiritual status symbol. You might find an evangelical magazine asking, 'My child, which have you: a *dusty* or a *well-worn* Bible?'[13] Dust on the cover means the volume has not been read, while 'well-worn' implies regular reading. But if some Bibles are well-worn, are there any that are worn wrongly? And who gets to decide what counts as 'wrong'?

What we can agree on is that a worn or damaged book often tells a story about its reader. I will focus on one novel, and one Bible described in it. If you take that material Bible and give it a material shake, a different set of meanings comes fluttering out (loose leaves, pressed flowers) than critical approaches discover without that emphasis. There will be a risk of seeming to read too much into one example: its potency will show that the material Bible is an Invisible Man of Victorian letters, wandering in and out of texts and histories without critics always noticing the meanings it carries. Even when placed simply as an appropriate prop, it might spill out into twenty-seven separate *brochures*. The Bible in question is a *new* New Testament; the novel is *Jude the Obscure*.

A re-arranged Bible

Jude the Obscure is a novel full of books and reading, and of biblical allusion and quotation. The Bible I consider here belongs to Sue Bridehead,

Jude's cousin and lover and the novel's other main character. Where Jude begins with a kind of dogged, dubious Christian faith, closely linked with his fantasies about scholarship, Sue begins with an assumed confidence of intellectual scepticism. She describes her '*new* New Testament' in a conversation early in their friendship, after making an illicit escape from her teaching training college and wading through a river in order to visit Jude at night. He is still pursuing theological study and regular devotional practices, so while he says his evening prayers, she turns away and looks through a small Bible as she waits for him.

> 'Jude,' she said brightly, when he had finished and come back to her; 'will you let me make you a *new* New Testament – like the one I made for myself at Christminster?'
>
> 'O yes. How was that made?'
>
> 'I altered my old one by cutting up all the Epistles and Gospels into separate *brochures*, and re-arranging them in chronological order as written, beginning the book with Thessalonians, following on with the Epistles, and putting the Gospels much further on. Then I had the volume rebound. My University friend Mr.——but never mind his name, poor boy – said it was an excellent idea. I know that reading it afterwards made it twice as interesting as before, and twice as understandable.'
>
> 'H'm,' said Jude, with a sense of sacrilege.[14]

'Brightly' she renews their conversation, but she is soon in tears again, and not much later he is 'rather more ruffled than she'. The scene is charged, not only with Jude's 'sense of sacrilege' and 'sense of her sex', but also with Sue's rapidly shifting feelings: she finds the chapter headings 'the drollest thing', then becomes 'spirited, and almost petulant', then besieged: 'nobody is ever on my side'. At the centre of this discussion are two Bibles: Jude's, and the restitched New Testament she describes (III.4, pp. 145–7).

Bibles are freighted in *Jude* with a threatening meaning. Earlier, the square-cut title page lettering of Jude's Greek New Testament expressed 'fixed reproach in the grey starlight' on his having left his desk to meet Arabella (I.7, p. 43). The scholarly credentials of this edition are given, and his feelings about it: '[h]e was proud of the book, having obtained it by boldly writing to its London publisher' (I.7, p. 38). It is his book specifically, unique and single, unlike Mercy Chant's 'armful of Bibles' in *Tess of the D'Urbervilles*, a superfluity of volumes savagely associated with an evangelicalism that '[sacrificed] humanity to mysticism'.[15] Jude's dogged labour is remembered in this dog-eared Testament after his death; the material Bible, 'roughened with stone-dust', is an emblem of his failed ideals (VI.11, p. 396).

For Sue, Bibles represent a different danger. Her '*new* New Testament' should be read with attention to her intellectual poise and complex sensitivities. Manuscript corrections show Hardy laboriously adding emotional nuance during composition. He changes his mind twice about 'moist' eyes (Figure 7.1). He allows Sue an emotion about her emotions, replacing 'tears running down her cheeks' with 'turning away her face that he might not see her brimming eyes' (Figure 7.2). And as Jude and Sue shake hands, their feelings are peeled apart so that each has a different realisation rather than sharing the same one (Figure 7.3). If some readers share Jude's surprise 'at her introducing personal feeling into mere argument', others might sympathise with Sue's hatred of 'humbug' and the intensity of her resistance to the interpretations of the powerful: 'nobody is ever on my side . . . You are on the side of the people in the Training School' (III.4, p. 146). Yet commentators on Hardy have favoured an iconoclastic reading of this scene. Elisabeth Jay says that Sue 'taunted' Jude; Mary Rimmer reads her activity as deconstructive, destructive: '[t]he characters subject the Bible to physical dismemberment as well as irreverent quotation: Sue Bridehead literally cuts it up, rearranging it in a textual parody'.[16] Rimmer

> great & passionate song!" Her speech had grown spirited, & almost petu-
> deary
> lant, ‸^at his rebuke,^ & her eyes ~~moist~~. "I wish I had a ~~fru~~ friend here to support me;
>
> but nobody is ‸^ever^ on my side!"

Figure 7.1. *Jude the Obscure:* Chapter One. Autograph manuscript. Hardy, Thomas (British, 1840–1928). 436 pages. Ink on paper, 26.5cm × 29cm, circa 1894, published 1895, p. 156. Quoted from the manuscript by permission of The Fitzwilliam Museum, Cambridge. MS 1-1911.

> turning away her face that he might
> "Yes you are, yes you are!" she cried, ~~tears running down her cheeks.~~
> not see her brimming eyes.
> ‸ "You are on the side of the people in the Training School __ at least you
>
> seem almost to be!

Figure 7.2. *Jude the Obscure:* Chapter One. Autograph manuscript. Hardy, Thomas (British, 1840–1928). 436 pages. Ink on paper, 26.5cm × 29cm, circa 1894, published 1895, p. 157. Quoted from the manuscript by permission of The Fitzwilliam Museum, Cambridge. MS 1-1911.

130   LUCY SIXSMITH

> to its softest note of
> "But you are not to say it now!" ~~say~~, " she replied, her voice ~~quite~~ changeding.
> severity.   like ~~smiled~~   cronies in a tavern, & ~~saw~~ Jude saw
> ∧ Then their eyes met, & they shook hands, ~~& laughed~~ ⟨ at the absurdity of quar-
>   a hypothetical
> relling on such ~~an abstr~~ subject., & she the silliness of crying about what was written
> in an old book like the bible.

Figure 7.3. *Jude the Obscure:* Chapter One. Autograph manuscript. Hardy, Thomas (British, 1840–1928). 436 pages. Ink on paper, 26.5cm × 29cm, circa 1894, published 1895, p. 157. Quoted from the manuscript by permission of The Fitzwilliam Museum, Cambridge. MS 1-1911.

draws on Joss Marsh's argument that the novel 'commits blasphemy with a vengeance' and on Marjorie Garson's vivid account of Sue, which construes her experiment as dissolution or 'antisacramental *sparagmos*' (that is, an act of tearing apart, or a ritual dismembering of a classical hero).[17] Without wishing to contradict these readings exactly, I would suggest that they are not the only possibilities. Alternative perspectives on Sue's character emerge if we examine her new New Testament as book-historical detectives, taking seriously the manual and intellectual work involved in making this new book.

Forensic bookbinding

One way to uncover alternative meanings of Sue's New Testament is to try the experiment oneself: forensic bookbinding, a parallel to Janet Stephens' work on ancient hairstyles using a professional hairdresser's techniques and skill.[18] I made the attempt with a cheap, modern, glued New Testament, a chopping-board and a vegetable knife (Figures 7.4–7.5), but a nineteenth-century woman working with a properly sewn text block would follow a meticulous process of unpicking. Turning back the front board and pressing down the text block with a ruler, she would gently force the binding outwards, then snip her way into the book's spine. Opening the first gathering, she would cut the thread and tease out stitching bit by bit, freeing each chunk of pages one by one. The New Testament books are all different lengths, so, having cut them apart, she would have a gathering here, a gathering and a half there, some stubs, some loose leaves. To reconstruct the text block Sue would have had to find ways of stitching all these together again, in a sort of amateur exercise in book conservation. It would be careful and precise work, with at least as much effort going into rearranging and reattaching as into detaching and dividing; not so much a destructive activity as a creative and constructive one.

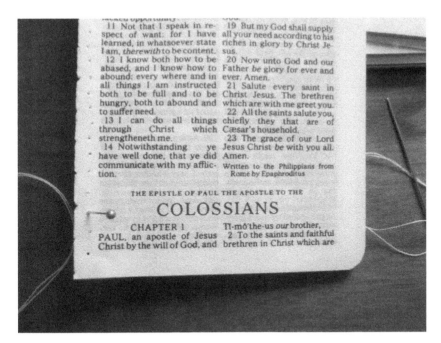

Figure 7.4. The Epistle to the Colossians as a separate brochure. Photograph: Lucy Sixsmith.

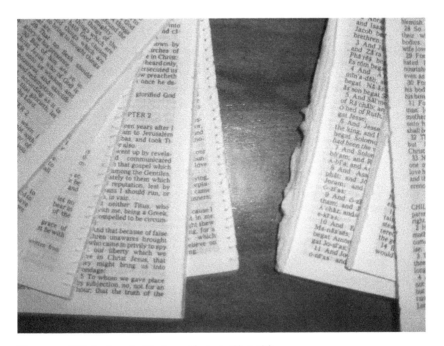

Figure 7.5. Stitched work. Photograph: Lucy Sixsmith.

That the task is constructive and requires skill is implied by Hardy's dialogue. Sue offers to 'make' the book for Jude, perhaps feeling that her artist-shop experience renders her more suited to the task than his as a stonemason. (One introduction to bookbinding states that 'the earlier operations' in the bookbinding process, 'from folding to sewing', were once known as 'the women's departments'.[19]) Jude picks up on the verb 'make', asking 'How was that made?' where he could have said, for example, 'What was that?' or 'What do you mean?' And when Sue speaks of 'cutting up all the Epistles and Gospels into separate *brochures*', the word derives from the French word for stitching: a brochure is 'a stitched work' or 'a few leaves stitched together'.[20] She is conscious of the tactile reality of the material text, and of a task that involves working with, through and between the pages in a controlled and thoughtful way. Jude's sense of sacrilege will come only later and may be read as creeping discomfort rather than outright horror.

This constructive emphasis puts a twist on 'taunt' as a reading of Sue's tone and pulls away from the idea that Sue's alterations are primarily iconoclastic. Rimmer and Garson probably think of 'physical dismemberment' because cutting up is mentioned by Sue, whereas restitching is not; a quickness to discover irreverence which is to take Sue's words on trust. A subtler indication of her attitude is given by punctuation: Sue uses a capital B for Bible twice in this chapter, whereas the narrator refers to 'the bible' as well as 'a bible', distinguishing Sue's earnestness from the narrator's impartiality (III.4, pp. 141, 145–6). The rebound Bible is an investment of labour, attempting to establish meaning more securely through the very risk of structural weakening. This could have been evidence in support of Rimmer's view that *Jude* holds the Bible vulnerably balanced between reverence and scepticism, affection and despair. In a way, Sue is engaging with the text, not recreating it; her project could be thought of as an accelerated version of the wear and tear caused by ordinary reading. Sue's fast-forwarding of the process, like her room-sharing arrangements with her undergraduate friend, is exposed to the readers' judgement or sympathy. Is she right or wrong? Who will throw the first stone?

'An apostle of culture'

The intellectual work that lies behind this project is also more about putting ideas together than taking ideas apart. Sue says in an easy way that she re-arranged the volume 'in chronological order as written, beginning the book with Thessalonians, following on with the Epistles, and putting the Gospels much further on'. But the biblical books do not come with their date of publication attached. By asking what the correct chronological order is, Sue is entering into a field of academic study where there were, and still are, differences of opinion. One modern study Bible suggests that Galatians may be placed in the late 40s or mid-50s AD, Philippians in the mid-50s, late 50s or early 60s, Hebrews between 60 and 95; Revelation contains conflicting evidence, II Corinthians consists of more than one letter, II Thessalonians could be early if written by Paul or impossible to date if not, and Jude is obscure.[21] It is plausible that Sue would have put serious research into this topic, weighing up the evidence and arguments on different sides, and forming her own conclusions.

Some readers have imagined that this must have been an act of resistance against organised, orthodox Christianity. Is her New Testament daringly rebellious in that it 'places the authority of the human reason . . . above any notion of revelation, or the authority of the Church in establishing the canonical order of the books'?[22] This is how J. Russell Perkin describes the scene's 'heretical' nature, while Matthew Bradley gives a differently loaded account: 'Sue Bridehead is an apostle of culture, whose knowledge . . . is sufficient to allow her to rearrange and cut up her New Testament into correct chronological order.'[23] But how sacrilegious is it, after all, to divide a Bible into parts? Some such portionings are taken for granted: as Sue Zemka points out, the circulation of the New Testament without the Old, rarely if ever questioned, is not inevitable given 'the supposed prevalence of typological interpretation'.[24] Divisions can be about resources and practicality. In 1804, Granville Sharp, a member of the Bible Society Committee, proposed that the Society's octavo Bibles could be printed in seven parts so that 'several persons may read & be instructed in different parts of the House or Garden with one single Copy of the Bible at one and the same time'.[25] While the Committee did not catch Sharp's enthusiasm, instalment-plan Family Bibles were being sold elsewhere.[26] Serialised, like Hardy's novel, these Bibles are a unity forcibly divided into time-staggered sections for the readers' convenience, while their adherence to the traditional book order, unlike Sue's Testament, produced an unconventional reading pattern compared to the cyclical reading plans given in lectionaries.[27]

Sue is not unusual, then, in dividing up her Bible, but it is difficult to find real-life parallels to her cutting and restitching procedure.[28] Her New Testament is somewhat like the Little Gidding Gospel harmonies, somewhat like Thomas Jefferson's Bible. But the Ferrar community and Jefferson were both cutting apart paragraphs within books, the former seeking to weave together, the latter preferring to select and omit, whereas Sue works in line with the existing book divisions.[29] The nearest real-life equivalent to Sue's project that I have found was the work of an ordained minister of the Church of England, Rev. Charles Hebert, a Doctor of Divinity, of Trinity College, Cambridge, who in 1882 published a slim volume entitled *The New Testament Scriptures in the Order in which they were Written: A Very Close Translation from the Greek Text of 1611, with Brief Explanations. The First Portion: The Six Primary Epistles to Thessalonica, Corinth, Galatia, and Rome, A.D. 52–58*.[30] Hebert never got beyond this first volume, but included a contents page for four that he had planned, gamely listing the books 'in what is assumed to be something like the chronological order in which they were written'.[31] Evidently rather a character, he also wrote a spirited defence of the 'actual superintendence of the authentic Scriptures (i.e. as originally written) by the Holy Ghost', responding to W. G. Clark: 'and now we live to be told by the Vice-Master of Trinity, that we don't believe the opinions for which we have been content to suffer loss'.[32] This belief in inspiration underpins his chronological New Testament: '[t]he one thing to which the writer clings more and more is the letter of the Scripture, with its Divine Plenary Superintendence and with all its historic human peculiarities'.[33] His pastoral and scholarly motive is that even readers with no Greek may be able to 'watch the first appearance of particular words, and trace their after-growth to a received meaning'.[34] For Hebert, his epigraph from St Jerome, 'The Holy Scriptures – in which even the order of words is a mystery', 'breathes such a spirit of strong confidence in the plenary inspiration of the Holy Scriptures that it sounds like a trumpet in this semi-sceptical age'.[35] It was not intellectual doubt that drove this real-life re-arrangement of the New Testament, but an earnest Christian faith rooted in academic study.

Sue is indeed semi-sceptical, while Charles Hebert was an ordained, scholarly figure of the sort that Jude would never become; orthodox, and not an apostle of culture. But her New Testament might not be a rebellion against the church so much as a simple assertion of her intellectual capacity. Arguments in favour of women's education were gaining traction at this time outside the novel's pages, and women's colleges had opened in Oxford and Cambridge (although women would not be able to take degrees there until 1922 and 1947 respectively). This context is mostly omitted from Sue's story: she does not have a stereotypical Girton girl's bicycle-riding vim, nor is she the severe 'bluestocking' imagined by those who believed that 'excessive intellectual activity conspicuously affect[ed] a woman's outward appearance'.[36] Nor does she ever turn to Christminster on her own account to say: 'I have understanding as well as you' (II. vi, p. 112). Instead, she asserts independence: 'I have no respect for Christminster at all, except, in a qualified degree, on its intellectual side' (III.iv, p. 141). In making her new New Testament, she positions herself as a student outside the college walls. And it is because she is outside that she works creatively with a physical object. She would never have the option of writing and publishing her own translation; cutting up a New Testament is not necessarily a destructive act, or glamorously heretical, but a practical matter of making use of the resources and skills she had to hand.

She is resisting authority, though; if not the church's authority to bind and loose, at least the binding authority of the Bible publisher. The Bible Society's history shows the usefulness of a binding to mediate reading: BFBS Bibles were sold pre-bound for shipping abroad, for lower-class customers unaccustomed to book-purchasing, and because there had been controversy about the inclusion or exclusion of the Apocrypha; pre-bound Bibles could not easily be combined with other texts.[37] By enforcing the BFBS rule of publishing Bibles 'without note or comment', the binding became a comment in itself.[38] Sue chooses not to have these decisions made for her.

Stitched work

But her home experiment would have been mired in practical obstacles. 'Twice as interesting as before, and twice as understandable' rightly has an Alice-like wistfulness, because Sue's idea cannot be realised with a single New Testament. With the end of Matthew printed on the same leaf as the beginning of Mark, the end of Mark on the same leaf as the beginning of Luke, and so on through the whole New Testament, it is impossible to divide one book from the next in a single printed volume. When I tried the experiment, I used two identical Testaments and took half the books from one, half from the other, alternating between the two copies. This means that my new New Testament is full of extra beginnings and ends of books, and its readability is compromised by bits and scraps of extra text appearing in the wrong place (Figure 7.6). I could paste blank paper over the superfluous passages, like the seventh Earl of Shaftesbury, who used two Bibles in this way to produce a single Bible in twenty-five easily portable volumes.[39] Still, it is likely that my new New Testament will be a little messy. In contrast to the neatly aligned edges of a newly cut book, Sue's home binding process draws together a jigsaw pattern of differently shaped pieces. However neatly she works, however firm her stitching, some evidence of the process will be visible, and the text block will have weak points where it did not have them before.

This New Testament, full of stubs and re-sewn leaves, would be like the copy of *The Imperial Family Bible* adapted with pasted-in manuscript

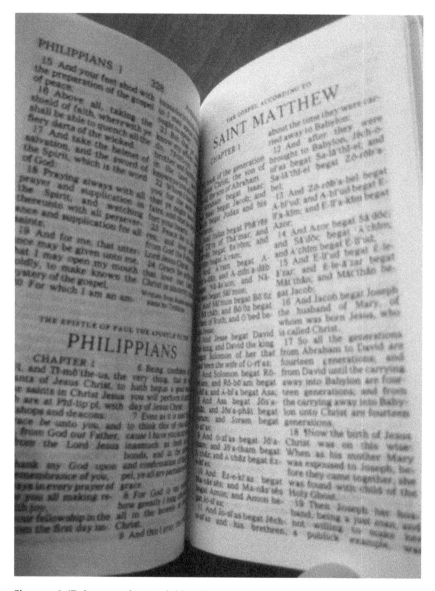

Figure 7.6. 'Twice as understandable'. Photograph: Lucy Sixsmith.

notes by Hester Thrale Piozzi.[40] Each of these Bibles is made materially patchy as its creator works with the text; paper, ink and paste are the visible signs of an intellect forced to operate within and around the parameters of the published book. Sue's Testament is also like Dinah Morris's 'small thick Bible, worn quite round at the edges': both Sue's Bible and Dinah's are marked in their 'physiognomy' by the earnestness of a young, serious, working, female owner.[41] The project proves Sue's mental agility, but she chooses it because it is accessible: she has to cut up her Bible because she has no opportunity to write a new translation from the Greek. 'Since I can do no good because a woman, / Reach constantly at something that is near it': without having Dorothea's idea that classical languages must be necessary 'to arrive at the core of things, and judge soundly on the social duties of the Christian', Sue too is a woman doing her best in uncongenial circumstances.[42] But something says 'you shan't' to a sparkling intelligence when she opens her Bible (VI.2, p. 327).

The new New Testament is a counterpart to the character who made it, then – both more vulnerable and more ferociously held together than a typical volume. It is risky to take a book apart and put it back together, just as it was risky for Sue to break out of her teacher training college and visit Jude against the rules and against social convention. While they have this conversation she herself is rebound in unusual covers, because while her wet clothes dry she is wearing Jude's Sunday suit. In Jude's eyes she is 'a slim and fragile being', 'pathetic in her defencelessness'; she seems physically vulnerable, and emotionally susceptible, although in intellectual acuity and self-reliance she is rather stronger than he is. By the end of Sue's story, another small Testament will symbolise a more explicit threat to her. Jude's 'small Bible' will reappear as 'a little brown Testament' on which her eventual husband Richard Phillotson will ask her to swear that she wishes to enter his bedroom, an act of submission that she has forced herself towards as a 'penance' and a 'duty' (VI.9; pp. 382–6). The contrast is sharp between Sue early in the novel, dressed in men's clothes, confidently turning pages, and Sue, later in the novel, dressed in nightclothes with her hand on the outside of the book. Jude's open book is associated with her well-informed, easy intelligence, her equal standing with men in her powers of mind. Closed, Phillotson's, it represents her impulse to 'drink to the dregs' (VI.9, p. 384). Phillotson is not like Dickens's Magwitch, whom Pip suspects of carrying his 'little black book about the world solely to swear people on in cases of emergency'.[43] He is all the more dangerous because he knows something of the inside of the book as well as the outside and still uses it as an instrument of coercion.

Indeed, in some contexts, binding Bibles was already recognised as a danger to women. High demand for cheap Bibles had driven down wages and the quality of working conditions: with bookbinder strikes on the one hand, there were outraged BFBS supporters on the other, talking of 'Scripture Slaves' and alarmed that these pressures would force female workers into prostitution. Howsam argues that playing upon middle-class anxieties about female sexual purity was a strategic move by advocates for the bookbinders: one memorial 'submit[ted] that the making it more difficult, and in some cases impossible, for females to earn an honest subsistence, by their labour, is in the same proportion to give potency to the seducers of female virtue'.[44] I have not found biographical evidence linking Hardy to these disputes, so it may be fanciful to imagine a connection between the women bookbinders and Sue. But it is a curious and sinister idea, that the binding of these fictional Bibles might have reminded some readers of the real exploitation of vulnerable women.

'I know something of the book'

It may be that all this is to perceive more in Sue's anecdote than Hardy did. He may have set her an impossible task simply because he did not think the project through. On the one hand, a revision to the dialogue shows a concern for accuracy: the serial and first editions offered Romans as the first book in Sue's Testament, which was later amended to the more probable Thessalonians.[45] But on the other hand, the slight clunk in the final rendering, implying that I and II Thessalonians are not Epistles, could indicate that for Hardy the details were not to be minutely weighed (III.4, p. 145). Perhaps, as Leah Price points out, a fictional book need not work the same way as a real one:

> We have a special word for persons when they're represented in fiction ('character'), but none for represented books. Yet both raise analogous questions. Is it legitimate to imagine an offstage life for either (for example, should we picture what news items Crosbie's newspaper contains)? What's the relation between the use we make of the represented object and the use we would make of its real-life referent?[46]

Sue's conversation with Jude flows smoothly enough without the reader imagining her rearranged Bible in full bibliographical detail. But a consequence of taking Sue's book seriously is taking Sue herself more seriously. In pursuing the probable life of the fictional object, even to the point of uncovering contradictions and impossibilities, we have been able to explore the complexities of the character handling it. This is a way to see through the façade if she seems to be 'putting on flippancy to hide real feeling, a common trick with her' (III.4, p. 145). As with the Hampshire woman who ate a New Testament, it may be unexpected earnestness, rather than irreverence, that kindles a 'sense of sacrilege' in the observer (III.4, p. 145). An unconventionally unironic commitment, too much respect rather than too little – her indignant feeling that 'people have no right to falsify the Bible!' – makes Sue 'spirited', 'almost petulant' and tearful (III.4, p.146). Her cutting and stitching of the material Bible is done in defence of the Bible, not as an act of destructive iconoclasm.

The complexity of Sue's relationship with Christianity is important to notice here if the crisis of her later religious breakdown is to be understood. 'But you are not to say it now!' she says to Jude in their early conversation about the Bible (III.4, p.146). After the trauma of their children's deaths, she corrects him in the same way, this time after she startles him by returning from a church service smelling of incense:

> 'You see, Jude, it is lonely here in the week-day mornings, when you are at work, and I think and think of – of my – ' She stopped till she could control the lumpiness of her throat. 'And I have taken to go in there, as it is so near.'

> 'O well – of course, I say nothing against it. Only it is odd, for you. They little think what sort of chiel is amang them!'

> 'What do you mean, Jude?'

> 'Well – a sceptic, to be plain.'

> 'How can you pain me so, dear Jude, in my trouble! Yet I know you didn't mean it. But you ought not to say that.' (VI.3, p.335)

On both occasions, Sue's emotions are further stirred up by Jude's accusations of scepticism: 'You are quite Voltairean!'; 'a sceptic, to be plain'. On both occasions, too, she is the one hampered in making her case by the physical manifestation of distress, whether 'brimming eyes' or 'the lumpiness of her throat' (III.4, p.146, VI.3, p.335). Jude can see that 'Sue and himself had mentally travelled in opposite directions since the tragedy . . . She was no longer the same as in the independent days, when her intellect played like lambent lightning over conventions and formalities which he at that time respected, though he did not now' (VI.3, p.333). It is true that she is no longer the same, declaring now that 'self-abnegation is the higher road. We should mortify the flesh – the terrible flesh – the curse of Adam' (VI.3, p.333). But this response to grief is not simply a neat reversal of her previous attitude, a dazzlingly heretical apostle of culture brought low by the events of the novel. Rather, it is the same Sue before and after, first made raw by her wish to resist 'humbug' and 'ecclesiastical abstraction' but worn down until she can say: 'I should like to prick myself all over with pins and bleed out the badness that's in me' (VI.3, p.334). There is by this time no vision of rearrangement and restitching; she imagines pins applied destructively to herself, rather than a needle applied constructively to the book.

'She had not her Bible before her for nothing.' This quotation has formed a sort of epigraph for this chapter in my mind, although it is not about Sue or any other Victorian reader, but Samuel Richardson's Clarissa Harlowe, whose Bible was opened so often at the book of Job that it developed a permanent inclination that way: '[o]ne opens naturally here, I see', says Sally; 'I make no doubt but you have doubled down the *useful places*, as honest Matt Prior says. . . . – You see, Miss Horton, I know something of the book.'[47] It takes a character who knows something of the book, though perhaps not so much of the text, to make the point that Clarissa's Bible has been shaped by her way of reading it: a mere forefinger of the right hand holding her place alters the book's physical character and shows that her reading of the volume is skewed.[48] The slight distortion of the object reflects a distorted interpretation. Whatever your theology, something must be missing if the only part of the volume being read is the book of Job. A reordered Testament, in contrast, shows an ambition to deal not only with the 'useful places', but with the whole thing. Sue's way of handling her New Testament is an attempt to do justice to the text, and even if, in fact, she had her Bible before her for nothing, it is right for Hardy's readers to do justice in turn, as far as possible, to her method of reading.

Notes

1. Matthew 4.4 (KJV).

2. David Cressy, 'Books as Totems in Seventeenth-Century England and New England', *Journal of Library History* (1974–87), 21(1) (1986), 92–106 (p. 99), citing *Notes and Queries*, 9th ser. 8 (1901), p. 103. (Cressy gives 'sides' for 'slices'.)

3. *Notes and Queries*, p. 103; Timothy Larsen, *A People of One Book: The Bible and the Victorians* (Oxford: Oxford University Press, 2011), pp. 262–3.

4. Larsen, *A People*, p. 1.

5. Leah Price, *How to Do Things with Books in Victorian Britain* (Princeton and Oxford: Princeton University Press, 2012), p. 40; Alyssa J. Currie, 'The Victorian Thumb Bible as Material Object: Charles Tilt's *The Little Picture Testament* (1839)', *Cahiers Victoriens et Édouardiens* [Online], 2016, https://doi.org/10.4000/cve.2910, accessed 10 February 2022; Leslie Howsam, *Cheap Bibles: Nineteenth-Century Publishing and the British and Foreign Bible Society* (Cambridge: Cambridge University Press, 1991) pp. 100, 122.

6. Price, *How to Do Things with Books*, pp. 107–35.

7. See note 5.

8. Benjamin Jowett, 'On the Interpretation of Scripture', in *Essays and Reviews* (London: John W. Parker and Son, West Strand, 1860), pp. 330–433 (pp. 338, 337–8).

9. Charles LaPorte, *Victorian Poets and the Changing Bible* (Charlottesville: University of Virginia Press, 2011); Norman Vance, *Bible and Novel: Narrative Authority and the Death of God* (Oxford: Oxford University Press, 2013).

10. Jane Austen, *Northanger Abbey*, ed. by Barbara M. Benedict and Deirdre Le Faye (Cambridge: Cambridge University Press, 2006), vol. 1, ch. 14, p. 109.

11. G. K. Chesterton, 'The Invisible Man', in *The Complete Father Brown* (London: Penguin Books, 1981), pp. 64–77.

12. Howsam, *Cheap Bibles*, pp. 124–5.

13. Price, *How to Do Things with Books*, p. 38.

14. Thomas Hardy, *Jude the Obscure*, ed. by Patricia Ingham, rev. edn (Oxford: Oxford University Press, 2002), Book III, ch. 4, p. 145. Based on the 1912 edition, with emendations, adopting the manuscript punctuation. Subsequent references are given in the text in the form 'III.4'.

15. Thomas Hardy, *Tess of the d'Urbervilles*, ed. by Juliet Grindle and Simon Gatrell (Oxford: Clarendon Press, 1983), ch. 40 (p. 370).

16. Elisabeth Jay, 'Introduction', in *The Blackwell Companion to the Bible in English Literature*, ed. by Rebecca Lemon et al. (Oxford: Wiley-Blackwell, 2009), pp. 465–81 (p. 478); Mary Rimmer, '"My Scripture Manner": Reading Hardy's Biblical and Liturgical Allusion', in *Thomas Hardy Re-Appraised: Essays in Honour of Michael Millgate*, ed. by Keith Wilson (Toronto: University of Toronto Press, 2006), pp. 20–37 (p. 28).

17. Joss Marsh, *Word Crimes: Blasphemy, Culture, and Literature in Nineteenth-Century England* (Chicago, IL: University of Chicago Press, 1998), pp. 269–327 (pp. 270–71); Marjorie Garson, *Hardy's Fables of Integrity: Woman, Body, Text* (Oxford: Oxford University Press, 1991), pp. 152–79 (p. 164); 'sparagmos, n.', *OED Online*, Oxford University Press, December 2021, https://www.oed.com/view/Entry /185634, accessed 10 February 2022.

18. Janet Stephens, 'Ancient Roman Hairdressing: On (Hair)Pins and Needles', *Journal of Roman Archaeology*, 21 (2008), 110–32. The phrase 'forensic hairdressing' is used in Stephens' videos, for example, https://www.youtube.com/watch?v =68LEUXw2QJU, accessed 10 February 2022.

19. Lionel S. Darley, *Introduction to Bookbinding* (London: Faber & Faber, 1965), p. 15.

20. 'brochure, n.', *OED Online*, Oxford University Press, December 2021, www.oed .com/view/Entry/23561, accessed 2 February 2022.

21. *The HarperCollins Study Bible Student Edition: Fully Revised and Updated*, ed. by Harold W. Attridge and Wayne A. Meeks (New York: HarperCollins, 2006).

22. J. Russell Perkin, 'Thomas Hardy's Apocryphal Gospels', in *Theology and the Victorian Novel* (Montreal and London: McGill-Queen's University Press, 2009), pp. 159–95 (p. 185).

23. Matthew Bradley, 'Religion and the Canon', in *The Oxford Handbook of Victorian Literary Culture*, ed. by Juliet John (Oxford: Oxford University Press, 2016), pp. 367–83 (p. 382).

24. Sue Zemka, *Victorian Testaments: The Bible, Christology and Literary Authority in Early-Nineteenth-Century British Culture* (Stanford, CA: Stanford University Press, 1997), p. 131.

25. Howsam, *Cheap Bibles*, p. 101.

26. Mary Wilson Carpenter, *Imperial Bibles, Domestic Bodies: Women, Sexuality, and Religion in the Victorian Market* (Athens, OH: Ohio University Press, 2003), pp. 1–47.

27. Wilson Carpenter, *Imperial Bibles*, p. 44.

28. David Pearson suggested to me that there could be homemade experiments extant in private archives. Also, the fragile results of such experiments would make them more vulnerable to damage than conventional books.

29. Little Gidding concordance, 1630. A 1275.5. Houghton Library, Harvard University, Cambridge, MA, http://nrs.harvard.edu/urn-3:FHCL.HOUGH:10090806, accessed 10 February 2022; Owen Edwards, 'How Thomas Jefferson Created His Own Bible', *Smithsonian*, January 2012, https://www.smithsonianmag.com/arts-culture/how-thomas-jefferson-created-his-own-Bible-5659505/, accessed 10 February 2022.

30. Charles Hebert, *The New Testament Scriptures in the Order in which they were Written: A Very Close Translation from the Greek Text of 1611, with Brief Explanations. The First Portion: The Six Primary Epistles to Thessalonica, Corinth, Galatia, and Rome, A.D. 52–58* (London: Henry Frowde, Oxford University Press Warehouse, Seeley, Jackson, and Halliday, 1882). Hereafter *New Testament Scriptures*.

31. *Historical Catalogue of Printed Editions of the English Bible, 1525–1961*, ed. by A. S. Herbert, T. H. Darlow, and H. F. Moule, 2nd edn (London: The British and Foreign Bible Society, 1968), p. 430; *New Testament Scriptures*, p. v.

32. Charles Hebert, *A Reply to the Pamphlet of The Rev. W. G. Clark, M.A., Vice-Master of Trinity College, Entitled The Dangers of the Church of England* (London: Macmillan and Co., 1870), pp. 5, 18.

33. *New Testament Scriptures*, p. ix.

34. *New Testament Scriptures*, pp. vii.

35. *New Testament Scriptures*, pp. i, xi.

36. Chris Willis, '"Heaven Defend Me from Political or Highly-Educated Women!": Packaging the New Woman for Mass Consumption', in *The New Woman in Fiction and Fact: Fin-de-Siècle Feminisms*, ed. by Angelique Richardson and Chris Willis (Basingstoke: Palgrave Macmillan), pp. 55–7; Jane Thomas, *Thomas Hardy, Femininity and Dissent: Reassessing the 'Minor' Novels* (Basingstoke: Macmillan, 1999), p. 31.

37. Howsam, *Cheap Bibles*, pp. 123, 129, 13–14.

38. Howsam, *Cheap Bibles*, p. 6.

39. *The Holy Bible* (London: printed by George Eyre and Andrew Strachan, 1828), Cambridge University Library, BSS.201.E28.19–43.

40. Wilson Carpenter, *Imperial Bibles*, p. 49.

41. George Eliot, *Adam Bede*, ed. by Stephen Gill (London: Penguin, 1985), ch. 15 (p. 204).

42. George Eliot, *Middlemarch*, ed. by Bert G. Hornback (London: W. W. Norton, 1977), p. 1 (ch. I epigraph from Beaumont and Fletcher's *The Maid's Tragedy*), ch. 7 (p. 42).

43. Charles Dickens, *Great Expectations*, ed. by Edgar Rosenberg (London: W. W. Norton, 1999), ch. 40 (p. 250).

44. Howsam, pp. 134–5.

45. See Timothy Hands, *Thomas Hardy: Distracted Preacher?* (New York: Palgrave Macmillan, 1989), p. 32.

46. Price, *How to Do Things with Books*, pp. 49–50.

47. Samuel Richardson, *Clarissa, or, The History of a Young Lady*, ed. by Angus Ross (Harmondsworth: Penguin, 1985), Letter 336 (p. 1071), Letter 333 (p. 1061).

48. Richardson, *Clarissa*, Letter 334 (p. 1065).

Bibliography of secondary literature

Attridge, Harold W. and Wayne A. Meeks (eds), *The HarperCollins Study Bible Student Edition: Fully Revised and Updated* (New York: HarperCollins, 2006)

Bradley, Matthew, 'Religion and the Canon', in *The Oxford Handbook of Victorian Literary Culture*, ed. by Juliet John (Oxford: Oxford University Press, 2016) pp. 367–83

Carpenter, Mary Wilson, *Imperial Bibles, Domestic Bodies: Women, Sexuality, and Religion in the Victorian Market* (Athens, OH: Ohio University Press, 2003)

Cressy, David, 'Books as Totems in Seventeenth-Century England and New England', *Journal of Library History* (1974–87), 21(1) (1986), 92–106

Currie, Alyssa J., 'The Victorian Thumb Bible as Material Object: Charles Tilt's *The Little Picture Testament* (1839)', *Cahiers Victoriens et Édouardiens* [Online], 2016 https://doi.org/10.4000/cve.2910

Darley, Lionel S., *Introduction to Bookbinding* (London: Faber & Faber, 1965)

Edwards, Owen, 'How Thomas Jefferson Created His Own Bible', *Smithsonian*, January 2012, https://www.smithsonianmag.com/arts-culture/how-thomas-jefferson-created-his-own-Bible-5659505/

Garson, Marjorie, *Hardy's Fables of Integrity: Woman, Body, Text* (Oxford: Oxford University Press, 1991), pp. 152–79

Hands, Timothy, *Thomas Hardy: Distracted Preacher?* (New York: Palgrave Macmillan, 1989)

Hebert, Charles, *A Reply to the Pamphlet of The Rev. W.G. Clark, M.A., Vice-Master of Trinity College, Entitled The Dangers of the Church of England* (London: Macmillan and Co., 1870)

Hebert, Charles, *The New Testament Scriptures in the Order in which they were Written: A Very Close Translation from the Greek Text of 1611, with Brief Explanations. The First Portion: The Six Primary Epistles to Thessalonica, Corinth, Galatia, and Rome, A.D. 52–58* (London: Henry Frowde, Oxford University Press Warehouse, Seeley, Jackson, and Halliday, 1882)

Herbert, A. S., T. H. Darlow, and H. F. Moule (eds), *Historical Catalogue of Printed Editions of the English Bible, 1525–1961*, 2nd edn (London: The British and Foreign Bible Society, 1968)

Howsam, Leslie, *Cheap Bibles: Nineteenth-Century Publishing and the British and Foreign Bible Society* (Cambridge: Cambridge University Press, 1991)

Jay, Elisabeth, 'Introduction', in *The Blackwell Companion to the Bible in English Literature*, ed. by Rebecca Lemon et al. (Oxford: Wiley-Blackwell, 2009), pp. 465–81

Jowett, Benjamin, 'On the Interpretation of Scripture', in *Essays and Reviews* (London: John W. Parker and Son, West Strand, 1860), pp. 330–433

LaPorte, Charles, *Victorian Poets and the Changing Bible* (Charlottesville: University of Virginia Press, 2011)

Larsen, Timothy, *A People of One Book: The Bible and the Victorians* (Oxford: Oxford University Press, 2011)

Marsh, Joss, *Word Crimes: Blasphemy, Culture, and Literature in Nineteenth-Century England* (Chicago, IL: University of Chicago Press, 1998)

Perkin, J. Russell, *Theology and the Victorian Novel* (Montreal: McGill-Queen's University Press, 2009)

Price, Leah, *How to Do Things with Books in Victorian Britain* (Princeton, NJ: Princeton University Press, 2012)

Rimmer, Mary, '"My Scripture Manner": Reading Hardy's Biblical and Liturgical Allusion', in *Thomas Hardy Re-Appraised: Essays in Honour of Michael Millgate*, ed. by Keith Wilson (Toronto: University of Toronto Press, 2006), pp. 20–37

Stephens, Janet, 'Ancient Roman Hairdressing: On (Hair)Pins and Needles', *Journal of Roman Archaeology*, 21 (2008), 110–32

Thomas, Jane, *Thomas Hardy, Femininity and Dissent: Reassessing the 'Minor' Novels* (Basingstoke: Macmillan, 1999)

Vance, Norman, *Bible and Novel: Narrative Authority and the Death of God* (Oxford: Oxford University Press, 2013)

Willis, Chris, '"Heaven Defend Me from Political or Highly-Educated Women!": Packaging the New Woman for Mass Consumption', in *The New Woman in Fiction and Fact: Fin-de-Siècle Feminisms*, ed. by Angelique Richardson and Chris Willis (Basingstoke: Palgrave Macmillan), pp. 53–65

Zemka, Sue, *Victorian Testaments: The Bible, Christology and Literary Authority in Early-Nineteenth-Century British Culture* (Stanford, CA: Stanford University Press, 1997)

Chapter 8

'A fire fed on books': books and reading in D. H. Lawrence's *Sons and Lovers*

Susan Watson

> *They began by talking books: it was their unfailing topic. Mrs Morel had said that [Paul's] and Miriam's affair was like a fire fed on books – if there were no more volumes, it would die out.*[1]

D. H. Lawrence's novel *Sons and Lovers* (1913) is liberally scattered with references and allusions to other works of literature. These begin with the Bible (Paul Morel, the novel's main protagonist, is named after St Paul) and go on to encompass the novels of Sir Walter Scott, the poetry of William Wordsworth and Thomas Hood, Charles Baudelaire's *Les Fleurs du Mal* and even the popular romances of Annie S. Swan. In addition, many of the main characters in the novel are described at least partly in terms of their attitude to books and to reading. Whether they read, what they read, and in some cases how well, or in what manner, they read provides crucial information about them and positions them in relation to the other characters. One of the central relationships in the novel, the ten-year friendship and later love affair of Paul Morel and Miriam Leivers, is said to be largely initiated and sustained through their shared reading. This chapter will examine the act of reading as it is represented in *Sons and Lovers*. It will also explore the significance of some of the specific works of literature cited in the novel, many of which are highly suggestive in the context of the narrative. In *Sons and Lovers* reading is sometimes a communal activity that signals a shared purpose or offers mutual support, but it is often a source of tension and conflict that divides the characters from one another, particularly where they cannot approach the texts together as equals.

Reading as cooperation

Sons and Lovers can be read in the context of some of the various movements concerned with working-class self-education in the late nineteenth century. Paul Morel's mother Gertrude is involved in the Co-operative Women's Guild, an organisation that brought working-class women together and encouraged them to help themselves and each other. The Guild encouraged wide reading: the concluding chapter of the 1931 anthology *Life As We Have Known It* is a collection of extracts from the writings of Guildswomen, many of which list and describe books that the authors have read.[2] When Paul leaves school it is the Co-op reading room that he visits to search the newspapers for job advertisements; earlier in the novel his elder brother William's first job was as a clerk in the Co-op office. Lawrence also describes the 'decent little library' in Bestwood: a subscription library open one evening a week in two small rooms in the Mechanics Hall, 'warm with a great fire in the corner' (ch. 7, p. 190), where Paul and Miriam meet each other when they go to change books for themselves and their families.[3] Clara Dawes, Paul's later lover, has acquired what Lawrence describes as 'a fair amount of education' (ch. 10, p. 306) through her involvement in the women's movement. Miriam Leivers owns a copy of *Palgrave's Golden Treasury of Songs and Lyrics*, a popular anthology first published in 1861 and compiled by Francis T. Palgrave and the then poet laureate, Alfred Tennyson. The *Golden Treasury* was highly influential in developing the tastes of the largely self-taught: 'Racing to make up educational deficits, autodidacts often resorted to prepackaged collections of classics.'[4] In her memoir *D. H. Lawrence: A Personal Record*, Jessie Chambers explains that the *Golden Treasury* became 'a kind of Bible' to them both: 'Lawrence carried the little red volume in his pocket and read to me on every opportunity, usually out in the fields.'[5]

In his book *The Intellectual Life of the British Working Classes*, Jonathan Rose describes what he calls 'mutual improvement': 'Education was a social activity, not essentially different from the fellowship of the pub, chapel, or trade union. Knowledge was something to be shared around.'[6] Paul and the Leivers family have 'bitter debates on the nationalising of the land, and similar problems' (ch. 7, p. 189). Later, they read *Macbeth*, using 'penny books' and taking parts. Together they go to meetings of the Literary Society in Bestwood. William Morel exchanges lessons with a Frenchman and Paul learns French and algebra from his godfather, who

BOOKS AND READING IN D. H. LAWRENCE'S *SONS AND LOVERS*   147

is a clergyman. He in turn attempts to teach these subjects to Miriam, with complicated and often painful results.[7]

Episodes where one character reads aloud to another are ostensibly an act of love or companionship but can be similarly complicated or unsuccessful. Paul's father makes 'an effort to come back somewhat to the old relationship of the first months of their marriage' by attempting to read the newspaper to his wife as she sews: 'slowly pronouncing and delivering the words like a man pitching quoits. Often she hurried him on, giving him a phrase in anticipation. And then he took her words humbly' (ch. 3, p. 63). The reading is an offering that Mrs Morel accepts reluctantly. She is impatient with Morel's clumsy attempt to enter into her world of words and ideas; she has already rejected him. Later in the novel, Paul reads a narrative poem that mentions Mablethorpe, the Morel family's holiday destination, aloud to Miriam, but of necessity the rest of the family also listen and their responses are lukewarm. Mrs Morel wishes that everything written were not so sad and then interrupts Miriam's attempts to discuss the poem with Paul, taking the conversation off at a tangent. Morel, who has listened as if the reading had been a sermon, responds dismissively: 'I canna see what they want drownin' theirselves for' (ch. 7, p. 212).

However, the act of reading itself is most often not shared and cooperative, but solitary and silent.

'She sat reading alone, as she always did'

There are several occasions in the novel where solitary reading is mentioned or described, usually quite briefly. These include glimpses of Gertrude Morel consulting books as she writes a paper for the Co-operative Women's Guild and of Clara Dawes sitting reading in the parlour during a visit to Miriam's family. These scenes illustrate the intellectual independence of both women, but they also subtly indicate their isolation. Mrs Morel is supported and mentally stimulated by the Guild, but it is resented by 'hostile husbands who found their wives getting too independent' (ch. 3, p. 69). Clara is apparently reading because she has momentarily been left alone and this points to her self-sufficiency and detachment, but she is separated from her husband; her situation is discussed and her unhappiness speculated on in detail later in the chapter. Miriam's elder brothers do not share or understand her literary tastes; they ridicule her for never daring to do anything except recite poetry. 'She can do nowt' but go about thinkin' herself somebody – "The Lady of the Lake" – yah!' (ch. 6, p. 156). Reading can also be a defensive measure or a deliberate means of shutting other people out. When during a seaside holiday Mrs Morel criticises Paul and Miriam for coming in late from a walk together, both of them retreat uncomfortably in this way: 'And she took no further notice of him that evening. Which he pretended neither to notice nor to care about, but sat reading. Miriam read also, obliterating herself' (ch. 7, p. 216). In the following chapter, Paul returns home from an evening with Miriam to his mother's (at first) silent reproaches: 'She sat reading, alone, as she always did' (ch. 8, p. 228). After Paul is late home yet again, he pretends to read in an attempt to avoid the inevitable confrontation with his mother and his sister: 'He knew his mother wanted to upbraid him' (ch. 8, p. 250). A book may be a weapon, as well as a shield.

It could also be argued that the readers in the book are themselves separated from the readers of the book. Many of the central characters in the novel have clearly done a great deal of silent, solitary and quite intense reading; this is implied by the titles of the books that Lawrence alludes to or that his characters mention in conversation, such as the works of Herbert Spencer, Ernest Renan's biography *Vie de Jésus* and the novels of Honoré de Balzac. Yet Lawrence never enters into the mind of characters as they engage with a text in the act of solitary reading. In contrast, James Joyce's hero Stephen Dedalus savours the sentences in Doctor Cornwell's Spelling Book that are 'like poetry'. As a student Stephen searches for 'the essence of beauty amid the spectral words of Aristotle or of Aquinas'. He remembers learning to construe the *Metamorphoses* of Ovid 'in a courtly English, made whimsical by the mention of porkers and potsherds and chines of bacon'; this leads him on to other memories of learning Latin and the 'ragged book' that he learned it from; he thinks that other human fingers touched the pages, fifty years ago. 'The dusky verses were as fragrant as though they had laid all those years in myrtle and lavender and vervain.'[8] In Virginia Woolf's novel *To the Lighthouse* Mrs Ramsay browses through an unnamed book of poetry, chanting the lines to herself and noticing the images that they call up: 'She felt that she was climbing backwards, upwards, shoving her way up over petals that curved over her, so that she only knew this is white, or this is red.'[9] In *Sons and Lovers* we may be told that characters are reading, but not *what* they are reading or what the physical text or the words themselves evoke for them in the moment of reading.

'He went on reading, but she did not hear'

On two occasions the novel enters into the mind of Miriam as Paul reads aloud to her. The first of these occurs in the chapter 'Strife in Love' and will be discussed later in this essay. The second occasion comes during a period

BOOKS AND READING IN D. H. LAWRENCE'S *SONS AND LOVERS*   149

of tension in their relationship, after they have agreed not to get engaged. One Sunday evening after chapel Paul reads a chapter of the Gospel of St John while the couple are momentarily alone in the Morel kitchen:

> As he sat in the arm-chair, reading, intent, his voice only thinking, she felt as if he were using her unconsciously, as a man uses his tools at some work he is bent on. She loved it. And the wistfulness of his voice was like a reaching to something, and it was as if she were what he reached with. She sat back on the sofa, away from him, and yet feeling herself the very instrument his hand grasped. It gave her great pleasure.
>
> Then he began to falter, and to get self-conscious. And when he came to the verse: 'A woman, when she is in travail, hath sorrow because her hour is come', he missed it out. Miriam had felt him growing uncomfortable. She shrank when the well-known words did not follow. He went on reading, but she did not hear. A grief and shame made her bend her head. Six months ago, he would have read it simply. (ch. 9, p. 268)

Miriam's response is to the act of Paul reading, rather than to the actual words being read. The first paragraph recalls the more positive and productive aspects of their literary relationship: sharing his own response to the Gospel and his thoughts about religion (they have been discussing the sermon) enables Paul to work out and clarify his own ideas. Miriam is content to be used in this way. She has realised that her ability to listen makes her of value to Paul. She is a tool and he has reached for her, he has reached out to her, he holds her. Yet this image of emotional connection and fulfilment follows closely after a passage written from Paul's point of view in which the language is aggressive and almost punitive. 'Miriam was the threshing floor on which he threshed out all his beliefs. While he trampled his ideas upon her soul, the truth came out for him . . . Almost impassive, she submitted to his argument and expounding' (ch. 9, p. 267). Paul *uses* Miriam in both senses of the word. And in the second paragraph above it is the words themselves, but words that must be suppressed, that recall them both to what divides them and obstructs their relationship: the issues of biology, birth and begetting.

Sometimes reading itself is obstructed or does not happen. Early in the novel Morel makes an attempt at housework so that his heavily pregnant wife can sit and read her books, but after he has left for the pit, Mrs Morel finds the house tidy but dirty and cannot rest until she has thoroughly cleaned it. William's fiancée, Lily, has to be left alone during a visit to the Morel family and Mrs Morel finds her 'a little thing of Annie Swan's' to read.[10] But Lily is a poor reader: 'It was pathetic to see her, on a wet afternoon, wading in misery through a few lines. She never got beyond the second page.' Morel sympathises with her: "Er canna see what there is i' books, ter sit borin' your nose in 'em for, no more can I' (ch. 6, pp. 160–161). Like Lily, Morel is virtually illiterate; he went into the pit when he was ten. He reads last night's paper while he eats his solitary breakfast before setting off to work, 'what of it he could, spelling it over laboriously' (ch. 2, p. 38). Lack of literacy links these characters and emphasises that they are both outsiders within the family, as well as unsuitable and potentially unsatisfying partners for those who do read.

The original book

The first book mentioned in *Sons and Lovers* is a Bible that was given to Gertrude Morel by John Field, a friend with whom she walked home from chapel and who (it is implied) she might once have hoped to marry. Instead, he married 'a woman of forty, a widow with property' (ch. 1, p. 17). Gertrude has 'preserved' his Bible – Lawrence uses that phrase twice – although she never speaks of him. The Bible is positioned in the novel as the original book: the one that comes before all the others, in both senses. But for Gertrude, the Bible is associated with disappointment: 'She understood pretty well what he might or might not have been.' It is also associated, in the early chapters, with an attempt to preserve something of the intellectual and spiritual life that she might have enjoyed, had she not made what is now clearly a disastrous marriage. Gertrude befriends the Congregational minister, who has recently lost his wife in childbirth; he becomes Paul's godfather. They discuss the wedding at Cana and the meaning of Christ changing water into wine: his ideas are 'quaint and fantastic' but she brings him 'judiciously to earth' (ch. 2, p. 45). This conversation enthuses them both, but it is then interrupted by the arrival home of Morel, drunk and in his pit dirt, demanding his dinner and more beer.

Later in the novel, religious belief ('the Orthodox creed') becomes something for Paul to question and debate with Miriam and a potential source of pain, yet biblical allusions and echoes sound through the whole narrative. During a childhood game in the street, Paul sees 'a big red moon lift itself up, slowly, . . . steadily, like a great bird. And he thought of the bible, that the moon should be turned to blood' (ch. 4, p. 101). Paul likens pine trunks glowing in the sunset to 'God's burning bush, that burned not away' (ch. 7, p. 183). Miriam is described as being 'like one of the women who went with Mary when Jesus was dead' (ch. 7, p. 184). A conversation about the nature of love 'remained graven in her mind, as one of the letters of the law' (ch. 7, p. 202). She 'suffered exquisite pain, as, with an intellect like a knife, the man she loved examined her religion in

BOOKS AND READING IN D. H. LAWRENCE'S *SONS AND LOVERS*   151

which she lived and moved and had her being' (ch. 8, p. 230; an echo of Acts 17.28) and later, when at last Paul confronts her with his need for physical intimacy, she thinks of an image that echoes the parable of the camel and the needle's eye: 'life forced her through this gate of suffering too, and she would submit' (ch. 11, p. 328). Clara is likened to the Queen of Sheba, while Paul remembers that as a boy he 'always thought that a pillar of cloud by day and a pillar of fire by night was a pit, with its steam, and its lights and the burning bank – and I thought the Lord was always at the pit-top' (ch. 12, p. 364). Even at the very end of the novel, outside at night after the death of his mother, Paul feels his grief and loss and despair in terms of an image from the Gospel of St John: he is 'less than an ear of wheat lost in the field' (ch. 15, p. 464). Paul has 'shovelled away all the beliefs that would hamper him' and yet he does not clear away the existence of the original book, the source of images and metaphors, the language that is so deeply embedded in the brain that it cannot be forgotten, although it can be appropriated for his (and Lawrence's) own purposes, as when he uses a Pentecostal metaphor to describe sexual ecstasy: 'a baptism of fire in passion' (ch. 11, p. 399).[11]

'A fire fed on books'

As might be expected, references and allusions to books feature most heavily in the five central chapters that concern the relationship between Paul and Miriam. The character of Miriam is based very closely on that of Lawrence's friend Jessie Chambers. Chambers's memoir *D. H. Lawrence: A Personal Record* devotes a whole chapter to the books that she and Lawrence read together in adolescence and Lawrence's responses to them. They read widely and voraciously: novels by authors ranging from George Eliot and Charles Dickens to R. L. Stevenson, Rider Haggard and R. D. Blackmore, poetry, essays and plays. Later they read French authors.[12] Chambers's account suggests that it was mostly Lawrence who chose the books they read, lending or occasionally giving them to her and finding others in the Mechanics' Institute library, but the actual reading was very much a shared enterprise. Lawrence and Chambers discussed the books on their walks home from the library:

> Our discussion was not exactly criticism, indeed it was not criticism at all, but a vivid re-creation of the substance of our reading. . . . The characters interested us most, and there was usually a more or less unconscious identification of them with ourselves, so that our reading became a kind of personal experience. Scott's novels in particular we

talked over in this way, and the scenes and events of his stories were more real to us than our actual surroundings.[13]

Later in her account, Chambers says: 'To say that we *read* the books gives no adequate idea of what really happened. It was the entering into possession of a new world, a widening and enlargement of life.'[14]

However, as John Worthen points out in his biography, there is considerably less emphasis on shared reading in Lawrence's fictional account than in Jessie Chambers's memoir; instead of being primarily an intellectual companionship, the relationship is presented as an incipient love affair from the very beginning. We are told that Paul and Miriam read and discuss a wide range of books intensely together, and titles and authors and the names of fictional characters are thrown easily and almost carelessly into the narrative, yet we almost never actually see the reading or discussion happening.[15] Lawrence does not attempt to describe or recreate the excitement and revelation or the sense of a widening world that Chambers recalls. Worthen also observes that the reference to Paul and Miriam's affair being like 'like a fire fed on books' comes relatively late in the novel. In fact, it comes after their brief attempt at a physical relationship – and with it their intellectual friendship – has actually ended and follows almost immediately after the episode in which Paul consummates his affair with Clara. And 'a fire fed on books' is a complex and troubling metaphor. It carries within it an echo of the 'baptism of fire in passion' or 'the real flame of feeling for another person' that Paul considers to be essential for the complete development of every human being. Fire can be life-affirming, but it can also be destructive. It is the books themselves that are consumed and reduced to ashes – in many authoritarian communities burning books is the means of condemning or suppressing them.

When we do see shared reading, it is clear that Paul and Miriam do not approach the texts as equals, but as teacher and pupil. Here Miriam is described, as Paul begins to become aware of her, in terms of her favourite reading and what it represents to her:

> The girl was romantic in her soul. Everywhere was a Walter Scott heroine being loved by men with helmets or with plumes in their caps. She herself was something of a princess turned into a swine girl, in her own imagination . . . Ediths and Lucys and Rowenas, Brian de Bois Guilberts, Rob Roys and Guy Mannerings rustled the sunny leaves in the morning . . .

> She hated her position as swine girl. She wanted to be considered. She wanted to learn, thinking that if she could read, as Paul said he could read, 'Columba', or the *Voyage Autour de ma Chambre*, the world would

BOOKS AND READING IN D. H. LAWRENCE'S *SONS AND LOVERS*   153

have a different face for her, and a deepened respect. She could not be princess by wealth or standing. So, she was mad to have learning whereon to pride herself. For she was different from other folk, and must not be scooped up among the common fry. Learning was the only distinction to which she thought to aspire. (ch. 7, pp. 173–4)

The works of Sir Walter Scott were still popular in the late nineteenth century when Lawrence was growing up and were greatly admired by the writer and critic Leslie Stephen among others. As adolescents, Lawrence and Jessie Chambers were enthusiastic readers of Scott and identified with the characters in the novels. However, here, Scott's novels (or Miriam's readings of them) are summed up in a perfunctory and dismissive way, details like plumes and helmets are used metonymically to evoke a romantic ideal of chivalry and courtly love; there is a hint of banal cliché; the plots are reduced to the names of characters. In this context it is significant that most of Scott's novels were historical novels; *Ivanhoe*, one of the best known and one of those to which Lawrence refers, was published in 1819 and is set during the reign of King John, while another, *The Bride of Lammermoor* (also published in 1819) is set in Scotland in the early sixteenth century. Lucy, one of Miriam's heroines, is a character in this novel. Lawrence interweaves the references to Scott's protagonists with tropes from fairy tales: the princess and the swine girl, King Cophetua and the beggar-maid.[16] Lawrence subtly criticises Miriam's approach to these texts by implying that the novels and poems are being used for consolation or as a means of escapism: Miriam views reading and learning at least partly as a means of self-advancement, as well as personal development. She hopes for a teacher who will also be a saviour.[17]

Paul helps Miriam to choose books in Bestwood library (although the reader is not told which ones) and teaches her French. One of the French lessons occurs on a very eventful evening during which Mrs Morel openly confronts Paul with her jealousy and resentment of Miriam and her misery in her marriage: 'she'd leave me no room, not a bit of room . . . she exults so in taking you from me' and which culminates in Paul almost coming to blows with his father (ch. 8, p. 252). The poets who are read and discussed, both French and English, underline the tensions, sexual and otherwise, that exist between Paul and Miriam and will eventually end their relationship.

'Shall we read, or is it too late?' he asked.
'It is late – but we can read just a little,' she pleaded.

She was really getting now the food for her life during the next week. He made her copy Baudelaire's 'Le Balcon'. Then he read it for her. His voice was soft and caressing, but growing almost brutal. He had a way of lifting his lips and showing his teeth, passionately and bitterly, when he was much moved. This he did now. It made Miriam feel as if he were trampling on her. She dared not look at him, but sat with her head bowed. She could not understand why he got into such a tumult and fury. It made her wretched. She did not like Baudelaire, on the whole – nor Verlaine.

> 'Behold her singing in the field
> Yon solitary highland lass – '

That nourished her heart – so did 'Fair Ines.' And:

> 'It was a beauteous evening, calm and pure,
> And breathing holy quiet like a nun – '

These were like herself. And there was he, saying in his throat, bitterly:

> 'Tu te rappelleras la beauté des caresses.' (ch. 8, p. 248)

Paul sometimes attempts to understand and explain the differences between himself and Miriam by placing qualities in opposition: a pine tree flaring up in the sunset rather than an ordinary tree, 'with fidgety leaves' (ch. 7, p. 183); the Gothic arch leaping up at heaven and losing itself in the divine (like Miriam), rather than the bowed Norman arch, the dogged leaping forward of the persistent human soul (like himself; ch. 7, p. 215). Here is another opposition: Romantic English poetry (Miriam's taste) placed alongside sensual French verse (Paul's taste). This scene in which Paul reads Baudelaire aloud is narrated from Miriam's point of view and she does not consciously attempt to rational-ise her feelings – for her, the difference between Wordsworth and Baudelaire is how they make her feel. Thomas Hood's 'Fair Ines' and Wordsworth's 'The Solitary Reaper' nourish her, but 'Le Balcon' does not. For Miriam, Baudelaire's verse is difficult to listen to because it makes Paul aggressive and transforms him into a cruel predator. Only one line of the poem is quoted, but this is enough to evoke the rest and to make its erotic nature quite clear.[18] There are other reasons why Miriam may prefer to concentrate on Paul, the reader, rather than on the words that he is reading. The poem begins:

> Mère des souvenirs, maîtresse des maîtresses,
> Ô toi, tous mes plaisirs! ô toi, tous mes devoirs!
> Tu te rappelleras la beauté des caresses,

BOOKS AND READING IN D. H. LAWRENCE'S *SONS AND LOVERS* 155

La douceur du foyer et le charme des soirs,
Mère des souvenirs, maîtresse des maîtresses!

(Mother of memories, loveliest of lovers,
You, all my pleasures, all the debts I owe,
Remember that perfection of caresses,
The evening charm, the gentleness of home,
Mother of memories, loveliest of lovers.)[19]

Later stanzas recreate softly firelit evenings, but also fragrant blood, the gathering night enclosing the lovers like a wall, sweetly poisonous breath and the lover clasping his mistress's knees like a child clasping his mother. The woman whom Baudelaire commemorates in gratitude conflates the figures of Miriam's two dangerous rivals for Paul's attention and his love: Gertrude Morel, the idealised mother figure, and Clara, the sensuous mistress who can offer the passion that the young woman who (according to Lawrence) imagines herself as a solitary reaper or a pure heroine, cannot give him.

When Miriam thinks about her favourite poems that they are like herself, what she may mean is that they are familiar: that they have been written about a world that she knows, the English countryside and the ordinary people who live and work there. In *Lyrical Ballads* and elsewhere Wordsworth deliberately wrote about marginalised figures, children and the poor, and used ordinary language that at that time was not considered consciously poetic. As well as 'The Solitary Reaper' and 'Lucy Gray', Miriam's copy of Palgrave's *Golden Treasury* would have included the more reflective and philosophical 'Ode on Intimations of Immortality'. However, the poems that Lawrence cites as her personal favourites are, like the Walter Scott novels, presented as a reflection of Miriam's idealised self-image:

Behold her, single in the field,
Yon solitary Highland Lass!
Reaping and singing by herself;
Stop here, or gently pass!
Alone she cuts and binds the grain,
And sings a melancholy strain;
O listen! for the Vale profound
Is overflowing with the sound.[20]

What the heroines of the Scott novels and the subjects of the Romantic poems appear to have in common is that they are either rescued or they are *recognised and acknowledged*. Fair Ines, in the poem of that name, is

156   SUSAN WATSON

mourned after her death in terms that, once again, adopt the language of chivalry:

> Would I had been, fair Ines,
> That gallant cavalier,
> Who rode so gaily by thy side,
> And whisper'd thee so near!
> Were there no bonny dames at home,
> Or no true lovers here,
> That he should cross the seas to win
> The dearest of the dear?[21]

The figure of the Solitary Reaper also continues to haunt the poet:

> I listened, motionless and still;
> And, as I mounted up the hill,
> The music in my heart I bore,
> Long after it was heard no more.[22]

A soul and a beast

Scott and Wordsworth may once have been Paul's favourite reading, too. In the early part of the novel he has admired and romanticised the red hair of one of the girls who winds stockings in the factory where he works. 'You remind me of Elaine in the *Idylls of the King*. I'd draw you if I could' (ch. 5, p. 137). The *Idylls of the King* was one of Tennyson's retellings of the Arthurian tales and it commemorates another virginal heroine. Elaine, the Fair Maid of Astolat, died of love for Sir Lancelot, and despite his dalliance with Guinevere, Sir Lancelot acknowledged her love for him and mourned her sorrowfully. And *Sons and Lovers* itself could be said to show the pervasive influence of Lawrence's poetic forebears, the Romantic poets that he read aloud 'over and over again' to Jessie Chambers.[23] It is about working people (or at least, some people of working-class origins), it uses dialect, and it is full of detailed evocations of the natural world.

But in *Sons and Lovers* French is the language of aspiration. It is Paul's ability to understand French that gets him his first job as a clerk at Jordan's, transcribing and translating orders from French customers: the job that saves him from having to follow his father into the pit and which eventually contributes to his social ascent. Paul begins to use French phrases as he thinks to himself and occasionally in conversation. Miriam's brothers seem to him like 'les derniers fils d'une race épuisée' (ch. 7, p. 180) and he believes that Clara has deliberately chosen to be 'une femme incomprise' (ch. 12, p. 361). After his mother dies, the weeks pass as a 'nuit blanche' (ch. 14, p. 445). Miriam reads Balzac with Paul and learns to write French compositions, which Paul corrects but also praises, albeit rather patronisingly. Paul accidentally observes that Miriam's rival Clara is reading *Lettres de mon Moulin*, by Alphonse Daudet and he then discovers that Clara has '*taught herself* French and could read in that language with a struggle' (ch. 10, p. 306, emphasis added). He later mocks her for not recognising an allusion to a poem by Victor Hugo, but Clara's openness to French literature is a sign that she may be more receptive to those aspects of his personality from which Miriam shrinks, even though *Lettres de mon Moulin* consists of light sketches and tales set in the French countryside, rather than darkly erotic poems. In the following chapter, 'Defeat of Miriam', Miriam picks up 'her favourite' Palgrave's *Golden Treasury*, but Paul instead chooses *Tartarin de Tarascon*, a satirical novel also written by Alphonse Daudet, to read aloud to her.[24] This is an ominous sign. Their subsequent conversation results in a temporary rift in their relationship. Later in the chapter he sends her a letter in which he says: 'See, you are a nun. I have given you what I would give a holy nun' (ch. 9, p. 292). This is a cruel echo of the William Wordsworth sonnet that is apparently one of Miriam's favourites, 'breathing holy quiet like a nun'.[25]

At the very beginning of their friendship, Miriam associates Paul with two French novellas, possibly without knowing more than their titles: Prosper Mérimée's 'Columba' and Xavier de Maistre's *Voyage autour de ma Chambre*. 'Columba' is set in Corsica and concerns a blood feud that ends in murder (possibly a veiled reference to Miriam's coming difficulties with Mrs Morel). In *Voyage autour de ma Chambre* the narrator, who is under house arrest, conducts an imaginary journey around his room, contemplating the furniture and other objects that the room contains and using them as the starting point for anecdotes and reminiscences and meditations. It is an exercise in seeing the familiar world differently and strangely, in making the best of the material to hand, which may be why it originally interested Lawrence and might conceivably have interested Miriam, if she read it. But it also contains a particularly suggestive passage:

> I have come to the conclusion, by way of various observations, that man is composed of a soul and a beast. These two beings are absolutely distinct, but so closely fitted together, or one on top of the other, that the soul must have a certain superiority over the beast to be in a position to draw a distinction between them. . . . The soul can make the beast obey it, and contrariwise, the beast often forces the soul to act against its inclination.[26]

The struggle between the soul and the beast – an idea to which de Maistre returns at intervals through the book – is one way of describing the conflict that often goes on within Paul himself, apparently caught between the values of his middle-class mother and his working-class father, between the life of the mind and the life of the body, between the Word and the Flesh. His mother may appear to have won the battle, but in Paul's taste for French literature the connection with his father persists and survives. His father, the sensual dancer, intemperate in both senses of the word, is part French, the grandson of 'a French refugee who had married an English barmaid – if it had been a marriage' (ch. 1, p. 17).[27]

Les fleurs du mal

It is not only books that Paul and Miriam share. As adolescents, they spend much time appreciatively contemplating a wren's nest, a sunset, daffodils, primroses, a manor garden with sheaves of shut-up crocuses. Celandines are 'scalloped splashes of gold' and Paul describes them as 'pressing themselves against the sun' (ch. 7, p. 179). A little later, Paul and Miriam look together at a wild rose bush:

> Its long streamers trailed thick, right down to the grass, splashing the darkness everywhere with great spilt stars, pure white. In bosses of ivory and in large splashed stars the roses gleamed on the darkness of foliage and stems and grass. Paul and Miriam stood close together, silent, and watched. Point after point, the steady roses shone out to them, seeming to kindle something in their souls. The dusk came like smoke around, and still did not put out the roses. (ch. 7, pp. 195–6)

These early flowers are sources of spiritual light, flowing generously outwards, golden, splashing, spilt stars, gleaming. The flowers are ivory and give off 'a white, virgin scent'. But the scene in which Paul finally decides to break off for good with Miriam, is, in one sense, his choice of Baudelaire's way of seeing the world rather than Wordsworth's. He makes his decision in the Morel garden, at night:

> And then, like a shock, he caught another perfume, something raw and coarse. Hunting round, he found the purple iris, touched their fleshy throats, and their dark, grasping hands. At any rate he had found something. They stood stiff in the darkness. Their scent was brutal. The moon was melting down upon the crest of the hill. It was gone, all was dark . . . Breaking off a pink he suddenly went indoors. (ch. 11, pp. 337–8)

These purple irises are *fleurs du mal*, decadent, embodied, livid, predatory.

BOOKS AND READING IN D. H. LAWRENCE'S *SONS AND LOVERS* 159

An ear of wheat lost in the field

By the end of the novel Paul has parted from Clara and his mother is dead. He cannot resume his old relationship with Miriam. He is alone. When Miriam briefly visits his lodgings, she looks to see what books he is reading: 'Evidently just an ordinary novel' (ch. 15, p. 459). If, earlier in the novel, reading could be a form of cooperation and mutual aid, of sharing, of making connections, by the end, at least for Paul, it has become a solitary activity, possibly little more than a way of passing the time. 'Where was he? – one tiny upright speck of flesh, less than an ear of wheat lost in the field' (ch. 15, p. 464). On the final page of the novel, mourning his mother, Paul returns, subconsciously, to the original book: 'except a grain of wheat fall into the earth and die, it abideth by itself alone'.[28] There follows an apocalyptic vision which seems to emerge from the Bible verse, even though that is not directly quoted:

> Stars and sun, a few bright grains, went spinning round for terror and holding each other in embrace, there in a darkness that outpassed them all and left them tiny and daunted. So much, and himself, infinitesimal, at the core a nothingness, and yet not nothing.
> . . . But no, he would not give in.

In the final paragraph of the novel, Paul turns away from the darkness, towards 'the city's gold phosphorescence'. No books are explicitly mentioned here, and Paul is walking, not reading, but the echo of the imagery and rhythms of the Bible seem to have inspired a resolution, an urge to survive, even though this takes the form of a reaction against the verse and the ideas that it evokes.

As a young man Lawrence 'read omnivorously, but books and ideas were never solitary experiences for him: he continually challenged the ideas he met, and discussed books and their ideas with others. He had thus come into full possession of his reading.'[29] For Paul Morel, as well as for Lawrence, books and reading hold the promise of drawing closer to others and creating communities, but in practice the act of reading makes differences more acute and divides people from one another. As John Worthen observes, Lawrence paid a price for his scholarship in 'loneliness and self-conscious difference'. In the novel, this seems to be most true of the female characters: Gertrude Morel, Clara Dawes and most of all Miriam Leivers are separated from others by their reading. It is Miriam, rather than Paul, who apparently pays the price; she gains a degree of independence but loses Paul's love and intellectual companionship.

In *Sons and Lovers*, the actual experience of engaging with a text is less important than what a book represents and how it can be used. Books can be a way of preserving a time that has been lost, or a means of self-education and social and worldly advancement. For Paul Morel they are sometimes the latter, but perhaps most of all they are something to respond to and challenge and, by doing so, develop his own ideas and define himself.

Notes

1. D.H. Lawrence, *Sons and Lovers*, ed. by Helen Baron and Carl Baron (Cambridge: Cambridge University Press, 1992), ch. 12, p. 360. All future references to *Sons and Lovers* will be given in the body of the text.

2. *Life As We Have Known It*, ed. by Margaret Llewelyn Davies (London: Hogarth Press, 1931), pp. 114–29. The books listed include novels of all kinds, poetry, biographies, history and scientific and political works, including Robert Tressell's *The Ragged-Trousered Philanthropists*, Carlyle's *The French Revolution*, Joseph Hyder's *The Case for Land Nationalisation* and Seebohm Rowntree's *Poverty: A Study of Life*.

3. The mechanics' institutes provided manual labourers with facilities for self-education, including libraries and night classes in reading, writing and practical subjects. They also provided some social facilities. William Morel plays billiards at the Mechanics Hall (ch. 3, p. 73).

4. Jonathan Rose, *The Intellectual Life of the British Working Classes* (New Haven, CT: Yale University Press, 2001), p. 128. Several of Rose's subjects include Palgrave's *Golden Treasury* among the books that were their favourite or formative reading. For the popularity of the *Golden Treasury*, see Martin Spevack, *The Golden Treasury*: 150 Years On, *eBLJ* (2012), article 2, especially pp. 1–4.

5. Jessie Chambers, *D. H. Lawrence: A Personal Record by E. T.*, 2nd edn (London: Frank Cass, 1965), p. 99.

6. Rose, *Intellectual Life*, p. 89 and ch. 2, 'Mutual Improvement'.

7. Informal teaching such as this was an important method of mutual improvement. William Morel also tutors pupils at home after learning shorthand at night school.

8. James Joyce, *A Portrait of the Artist as a Young Man* (1916) (London: Jonathan Cape, 1968), pp. 10, 180, 182–3.

9. Virginia Woolf, *To the Lighthouse* (London: Hogarth Press, 1927), pp. 183–4.

10. Annie S. Swan (1859–1943) was a prolific romance novelist, many of whose books appeared in serial form in the women's magazine *The People's Friend*. Her novels and stories were generally undemanding and sentimental, dealing with women's domestic lives and hardships. See B. Dickson, 'Swan [married name Burnett Smith], Annie Shepherd (pseud. David Lyall)' (1859–1943), *Oxford Dictionary of National Biography* (2004), https://doi.org/10.1093/ref:odnb/40374. By showing that Lily is unable even to read 'a little thing of Annie Swan's', Lawrence confirms that her standard of literacy is very low indeed.

11. One very striking example of Lawrence's appropriation of the Bible comes in the foreword to *Sons and Lovers*, which was omitted from the original 1913 edition but has been included in the 1992 Cambridge edition (Appendix 1, pp. 467–73). Here, Lawrence adopts not only the language but the rhythms of Bible verses in a response to, or a reversioning of, the beginning of the Gospel of St John.

12. See Chambers, *D. H. Lawrence*, ch. 4 'Literary Formation', pp. 91–123.

BOOKS AND READING IN D. H. LAWRENCE'S *SONS AND LOVERS*   161

13. Chambers, *D. H. Lawrence*, pp. 93–4.

14. Chambers, *D. H. Lawrence*, p. 96.

15. John Worthen, *The Cambridge Biography (Vol. 1): D. H. Lawrence: The Early Years 1885–1912* (Cambridge: Cambridge University Press, 1991), pp. 351–2. A further point to note is that Edward Garnett made significant cuts to Lawrence's manuscript when he published the original edition in 1913 and these tended to strengthen the emphasis on the love affair at the expense of the intellectual companionship. For example, Garnett excised the account of Paul's and Miriam's choosing their books in Bestwood Library and abridged some of their conversations about books and ideas.

16. This is probably intended as a reference to Tennyson's poem 'The Beggar Maid', which Miriam might well have read (and which inspired Pre-Raphaelite paintings), see note by Helen Baron and Carl Baron in *Sons and Lovers*, p. 534).

17. 'Even in those days Lawrence used to declare that the main purpose of education was to teach people how to use their leisure, or rather how to use themselves' (Chambers, *D. H. Lawrence*, p. 80).

18. *Les Fleurs du Mal* was condemned as offensive to public morality when it first appeared in 1857.

19. Charles Baudelaire, *The Flowers of Evil*, trans. by Anthony Mortimer (Richmond, UK: Alma Classics, 2016), pp. 70–1.

20. *The Golden Treasury of the Best Songs and Lyrical Poems in the English Language*, ed. by Francis T. Palgrave, 4th edn (London: Oxford University Press, 1940), p. 287.

21. *The Oxford Book of Victorian Verse*, ed. by Arthur Quiller-Couch (Oxford: Clarendon Press, 1913) p. 43.

22. *Golden Treasury*, pp. 287–8.

23. Chambers, *D. H. Lawrence*, p. 99.

24. *Tartarin de Tarascon* is the story of a native of Provence who boasts of his ability as a hunter. He only succeeds in shooting an old, blind lion, but this is presented as a triumph.

25. *Golden Treasury*, p. 303.

26. Xavier de Maistre, *A Journey around My Room*, trans. by Andrew Brown (Richmond, UK: Alma Classics, 2013), p. 10.

27. '(Lawrence) tended to make France, and French – like the vermouth and absinthe he drank in cafes – symbolic of the decadent poet's life, of witty cultivation and an amoral pose; but still more it was a reminder of how far he aimed to travel from the limitations (and language) of Eastwood, and of how cultivated (in a non-Eastwood sense) he was' (Worthen, *Early Years*, p. 62). Lawrence liked to imagine that he had a French ancestor and Chambers recalls him saying: 'If English people don't like what I write . . . I shall settle in France and write for the French' (Chambers, *D. H. Lawrence*, p. 106).

28. John 12.24.

29. Worthen, *Early Years*, p. 346.

Bibliography of secondary literature

Chambers, Jessie, *D. H. Lawrence: A Personal Record by E. T.*, 2nd edn (London: Frank Cass, 1965)

Davies, Margaret Llewelyn (ed.), *Life As We Have Known It* (London: Hogarth Press, 1931)

Dickson, B., 'Swan [married name Burnett Smith], Annie Shepherd (pseud. David Lyall' (1859–1943), *Oxford Dictionary of National Biography* (2004), http://doi.org/10.1093/ref:odnb/40374

Rose, Jonathan, *The Intellectual Life of the British Working Classes* (New Haven, CT: Yale University Press, 2001)

Spevack, Martin, *The Golden Treasury*: 150 Years On, *eBLJ* (2012), article 2

Worthen, John, *The Cambridge Biography (Vol. 1): D. H. Lawrence: The Early Years 1885–1912* (Cambridge: Cambridge University Press, 1991)

Chapter 9

'I sometimes like to read a novel': books and reading in Victorian adventure romance

Andrew Nash

> [I]t only remains for me to offer my apologies for my blunt way of writing. I can only say in excuse for it that I am more accustomed to handle a rifle than a pen, and cannot make any pretence to the grand literary flights and flourishes which I see in novels – for I sometimes like to read a novel.[1]

Allan Quatermain's disavowal of his writing ability in Henry Rider Haggard's *King Solomon's Mines* (1885) is a common trope of adventure fiction narratives. It might be assumed that this elephant hunter and trader is no more comfortable holding or reading a book than he is holding a pen. Quatermain's resolution to tell his story 'in a plain, straightforward manner' appears consistent with a character who often misquotes works of literature from memory, ascribing lines from Shakespeare to the Bible, for instance. As he informs us in the very first paragraph of his narrative, Quatermain is 'not a literary man' (ch. 1, p. 9). Fittingly, in this tale of a Biblical legend, his only professed devotion in reading is to the Old Testament and the *Ingoldsby Legends*, R. H. Barham's collection of ghost stories and verse myths first published serially in 1837. Yet Quartermain's passing admission to sometimes reading a novel points to a surprising engagement with books and reading in romance narratives of the late nineteenth century.[2] As a genre that explicitly rejects the domestic environment for the bodily passions of outdoor activity, and which rhetorically elevates oral forms of storytelling above the printed word, adventure romance can hardly be expected to embrace at any length the world of books and letters, least of all the enclosed mental space of reading. As this chapter will show, however, for all its surface rejection of the literary, books and textual documents – both as material objects and vehicles for reading – are written into the form and content of the genre in at least three discernible ways. Focusing on the work of three writers – Rider Haggard, Robert Louis Stevenson and John Buchan – the chapter will show how books and documents of various kinds are presented as the material containers of the stories that lie behind the adventures; how the process of reading emerges as the very substance that forms the appetite for adventuring; and how metaphors of the book are used to articulate some of the moral ambivalences inherent in the narratives.

Leaving the books behind

Reading's sedentary nature makes it naturally at odds with the adventurer's physical journeying. In the opening scene of Buchan's *Salute to Adventurers* (1915), set in the religious wars of late seventeenth-century Scotland, the eighteen-year-old hero, who has set out on foot from the south-west of Scotland to complete his education in Edinburgh, is immediately assaulted by driving rain, making him thank Providence that 'I had left my little Dutch *Horace* behind me in the book-box.'[3] Andrew Garvald's journey is quickly overtaken by events as he falls among religious fanatics and is arrested by a troop of passing dragoons. He never makes it back to college; his book (almost certainly an Elzevir duodecimo), which has already travelled from the continent to Scotland, must journey without him.[4] The opening scene of Stevenson's *Kidnapped* (1886) presents a similar picture of books being left behind. David Balfour locks the door of his dead father's house and sets forth on his journey to the House of Shaws, taking leave of Mr Campbell, the local minister. Campbell has already purchased David's father's books and plenishing so that he can resell them at a profit to the local dominie. Books are part of the fixtures of life the orphaned David must forsake for the fluidity of uncertain adventure – the 'pickle money' from the proceeds of the sale being more useful to him on his journey.[5] Among the other items Campbell hands him is a Bible – his prayerful wish being that it will see David 'into a better land' (ch. 1, p. 9). Though he quotes from the Bible at one point in his adventures, there is no evidence that David reads the volume given to him by the minister or keeps it with him during his travels. The lands over which he must travail are a test of the body and of the inner conscience, not of studied moral learning.

As has often been remarked, *Kidnapped* observes the standard pattern of the romance form by commencing with a journey away from home, only to undercut it with the title of the second chapter – 'I come to my journey's end'. In his uncle's house David finds 'a great number of books, both Latin and English'. We are told little about these, other than they afford David 'great pleasure all the afternoon', until he discovers an inscription in his father's hand on the 'fly-leaf of a chapbook (one of Patrick Walker's)' (ch. 4, p. 22). Patrick Walker, known as 'the Cameronian pedlar', wrote popular biographies of leading Covenantors of the seventeenth century which were a favourite of Stevenson's own reading – his heavily marked copy of Walker's *Biographia Presbyteriana* (1728) survives.[6] Just as tales and histories of the persecution of the Covenanters fuelled the author's imagination, we might conceive David's imagination being fuelled by the chapbook. It might even serve as a warning for the persecution that awaits him at the hands of his uncle. But David is a poor reader. He fails to detect that the inscription on the flyleaf discloses his uncle's deception: his usurpation of his elder brother's (and so David's) rightful inheritance. In an effort to get the baffling image 'out of my head', David pulls down other books from the shelf – 'many interesting authors old and new, history, poetry and story-book' (ch. 4, p. 22), but the riddle of the flyleaf inscription sticks to him. Naively, he confronts his uncle with innocent questions that lead first to an attempt on his life and then to his kidnapping. The alert reader of Stevenson's romance must pick up the clues David misses.

As a passive adventure hero, it is appropriate that David should prove a naive reader of books and situations – at least at first. More successful adventurers are those better able to interpret the linguistic and bibliographic codes of the books and documents they encounter.[7] In Rider Haggard's *She* (1887), the whole mystery and purpose of the quest depends upon a successful reading of texts. Horace Holly is entrusted with the care of a locked iron chest given to him by the father of his ward Leo Vincey. On Leo's father's instructions, the box is opened on the son's twenty-fifth birthday and is found to contain a letter, an Egyptian potsherd bearing some Greek uncial writing and two rolls of parchment carrying translations of the writing on the potsherd, one in English and one in black-letter Latin. The letter and the English and Latin translations of the text on the potsherd are presented verbatim to the reader, the Latin translation in an appropriately Gothic Victorian type. Holly also presents his own transcription of the uncial Greek writing and, 'for general

convenience in reading', a further transcription into the 'cursive character'.[8] The potsherd, in addition, has other markings in Greek, Latin and
English, which Holly again both translates and presents to the reader in
their original script. It is from this relic of the past – carefully interpreted
by the scholar Holly – that Leo Vincey learns his strange line of descent,
a discovery that prompts the quest to Africa to find, and as it transpires to
slay, the evil woman who killed his ancestors.

On one level, the presentation of these documents in their original
forms recreates the textual substance of the mystery that forms the object
of the quest, placing Haggard's reader in the same position as his characters. On another level, however, the various transcriptions of the ancient
writing – both those on the parchment and Holly's own – reinforce how
the text on the potsherd is, in Robert Fraser's words, a 'cultural reincar-
nation' of a lost civilisation which survives in encoded form.[9] The legend
that unfolds in *She* has already been written in – or rather on – an ancient
form of the 'book'. The transcriptions and, by extension, both Holly's narrative and Haggard's novel are thus further cultural reincarnations, part
of what Fraser calls the 'textual recycling'[10] that preserves the legend.

A similar pattern is followed in *King Solomon's Mines*, where the map
that leads the adventurers to the mines has been handed to Quatermain
by José Silvestre, the descendant of a Portuguese explorer. The map is
drawn on a torn linen rag which also contains some text 'written in rusty
letters' – the blood of the explorer (ch. 2, p. 20). The documents convey the
location of Solomon's treasure, preserving the legend of the mines which
has been passed down through oral tradition. As Thomas Vranken has
argued, it is surely not coincidental that the map and the explorer's story
are written on a substance used for pre-industrial paper production –
linen rag.[11] Readers of early editions of the work were supplied with a
fold-out facsimile of the map as a frontispiece – simulated ancient paper
printed on industrial Victorian paper.[12] In this instance, however, reading is fraught with danger. The dying Silvestre explains that the rag has
been in the family for centuries 'but none have cared to read it till at last
I did. And I have lost my life over it' (ch. 2, p. 20). Quatermain, for his
part, explains that he has never shown the document or the map to anyone before, 'except my dear wife, who is dead . . . and a drunken old
Portuguese trader who translated it for me, and had forgotten all about it
next morning' (ch. 2, p. 21). The textual instantiation of the truth of the
legendary mines becomes a Pandora's box for whoever opens the book of
mystery, inside or outside of the novel.[13]

What these examples show is that in adventure romance it is invariably documents of one kind or another that trigger the quest. Fragments of
text written in fly leaves, on Egyptian pots, or on scraps of the raw

material of paper carry the mysteries or legends that have been passed down through time. We are encouraged to believe that no adventurer would set out in search of King Solomon's mines without documents to verify their existence and location. Books and texts may get left behind in adventure romance, but their careful reading matters.

'This is no furniture for the scholar's library'

In his Dedication to *Kidnapped*, Stevenson draws a distinction between romance-reading and scholarly pursuits. Cautioning his friend Charles Baxter not to look for historical accuracy in his story, he writes:

> This is no furniture for the scholar's library, but a book for the winter evening school-room when the tasks are over and the hour for bed draws near; and honest Alan, who was a grim old fire-eater in his day, has in this new avatar no more desperate purpose than to steal some young gentleman's attention from his Ovid, carry him awhile into the Highlands and the last century, and pack him to bed with some engaging images to mingle with his dreams.

Romance-reading is presented here as a distraction from another kind of reading experience, its intensity carried over beyond the moment into dreams. Stevenson explored the connections between reading and dreaming in several of his critical essays, notably 'A Gossip on Romance', written in 1882, shortly after the serialisation of *Treasure Island*. His arguments in this essay – which amount to a manifesto for the romance form – create a complex dynamic for understanding the portrayal of books and reading in his texts, one that underpins the work of other romance writers. On the one hand, an art that advocates the primacy of 'the problems of the body and of the practical intelligence, in clean, open-air adventure', as Stevenson puts it, must of necessity eschew the enclosed solitary world of *actual* reading undertaken 'when the hour for bed draws near' as it does for the young gentleman reading *Kidnapped*.[14] On the other hand, Stevenson's argument that the act of reading is what prompts 'the realisation and the apotheosis of the day-dreams of common men', and that the true mark of 'the great creative writer' is 'to satisfy the nameless longings of the reader, and to obey the idea laws of the day-dream', leads him to cast the adventure narrative into close alignment with the act of reading.[15] Adventure stories may reject reading at the level of narrative, but they retain at the level of form a self-awareness of how the narrative should be read and what the implications of that reading should be.

Like Stevenson's image of the distracted young gentleman, romance narratives commonly open with a rejection of other forms of reading. In the first chapter of *She*, we find Holly – who wishes he could do something with the outside rather than the 'inside of my head' – in his rooms at Cambridge, flinging down a mathematical textbook on which he has been 'grinding away' (ch. 1, p. 7). One reading experience is flung aside to make way for a narrative that will subordinate mental experience – the 'inside of my head' – for outside adventure. This simple dichotomy underpins the whole structure of Buchan's early historical romance *John Burnet of Barns* (1898). Although the adventuring hero claims that 'the making of tales is an art unknown to me', John is an accomplished scholar who during the course of the tale informs us that he has produced a written exposition of the works of Descartes with his own additions 'which I intend, if God so please, to give soon to the world'.[16] In this instance, the traditional caveat warning the reader not to 'look for any great skill in the setting down' of his tale (ch. 1, p. 13) is convincing only at the level of genre: a mind attuned to critical exegesis may legitimately approach the task of writing adventure fiction with uncertainty. John describes himself as 'born between two stools; for, while I could never be content to stay at home and spend my days among books, on the other hand the life of unlettered action was repugnant' (bk 2, ch. 8, p. 191). Throughout the narrative, he oscillates between a scholarly and soldiering life as the events shift between scenes of college learning in Glasgow and Leiden and the field of battle. In the early chapters Buchan subjects the reader to a lengthy summary of John's reading in Greek, Latin and natural philosophy, but the sight of his fearsome yet graceful cousin Gilbert – who becomes the rival to the hand of his sweetheart Marjory – leading his troop off to battle unlocks his wish to 'fling' his books into the Clyde and head off to the wars (bk 1, ch. 4, p. 54).

The image in this novel of the adventuring hero as a reluctant reader and scholar is not, however, as simple as it first seems. In contrast to Haggard, Buchan does not set up a simple dichotomy between the battlefield and the library or university. John's taste for the 'profession of arms' is fostered by the 'many martial tales' he reads in childhood – chronicles of Froissart, a history of the Norman kings, Tacitus and Livy, and Homer (bk 1, ch. 2, p. 30). Reciprocally, his scholarly ambitions take their inspiration from an inner lust for adventure. Tired of the 'contradictions and phantasies' he finds in the followers of Aristotle, and critical of the disparaging of the mind he detects in 'Bacon and Galileo and the other natural philosophers', he is inspired by a reading of Descartes to put aside his doubts and commit himself to physical action. Towards the end of the novel he advances the claims of his own writings on the philosophy

BOOKS AND READING IN VICTORIAN ADVENTURE ROMANCE   **169**

of the Greeks in opposition to those with deeper learning, averring: 'my mind, since it has ever been clear from sedentary humours and the blunders which come from mere knowledge of books, may have had in sundry matters a juster view and a clearer insight' (bk 4, ch, 9, p. 442). A moderate among religious and political extremists, John's reading tempers the fanaticism of the adventuring spirit embodied in his cousin, just as his own appetite for adventure leads him to a worldly insight beyond the 'blunders' of philosophical theorising. In a novel about reconciliation at the personal and national level, books and adventure are codependent and essential to resolving the conflict of a man and a nation caught between 'two stools'.

A further episode illustrates the symbolic function of books in Buchan's romance. Summoned home from university in Leiden, having temporarily retreated from the battlefield, John becomes a fugitive when he finds his reputation sullied and his lands seized by government forces. He takes to the hills but is one day struck by a great desire 'for some book to read in' (bk 3, ch. 13, p. 314). Risking his life, he sets out for Barns pursued by soldiers. With 'mad recklessness' (bk 3, ch. 13, p. 315) he enters the library, seizing the first volume he lays his hands on. Essentially, this episode is just another thrilling incident in the larger set of adventures, but it is also a reminder that for this scholar-adventurer a life of solitude in the moorland hills is not easy to endure without the comforts of reading. The death-defying trip to the library is symbolic of what John has lost at this stage of the narrative – the stability of home and the rights of ownership. The final chapter pictures John restored to his home sitting in his study 'looking forth of the narrow window over the sea of landscape' surrounded by 'the mellow scent of old books and the faint fragrance of blossoms' (bk 4, ch. 9, pp. 444–5) – proper furniture for an *adventurer's* library.

'A story like some ballad'

When Allan Quatermain reads José Silvestre's document containing the blood-written testimony of his ancestor Captain Good, one of his adventuring companions, declares: 'I have been round the world twice, and put in at most ports, but may I be hung if I ever heard a yarn like that out of a story book, or in it either, for the matter of that' (ch. 2, p. 22). The current online edition of the *OED* defines 'yarn' in its secondary sense of storytelling as to "spin a yarn", tell a story; also, to chat or talk'. The usage, which interestingly dates from the early nineteenth century, underlines the primacy of the oral in the romance form, even when it is used in relation to the written word. As Fraser argues, 'romance seems to have approximated in the eyes of late-Victorian people to what we now call "orature", something handed down by word of mouth'.[17] Orality is written deep into the lexical fabric of romance narratives of this period. 'I am going to tell you a story' (ch. 1, p. 19) is how Sir Henry Curtis begins his account of his brother's expedition into Africa in search of King Solomon's mines, and the men are frequently pictured 'yarning away' (ch. 4, p. 54) while on their journey into the interior. This characteristic is developed in a more pervasive way in *Kidnapped*. The turbulent relationship between the Jacobite Alan Breck and the Whig David Balfour is built on a constant exchange of stories. When Alan recounts the persecution of the Jacobites at the hands of the Campbells, David's response is to call it 'a strange story' (ch. 13, p. 77). Later when he hears Mr Henderland's view on the matter he calls it 'a poor story' (ch. 16, p. 100). Stories capture the moral complexity that political allegiances elide. At the height of their conflict, when David judges Alan 'blood-guilty in the first degree', Alan invokes fairy lore – 'the story of the Man and the Good People' (ch. 18, p. 108) – to persuade him of the requirement for personal loyalty above political allegiance. Significantly, the other narrative layer of *Kidnapped* – David's wrongful disinheritance – is likewise cast in a form that draws on oral folklore. Having failed to pick up the truth of his uncle's deception from the evidence in the books, David obliquely discloses the mystery to himself when he recalls how 'there came up into my mind (quite unbidden by me and even discouraged) a story like some ballad I had heard folks singing, of a poor lad that was a rightful heir and a wicked kinsman that tried to keep him from his own' (ch. 4, p. 23). The tale of David's journey towards his 'kingdom', as the heading of the penultimate chapter has it, is thus framed as a re-enactment of a sung ballad – the unfolding of a legendary tale that has sung its way into David's head.

The appeal to oral traditions of storytelling in these texts nevertheless carries a paradox. At a basic level, orality and writing are entwined because the oral is inscribed in the written – the printed form of the texts themselves.[18] In this context, it is significant that the romance revival of the late nineteenth century took place alongside an extended critical debate about fiction and reading which, as Stephen Arata notes, was characterised by a new interest in the activity of reading itself – 'what it is, how it is best done, and to what ends'.[19] Stevenson's large body of critical writing was a major contribution to this debate.[20] In one essay from 1887 he presents the experience of reading in terms of physical enclosure leading to a mental awakening. Recalling his repeated readings of Dumas's *The Vicomte of Bragelonne* (1847–50) when he lived alone among the Pentland hills during the winter, Stevenson writes:

> I would return in the early night from one of my patrols with the shepherd . . . and I would sit down with the *Vicomte* for a long, silent, solitary lamplight evening by the fire. And yet I know not why I call it silent, when it was enlivened with such a clatter of horse-shoes, and such a rattle of musketry, and such a stir of talk; or why I call those evenings solitary in which I gained so many friends.[21]

The 'silent, solitary' venue of reading becomes in the mind 'a place as busy as a city, bright as a theatre, thronged with memorable faces, and sounding with delightful speech'.[22] In other essays, this mental awakening is linked explicitly to the creative imagination. In 'The Genesis of *The Master of Ballantrae*' (an essay posthumously published in 1896), Stevenson recalls how the idea of writing such a story came to him during an isolated walk on a 'fine frosty night', straight after having 'finished my third or fourth perusal of *The Phantom Ship*'. The sense of one story preceding another is recognised as the very substance of writing and reading romance: 'I saw that Marryat, not less than Homer, Milton, and Virgil, profited by the choice of a familiar and legendary subject; so that he prepared his readers on the very title-page.'[23] Stevenson here anticipates modern theories of genre fiction, which emphasise how certain forms of literature rely on a set of conventions that are anticipated by a reader before and during the process of reading: just as in detective fiction there will be a body, so in adventure romance there will be a journey or quest and a legend. As Stevenson writes in 'A Gossip on Romance':

> It is not character but incident that woos us out of our reserve. Something happens as we desire to have it happen to ourselves; some situation, that we have long dallied with in fancy, is realised in the story with enticing and appropriate details. Then we forget the characters; then we push the hero aside; then we plunge into the tale in our own person and bathe in fresh experience; and then, and then only, do we say we have been reading a romance.[24]

The requirement in romance to echo a pre-existing tale – whether directly through conscious allusion or indirectly through the deployment of familiar tropes – is what allows Stevenson, in his essay on the genesis of *Treasure Island*, to excuse himself of the plagiarisms contemporary readers detected in the work. Other writers leave behind them 'footprints on the sands of time' into which all writers of romance must tread.[25] Romance narratives may be couched in ballad form or re-enact legendary tales passed down orally, but the spectre of reading and other books hover perceptibly behind these apparently anti-literary works.

172   ANDREW NASH

For Stevenson this crucial dynamic was more than a simple matter of genre and intertextuality. In a late, fragmentary essay, 'Rosa Quo Locorum', he meditates on childhood reading, positing that a child's apprehension of life arises from a response to hearing and reading stories: 'The child is conscious of an interest, not in literature but in life. A taste for the precise, the adroit, or the comely in the use of words, comes late; but long before that he has enjoyed in books a delightful dress rehearsal of experience.'[26] A common trope of adventure romance is to contrast the realism of a scene with the hero's prior apprehension of reality through books. During the flight in the heather in *Kidnapped*, David comments: 'By what I have read in books, I think few that have held a pen were ever really wearied, or they would write of it more strongly' (ch. 22, p. 139). These scenes form the most intensely physical part of David's narrative, as the bodily conditions of his plight are rendered in close sensory detail. Yet David still reaches for metaphors, finding one in the act of reading. When he wishes to describe the darkening of a July night sky in the far north of the Highlands, he informs his readers: 'you would have needed pretty good eyes to read, but for all that, I have often seen it darker in a winter midday' (ch. 22, p. 138). Evoking the physical sensation of reading is necessary for Stevenson's attempt at verisimilitude – the readers' own eyes, fixed on the pages of the story, must be made to *see* the darkness. Reading has been a 'dress-rehearsal' for David's experience, but for the reader of his story, in their enclosed space like Stevenson with Dumas, it must *be* the experience.

'A mine of suggestion'

In the remainder of this chapter, I want to bring together the various threads of the discussion into a reading of some key scenes in *Treasure Island*. Serialised in *Young Folks* from 1 October 1881 to 28 January 1882, Stevenson's 'story for boys'[27] was the pioneering work of the romance revival, inspiring Haggard to write *King Solomon's Mines* and influencing the form and style of many lesser works of adventure fiction aimed at a juvenile audience in the closing decades of the nineteenth century. At first glance, the work appears to follow the structural patterns mentioned above where books are left behind as the adventurers take to their journey. Jim Hawkins's first meeting with Dr Livesey and Squire Trelawney takes place in the Squire's library – 'all lined with bookcases and busts upon the top of them'.[28] If the cases contain any books, Jim appears not to notice them; or perhaps he decides they are of no consequence to the story he has been asked to 'write down' (ch. 1, p. 1). Later, during the

BOOKS AND READING IN VICTORIAN ADVENTURE ROMANCE 173

island adventure, when Jim returns to the Hispaniola just before his encounter with Israel Hands, he notices one of the doctor's medical books 'with half of the leaves gutted out' – for 'pipelights', he supposes (ch. 25, p. 201–2). The image seems symbolic of the redundancy of reading in this 'boy's game' (ch. 26, p. 214), which is about to take a deadly turn.

These instances of the absence or destruction of books underline the importance of orality to *Treasure Island* which both pervades the narrative and lies behind the work's composition. Stevenson's initial audience for the story was his stepson Lloyd Osbourne and the circle of family and friends who visited the Stevensons in Braemar in the wet summer and autumn of 1881. According to his own and his wife's testimonies, the author 'read aloud' instalments of the story daily, and among the captive audience was his father who 'not only heard with delight the daily chapter, but set himself acting to collaborate'.[29] Stevenson claimed that his father was responsible for the inventory of contents in Bones's chest along with other descriptive elements of the story. This picture of oral exchange and collaborative authorship typifies the notion of textual recycling discussed above – the interdependency of reading or listening to stories and writing romance.

Oral exchange is also prominent in the text itself. Linking the work to Stevenson's two-part essay 'Talk and Talkers' – where the author 'elevates the activity of talk above any kind of literary endeavour' – Amy R. Wong emphasises the recurrent interest in talk in *Treasure Island*: 'Squire John Trelawney fatefully "blabs" secrets away, the marooned Benn Gunn is impossibly loquacious, Long John Silver is a smooth talker with a pet parrot.'[30] One might go further and note how talking in the form of stories creates the necessary anticipation of adventure: Billy Bones's stories about hanging, walking the plank, and storms at seas are what 'frightened people worst of all' in the Admiral Benbow Inn (ch. 1, p. 5), and it is Bones who puts the image of 'the seafaring man with one leg' into Jim's mind so that it haunts his dreams before he actually meets Long John Silver – at which point the story becomes reality.

It would be wrong to read *Treasure Island* as exclusively concerned with orality, however. Books and other written and printed documents play a significant part in the adventure, both as literal markers of reading and misreading, and as metaphors for channelling the text's preoccupation with the moral problem of duty and allegiance. For one thing, it is not only Billy Bones's stories that fuel Jim's imagination. The map he secretes from Bones's possessions performs a similar function. Before the voyage commences, Jim recalls how he 'brooded' over the map 'in charming anticipations of strange islands and adventures . . . Sitting by the fire in the house-keeper's room, I approached that island in my fancy, from every possible direction' (ch. 7, p. 54). In his essay on the genesis of the story, Stevenson identifies the drawing of the map as the true inspiration for writing *Treasure Island* and 'the chief part of my plot'.[31] A map, he argues, provides an author with 'a mine of suggestion' – a threshold into an imaginative world: 'The tale has a root there, it grows in that soil.'[32] Like his author, Jim's finds the map 'a mine of suggestion', and his brooding over it provokes an imaginative encounter with the island before the adventure has taken place.

Jim's actions can be linked to Stevenson's own childhood experiences recalled in the essay 'Popular Authors' (1888). Here Stevenson recounts how, when he had been unable to obtain the latest penny number of a favourite author, he would 'study the windows of the stationer and try to fish out of subsequent woodcuts and their legends the further adventures of our favourites'.[33] A similar situation is explored in another essay, '"A Penny Plain and Twopence Coloured"' (1884), where Stevenson recalls his childhood love of Skelt's Juvenile Drama, the interactive model toy theatres packaged in magazine form. Here it is the materiality of the printed illustrations that triggers the creative imagination, and the material destruction of the prints – their disintegration into 'dust' – that signals the nightmare of imagination's extinction.[34] In each case, it is images inspired by a pre-existing story that fuel the creative imagination and allow the story to continue. Crucially, however, that continuation depends upon the existence of print or illustration. Without a material text, there is no 'mine of suggestion', and no story.

Captain Flint's map plays a crucial part in the narrative of *Treasure Island* as well, despite the fact that it proves ultimately useless – Ben Gunn having already moved the treasure from its original location. On the island, reading the map becomes less about finding treasure and more about discovering the truth about character and motive. This is evident in Silver's first encounter with the map. Captain Smollett presents him not with the original document but an 'accurate copy', lacking the all-important red marks and written notes. Jim recognises it as a copy because it is printed on paper which has a 'fresh look' (ch. 12, p. 95). His reading of the materiality of the document is what allows him to follow the course of the game that subsequently takes place between Silver and the Captain: 'Sharp as must have been his annoyance, Silver had the strength of mind to hide it' (ch. 12, p. 95). Yet Jim picks up the bibliographical cue and sees beyond the hidden gaze. In his reading of this passage, Vranken highlights the difference between this document and the reproduction of Flint's map printed as a frontispiece to the volume edition of the story in 1883. Emphasising the 'strict eighteenth-century guise' of the frontispiece, which in the first edition printed Flint's crosses in red ink, Vranken argues that the reproduction, printed on industrial-made paper that would yellow over time, helps its readers to 'imagine the materiality' of Jim's map, 'the worn, yellowed paper on which it is drawn, and the world of pre-industrial print culture that it metonymically represents'.[35] Reader and character are placed in the same position of having to read the bibliographical features of a document as well as its actual content.

'Speak like a book'

In *Treasure Island* books and documents have a metaphorical as well as a material significance. On the sea voyage, the coxswain, a 'great confidant' of Silver, tells Jim that the sea cook is 'no common man . . . He had good schooling in his young days, and can speak like a book when so minded' (ch. 10, p. 80). The estimate of Silver's rhetorical powers ascribes to print a power and authority beyond orality. The scarcely literate coxswain is easily influenced by Silver's eloquence. Elsewhere in the text, print is used as a metaphor for certainty. Bones tells Jim that in his moments of delirium – which only rum can hold at bay – he sees old Flint in the corner of the room 'as plain as print' (ch. 3, p. 20); later, when Jim has become attuned to Silver's duplicity, he claims to be able to read the pirate's thoughts 'like print' (ch. 32, p. 273).

For all the emphasis on talk, therefore, the 'remarkable game' (ch. 29, p. 246) played out on Treasure Island is articulated through metaphors of the book, as another pivotal scene illustrates. After Jim has cut loose the *Hispaniola* and shot Israel Hands, he returns to the stockade, only to find it has been taken by the pirates. Stranded in the enemy camp, he realises he must temporarily side with Silver. The pirates, mistakenly thinking Silver knows the location of the treasure because he has possession of the map, turn against him. From a distance, Jim observes the pirates in conference:

> About halfway down the slope to the stockade, they were collected in a group; one held the light; another was on his knees in their midst, and I saw the blade of an open knife shine in his hand with varying colours, in the moon and torchlight. . . . I could just make out that he had a book as well as a knife in his hand; and was still wondering how anything so incongruous had come in their possession, when the kneeling figure rose once more to his feet, and the whole party began to move together towards the house. (ch. 29, p. 238)

The book is a Bible, out of which one of the pirates has torn a leaf to mark the 'black spot' – the signal that a pirate crew has turned against its captain. The leaf is handed to Silver. 'Where might you have got the paper?' Silver asks before quickly detecting traces of the final verses of *Revelation*: 'Why hillo! look here, now: this aint lucky! You've gone and cut this out of a Bible. What fool's cut a Bible?' (ch. 29, p. 239). At the end of the scene, Silver tosses the paper to Jim, who describes it as 'round about the size of a crown piece. One side was blank, for it had been the last leaf; the other contained a verse or two of Revelation – these words among the rest, which struck sharply home upon my mind: "Without are dogs and murderers"' (ch. 29, p. 245). The King James Version known to Stevenson has: 'For without are dogs, and sorcerers, and whoremongers, and murderers, and idolaters, and whosoever loveth and maketh a lie' (Rev. 22.15). Jim may only have read or recalled the words that struck his mind most sharply, but it appears that the torn page, blackened with the wood ash the pirates have used for ink, cuts through the quotation.

For Silver, the desecration of the Bible is a sign that nothing good will come of the pirates' actions; its owner, Dick, has 'crossed his luck and spoiled his Bible' (ch. 29, p. 245). In playing on Dick's fears about having destroyed the word of God, however, Silver seizes on the book's broken materiality as a metaphor for the now broken association between the mutineers:

> 'It'll do to kiss the book on still, won't it?' growled Dick, who was evidently uneasy at the curse he had brought upon himself.
> 'A Bible with a bit cut out!' returned Silver derisively. 'Not it. It don't bind no more'n a ballad-book.' (ch. 29, p. 245)

As Alex Thomson points out, Stevenson is referring here to the pirate tradition of swearing an oath of allegiance on a Bible.[36] The disbound book symbolises the breaking of bonds among the pirates. Critics have made much of Stevenson's pun on 'duty' in this critical scene, but we should be alert to the complexity of the verb 'to bind' as well. When Silver is handed the black spot, a crew member challenges him by the code which apparently makes him duty 'bound' to accept the deposition: 'This crew has tipped you the black spot in full council, as in dooty bound; just you turn it over, as in dooty bound, and see what's wrote there' (ch. 29, p. 240). Silver's response continues the metaphor: turning over the paper and seeing the word 'Deposed', he reacts calmly: 'Very pretty wrote to be sure; like print, I swear' (ch. 29, p. 240). In fact, as Jim later reveals when Silver tosses him the paper, not only is the written word on the document – 'Depposed' – misspelt, but the makeshift ink is already fading, blackening Jim's fingers as he turns over the paper. And as *he* writes, Jim observes: 'I have that curiosity beside me at this moment; but not a trace of writing now remains beyond a single scratch' (ch. 29, p. 245). As Thomson argues, the disintegration of their document 'confirms the insubstantial nature of the pirate's access to textual authority'.[37] Crucially, however, it is the textual authority embedded in Stevenson's deployment of bibliographical terminology that marks out the superiority of Silver, the man who can 'speak like a book'. Silver's reference to a ballad-book is telling, because a ballad-book, if it is a broadside, would not be bound at all, but printed on a single sheet and folded. His careful pun clinches his message that the pirates' case for deposition is no more binding than a book without a binding.

The apparent fixity of print and the bound book, then, becomes a metaphor for the pervasive ambiguity that surrounds the problem of authority in *Treasure Island*, a problem that can be crystallised into a simple question: who has a right to the treasure? That question has provoked a host of critical responses to this deceptively simple 'story for boys'. Close attention to the role of books and reading in the story, and in the adventure romance genre more widely, can offer new ways of approaching the matter, and to understanding the interplay between the written and the oral in the romance form.

Notes

1. H. Rider Haggard, *King Solomon's Mines* (1885), ed. by Roger Luckhurst (Oxford: Oxford University Press, 2016), 'Introduction', p. 8. Further references are in the text.

2. In the Revised New Illustrated Edition of 1905, Haggard inserted a further reference to Quatermain's reading when he makes his adventurer use a highfalutin phrase drawn 'from the pages of a popular romance that I chanced to have read recently' (H. Rider Haggard, *King Solomon's Mines* (London: Cassell, 1905), p. 165).

3. John Buchan, *Salute to Adventurers* (1915; London: Thomas Nelson, 1922), ch. 1, p. 12.

4. Andrew later completes his education in Glasgow before sailing to America where the main adventures take place against the backdrop of the newly settled plantations in Virginia.

5. Robert Louis Stevenson, *Kidnapped* (1886), ed. by Ian Duncan (Oxford: Oxford University Press, 2014), ch. 1, p. 9. Further references are in the text.

6. See Barry Menikoff, *Narrating Scotland: The Imagination of Robert Louis Stevenson* (Columbia: University of South Carolina Press, 2005), p. 189.

7. The terms 'linguistic codes' and 'bibliographic codes' are taken from Jerome J. McGann, *The Textual Condition* (Princeton, NJ: Princeton University Press, 1991), p. 77.

8. H. Rider Haggard, *She* (1887), ed. by Daniel Karlin (Oxford: Oxford University Press, 1991), ch. 3, p. 33. Further references are in the text.

9. Robert Fraser, *Victorian Quest Romance: Stevenson, Haggard, Kipling, and Conan Doyle* (Plymouth: Northcote House, 1998), pp. 44.

10. Fraser, *Victorian Quest Romance*, p. 45.

11. Thomas Vranken, *Simulating Antiquity in Boys' Adventure Fiction: Maps and Stains* (Cambridge: Cambridge University Press, 2022), pp. 16–18.

12. Reproduced in Vranken, *Simulating Antiquity*, p. 17.

13. As discussed below, the map in Stevenson's *Treasure Island* performs a similar function.

14. Robert Louis Stevenson, 'A Gossip on Romance' (1882), repr. *Memories and Portraits* (London: Chatto & Windus, 1887), pp. 247–74 (p. 251).

15. Stevenson, 'A Gossip on Romance', p. 255.

16. John Buchan, *John Burnet of Barns: A Romance* (1898; London: Thomas Nelson, 1922), bk 1, ch. 1, p. 13; ch. 4, p. 52. Further references are in the text.

17. Fraser, *Victorian Quest Romance*, p. 7.

18. For a deeper exploration of this topic, see Penny Fielding's chapter 'Bookmen: Orality and Romance in the Later Nineteenth Century', in her *Writing and Orality: Nationality, Culture and Nineteenth-Century Scottish Fiction* (Oxford: Oxford University Press, 1996), pp. 132–52. Fielding usefully reminds us that one of the main advocates of the romance revival, Andrew Lang, was a prominent bibliophile.

19. Stephen Arata, 'Stevenson Reading', *Journal of Stevenson Studies*, 1 (2004), 192–200. For an account of the critical debate itself, see Kenneth Graham, *English Criticism of the Novel 1865–1900* (Oxford: Clarendon Press, 1965), pp. 61–70.

20. For a detailed study, see Glenda Norquay, *Robert Louis Stevenson and Theories of Reading* (Manchester: Manchester University Press, 2007).

21. Robert Louis Stevenson, 'A Gossip on a Novel of Dumas's' (1887), repr. *Memories and Portraits*, pp. 228–46 (pp. 231–2).

22. Stevenson, 'A Gossip on a Novel of Dumas's', p. 232.

23. Robert Louis Stevenson, *Essays in the Art of Writing* (London: Chatto & Windus, 1905), pp. 135–42 (pp. 135–7).

24. Stevenson, 'A Gossip on Romance', p. 268.

25. 'My First Book: *Treasure Island*' (1894), repr. *Essays in the Art of Writing*, pp. 111–32 (pp. 120–1).

26. '*Rosa Quo Locorum*', in *The Works of Robert Louis Stevenson. Miscellanies, vol. 4* (Edinburgh: T. and A. Constable, 1896), pp. 302–12 (p. 302).

27. The appellation is Stevenson's own. See 'My First Book', p. 118.

28. Robert Louis Stevenson, *Treasure Island* (London: Cassell, 1883), ch. 6, p. 46. Further references are in the text.

29. Stevenson, 'My First Book', p. 121–2. Stevenson's account of the genesis of the work has provoked a lot of enquiry and contradictory opinion. For a summary of the debate, see the introduction to Centenary Edition of the work, ed. by Wendy R. Katz (Edinburgh: Edinburgh University Press, 1998).

30. Amy R. Wong, 'The Poetics of Talk in Robert Louis Stevenson's *Treasure Island*', *Studies in English Literature 1500–1900*, 54(4) (2014), 901–22 (pp. 901, 902).

31. 'My First Book', p. 127. In his introduction to the *Tusitala* edition of Stevenson's works, Lloyd Osbourne maintains that he, not Stevenson, drew the original map. Robert Louis Stevenson, *Treasure Island* (London: William Heinemann, 1923), p. xviii.

32. Stevenson, 'My First Book', p. 131.

33. Robert Louis Stevenson, 'Popular Authors', *Scribner's Magazine* 4 (July 1888), 122–8 (p. 125).

34. Repr. *Memories and Portraits*, pp. 213–27 (p. 227).

35. Vranken, *Simulating Antiquity*, p. 15.

36. Alex Thomson, '"Dooty Is Dooty": Pirates and Sea-Lawyers in *Treasure Island*', in *Pirates and Mutineers of the Nineteenth Century*, ed. by Grace Moore (Farnham: Ashgate, 2011), pp. 211–22 (p. 212). It is worth noting that while, according to Silver, the Bible is no longer of use for the purpose of oath-swearing, Dick clutches it and prays when the pirates think they hear Captain Flint's voice come back from the dead (see ch. 32, pp. 270, 272).

37. Thomson, 'Dooty', p. 213.

Bibliography of secondary literature

Arata, Stephen, 'Stevenson Reading', *Journal of Stevenson Studies*, 1 (2004), 192–200

Fielding, Penny, *Writing and Orality: Nationality, Culture and Nineteenth-Century Scottish Fiction* (Oxford: Oxford University Press, 1996)

Fraser, Robert, *Victorian Quest Romance: Stevenson, Haggard, Kipling, and Conan Doyle* (Plymouth: Northcote House, 1998)

Graham, Kenneth, *English Criticism of the Novel 1865–1900* (Oxford: Clarendon Press, 1965)

Katz, Wendy R., 'Introduction', in Robert Louis Stevenson, *Treasure Island*, ed. by Wendy R. Katz (Edinburgh: Edinburgh University Press, 1998), pp. xix–xli

Luckhurst, Roger, 'Introduction', in H. Rider Haggard, *King Solomon's Mines* (1885), ed. by Roger Luckhurst (Oxford: Oxford University Press, 2016), pp. vii–xvii

McGann, Jerome J., *The Textual Condition* (Princeton, NJ: Princeton University Press, 1991)

Menikoff, Barry, *Narrating Scotland: The Imagination of Robert Louis Stevenson* (Columbia: University of South Carolina Press, 2005)

Norquay, Glenda, *Robert Louis Stevenson and Theories of Reading* (Manchester: Manchester University Press, 2007)

Osbourne, Lloyd, 'Introduction', in Robert Louis Stevenson, *Treasure Island* (London: Heinemann, 1923), pp. ix–xix

Stevenson, Robert Louis, *Essays in the Art of Writing* (London: Chatto & Windus, 1905)

Stevenson, Robert Louis, 'A Gossip on a Novel of Dumas's' (1887), repr. *Memories and Portraits* (London: Chatto & Windus, 1887), pp. 228–46

Stevenson, Robert Louis, 'A Gossip on Romance' (1882), repr. *Memories and Portraits* (London: Chatto & Windus, 1887), pp. 247–74

Stevenson, Robert Louis, 'Popular Authors', *Scribner's Magazine* 4 (July 1888), 122–8

Stevenson, Robert Louis, '*Rosa Quo Locorum*', in *The Works of Robert Louis Stevenson. Miscellanies, vol. 4* (Edinburgh: T. and A. Constable, 1896), pp. 302–12

Thomson, Alex, '"Dooty Is Dooty": Pirates and Sea-Lawyers in *Treasure Island*', in *Pirates and Mutineers of the Nineteenth Century*, ed. by Grace Moore (Farnham: Ashgate, 2011), pp. 211–22

Vranken, Thomas, *Simulating Antiquity in Boys' Adventure Fiction: Maps and Stains* (Cambridge: Cambridge University Press, 2022)

Wong, Amy R., 'The Poetics of Talk in Robert Louis Stevenson's *Treasure Island*', *Studies in English Literature 1500–1900*, 54(4) (2014), 901–22

Chapter 10

When it isn't cricket: books, reading and libraries in the girls' school story

Karen Attar

The girls' school story has been claimed to account for some forty per cent of girls' reading and publishing in Britain in the 1920s and 1930s.[1] It remained the most popular type of fiction for eleven to fourteen-year-old girls for whom boarding school was an exotic unreality in the 1940s.[2] Angela Brazil, Elinor Brent-Dyer, Dorita Fairlie Bruce and Elsie J. Oxenham, the 'big four', were joined by myriad other writers.[3] A late twentieth- and twenty-first-century interest both in children's literature and in popular fiction has led to academic interest in the girls' school story, under the lens of social class, the latent feminism of an empowering all-female environment in which women govern their own lives, and sexological interpretations of that same environment which can include close female friendships.[4] Scholarly interest in the reading of fiction, extending sometimes to intradiegetic reading, has barely extended to girls' school stories.[5] This chapter seeks to fill the lacuna, with particular focus on Elinor Brent-Dyer's Chalet School series.

Intertextually, the genre itself seldom promotes reading. Like some actual boarding schools, the school story seldom celebrates cerebral activity. Girls, if not mistresses – and stories tend to be related from the girls' perspective – regard lessons as being of secondary importance to sports. Dorita Fairlie Bruce's *The Senior Prefect* (1921), in which the girls resent a new headmistress's decision to curtail the time spent on games, summarises trenchantly fictional girls' typical values:

> 'Of course, we know she's very clever and all that,' began Meg, reviving again. 'She's an M.A., and – and other things – '

> 'M.A.!' the head girl's tone was even more scornful than before, as she slipped off the desk on which she had been sitting and prepared to leave the room. 'M.A., indeed! She's a hockey-blue of Cambridge, and she played for England two years ago!'[6]

General reticence concerning reading has an even more deep-rooted reason in the underlying values of the school story and of its structure. The school is a community, whose values are communal. A recurrent overarching theme concerns 'forming, storming and norming'[7] as a new element introduced at the beginning of the book either adapts to that community or, more seldom, leaves it: usually an individual new girl or a small group of new girls; sometimes a new mistress, generally a headmistress with particular ideas and the power to execute them; a new house; or even an entire additional school. The emphasis is on relationships, whether feuds or friendships, and is social.[8] Societal values are courage and resourcefulness, helping the weak and above all a sense of honour, understood as being truthful in word and deed and in never sneaking.[9] The explicit importance of games is to foster team spirit, with praise for girls who know not to poach their partners' tennis balls and when to pass a hockey ball. What matters is putting the society – team or school – before self. Girl Guides or similar institutions (Guildry, Camp Fire) are likewise common as character-building, communal activities.

In such a world, reading has little place. It does not lend itself plot-wise to the exhibition of bravery or honour. Moreover, reading in the modern period is primarily an individual activity and as such is at odds with community values, acceptable as it may be outside the school environment. External reading which can be made to serve the school community is welcomed: for example, when girls are acting a play based on a book and want to know the plot.[10] Biblical readings at morning prayers for the assembled school are a communal activity which is taken for granted. Reading on the whole, being individual, is either marginalised or is portrayed negatively. Explanation is required to render it acceptable: for example, Petronella in Irene Mossop's *Well Played, Juliana!* (1928) is permitted to be a bookworm because severe illness prevents her from playing games.[11] Notwithstanding, Mossop portrays Petronella as oversensitive, jealous and sarcastic, scarcely an ideal role model. Gwendoline Courtney's Rosalind in *At School with the Stanhopes* (1951) puts her reading of Lord Chesterfield's letters to his son to a social use when the girls stage an eighteenth-century evening, but although clever and a natural reader, she resents the circumstances which threw her upon the works of Jane Austen, Fanny Burney, Boswell, Smollett, Sheridan and Goldsmith: the older brother with whom she was sent to live after her aunt died is a

BOOKS, READING AND LIBRARIES IN THE GIRLS' SCHOOL STORY   **183**

scholar who neglects her, and: '"there's nothing else I can do when I'm at home," Rosalind said, the interest in her tone changing to bitterness.'[12]

Even worse, reading is imposed as a salutary punishment. Barbara in *The New Head – and Barbara* spends two hours in detention reading.[13] In a late, superior example of the genre, Nicola Marlow, an excellent all-rounder who enjoys reading during the holidays, is discovered to have smuggled an unfinished library book of questionable content back to school with her, and is set to read a list of classics before embarking again upon a book of her own choice.[14] The message is mixed. Barbara has previously read and enjoys the book set, yet she would rather be outside. Nicola relishes some of the books on her list and must force herself through others.

Whereas in the above examples negativity lies in the circumstances of reading, sometimes the reading matter is what is objectionable. In such instances it combines with other elements to indicate unacceptable character. Hazel Simmons reads one stereotypical magazine story after another about a lord who marries a secretary, and her superficial reading is of a piece with general flouting of rules, bullying, forgery, and bad behaviour.[15] Worse again is forbidden, salacious literature: novels which remain unnamed, to prevent actual readers of school stories from pursuing them. Smuggling such books into school and reading them is one of several signs of moral depravity, and possession of such reading matter is liable to be the proof which seals girls' expulsion. One of Elinor Brent-Dyer's headmistresses sums up the general thought, which applies to girls within school stories and beyond them: 'We want you girls to retain your purity of mind as long as possible. Do you think that you can soil your minds with the thoughts and deeds recorded in such a story and yet retain that purity? It is impossible, for you are not little children now.'[16]

Particularly obvious and common, whether incidental or a strong plot element, is the intradiegetic reading of school stories.[17] In an atypically mature treatment of the scenario, underlying the falseness of the story within the story, twenty-three-year-old Nicola is a successful authoress whose publishers have asked her to write a school story. Having been educated privately and hence having no knowledge of schools, she turns to school stories to learn about the environment, only to become increasingly bewildered: 'I got heaps of school stories out of the library and soaked myself in them, but I wasn't satisfied. Most of them seemed to me frightfully unnatural. I liked some of them, but I got so mixed I couldn't make up my mind which kind was nearest to the real thing.'[18] She masquerades as a late teenager to spend a term as a schoolgirl and gain experience to inform her writing. At one point in the story girls criticise the standard school story as unrealistic – 'real schools aren't a bit like those in books' – and suggest ideas for a more credible plot.[19] Nicola provides an additional narratorial level which the standard school story lacks, able to point out the artificiality of the schoolgirl world: for example, the intense keenness on sports and the complete indifference to young men.[20]

Whereas Nicola is open-minded, usually the context is of new girls who have conceived false expectations of schools from their reading and must adjust their views. The distinction is especially strong when the preconceptions are based on penny or tuppeny weeklies, a cheaper and hence 'lower' form of literature than the hardbound novel, as in Winifred Darch's *Heather at the High School* (1924) and Elinor Brent-Dyer's *A Problem for the Chalet School* (1956).[21] Heather's integration takes place over a prolonged period as she realises the senselessness of the schoolgirl periodical on which at first she based both her expectations and her behaviour. In Brent-Dyer's novel, Rosamond Lilley, of a working-class family, fears snobbery on the basis of the cheap schoolgirl papers she has read and must be disabused in word and deed.[22] Reading is divorced from reality, so is unhelpful and misleading. In all such situations, the writer validates her supposedly mimetic story by distinguishing strongly between it and the false intertextual one.

Against this non-portrayal or negative portrayal of reading within girls' school stories, Elinor Brent-Dyer's books are remarkable for promoting reading.[23] The remainder of this chapter focuses on books and reading in her Chalet School series. Brent-Dyer's series stands out among girls' school stories for several reasons, most prominent of which are length and enduring popularity. It comprises fifty-nine books published between 1925 and 1970 (the year after Brent-Dyer's death), which continued to flourish after the genre in general had died; values remain static throughout the series. The entire series was republished in paperback abridgements in the 1990s and continues to be reissued unabridged. Whereas other authors set single books on the Continent, only Brent-Dyer placed most of a series there. In some ways the Chalet School appears distinctive because the sheer quantity of books underlines elements which are inevitably less marked when present in single books, such as the depiction of staff in their quarters without the girls. Brent-Dyer, carving out her place in a crowded genre, consciously sought to stand out: for example, by giving her protagonist Jo triplets, who, with their siblings, call their parents 'Mamma' and 'Papa'; and by the convention of pupils curtseying to the headmistress, to the astonishment of new English girls – features emphasised repeatedly in the books. The values of the Chalet School differ from those of a standard boarding school. Pupils underline merely the school's exceptionally caring nature and its emphasis on health.[24] But the Chalet School also stands apart for following criteria for new, state-funded (day)

BOOKS, READING AND LIBRARIES IN THE GIRLS' SCHOOL STORY   185

girls' high schools more than it does the typical boarding school images: preparing substantial numbers of girls for university; fostering meritocracy; providing academically rigorous instruction in 'boys' subjects (mathematics, science, the classics); and professionalising the traditional girls' subjects.[25]

The Chalet School is more academic than most fictional schools.[26] A *leitmotif* is that pupils are expected to work hard during lessons and prep, although for their health they are not to work beyond them – a ban which disappoints some girls. Several stories note the school's academic credentials, on the basis of which the headmistress is chosen to spend a term as a school inspector.[27] A couple of books describe girls of a certain age as 'marks hunters', while in a third, a new girl who is moved up mid-term in preference to longer-standing form members is reassured that nobody will grudge her the honour, as being moved up at that time will mean forfeiting the hope of a form prize.[28] The plot of *Adrienne and the Chalet School* (1965) centres partly around an established pupil disliking a newcomer for joining her as top of the class. Concomitantly, the role of games is minor. Although interschool matches in tennis, cricket, hockey and lacrosse are played in the Chalet School as elsewhere, games are seldom described in detail, nor is the choice of teams a significant plot element.[29] Such an unusually academic emphasis renders it natural for books, reading and libraries to be valued far more in the Chalet School series than in the average school story and for their presentation to be more positive. The challenge remains of how to foreground them.

In a communal world, Brent-Dyer, unlike other authors, achieves this by presenting reading as a communal activity. From the first book in the series to the last, staff regularly read aloud to the juniors during rest periods and to girls of all ages while they are sewing or engaged in hobbies. Titles are occasionally mentioned: *The Little Flowers of St Francis*; George MacDonald's *At the Back of the North Wind*; Rudyard Kipling's *Stalky and Co.*; Florence Converse's *The House of Prayer*; *Swiss Family Robinson*.[30] When reading to themselves, girls are often congregated: resting in hall after lunch, or in the grounds in hot weather. They are allied by enjoying the same books: 'Half the form had already revelled in *Shadows on the Rock* which gives such a vivid picture of life in Quebec at that time, and the other half was waiting anxiously for it.'[31] Past as well as current reading welds them in a shared culture, with allusions which the characters expect each other to understand: 'You sound exactly like the Red Queen out of Alice',[32] for example, or: 'The next day "Mrs Squeers", as naughty Jo promptly christened her sister, appeared again with her medicine.'[33]

Books unite girls in multiple voluntary, sometimes mischievous activities. The younger girls study an encyclopaedia together in order to reset a clock whose slowness results in a slight increase of lesson and decrease in break time.[34] They pore over Roget's *Thesaurus* for alternatives to forbidden slang, relishing the unusual words they find.[35] Unnervingly, they devour Martha Finlay's *Elsie's Motherhood* with each other to learn about the Ku-Klux-Klan for ideas of how to treat the pupils of a rival school.[36]

Educationalists deplored school stories partly for their use of slang.[37] Writers, on the other hand, believed that slang appealed to the books' target audiences and promoted a sense of realism. Brent-Dyer addressed the problem by allowing girls to speak slang while having the staff crusade regularly against it, and drew intertextual reading into her defence. Sent to school to reform for talking too slangily, Prunella takes revenge by speaking unnaturally stilted English. Series heroine Mary-Lou recounts the plot of Fanny Burney's *Evelina* and compares Prunella's language with that of a Burney heroine.[38] Brent-Dyer defends her own reproduction of colloquial language in an explicit message aimed at the censors of girls' fiction as much as at the readers when Mary-Lou tells Prunella:

> No modern girl would read them [Jo Bettany's books] if they weren't written in – in modern idiom. You couldn't expect it. . . . People must talk like their neighbours or else other folk will think there's something wrong with them. . . . Anyhow, the people in Aunt Joey's books are just like real people and there's precious few real people nowadays who go around talking as if they'd just had a session with Elizabeth Bennet or Evelina Belmont![39]

Twice slang is used in conjunction with communal reading as a significant plot element. In Chapter 9 of *Jo of the Chalet School*, heroine Jo and her friends retaliate to an attack on slang by speaking Shakespearean English for a day, a prank which requires a week of preparatory reading of Shakespeare's plays. Several books later the next generation of pupils, having heard of the Shakespearean escapade and inspired by the moan 'It's hard lines to have to talk like a Jane Austen heroine',[40] decides to speak Regency English in protest. Too lazy to read early nineteenth-century novels in full, they make do with abridgements and with Georgette Heyer. In a lesson that idiom is of its time, the prefects make the Regency speakers behave like Regency girls for a weekend, imitating physically and uncomfortably a world in which they had chosen not to immerse themselves intellectually by reading.[41]

In an environment in which reading contributes to the community atmosphere, girls who dislike reading exclude themselves from communal enjoyment. Games depend on books. In *Shocks for the Chalet School*, mistresses dress as book titles for Saturday evening entertainment, for all to guess: a pleasure for those within a book culture and an impossibility

BOOKS, READING AND LIBRARIES IN THE GIRLS' SCHOOL STORY 187

for those outside one, especially as the eclectic titles used are mainly out-side the curriculum (J. M. Barrie's *The Little Minister*; Dorothy Sayers's *Whose Body*; Wilkie Collins's *The Woman in White*).[42] In *A Leader in the Chalet School* girls compete to guess the names of charades based on books, mainly of books mentioned elsewhere in the Chalet School series: *Das Buch von Trott*; *Little Women*; *Anne of Green Gables*; *Heidi*; *Nicholas Nickleby*; *Swiss Family Robinson*; *Oliver Twist*; *Sans famille* (Hector Malot) and *Vanity Fair*.[43] One character, Jack, is seriously disadvantaged by not being a reader. Competitions involve impersonating characters, either historical or fictitious (Alice in Wonderland; Mrs Malaprop) and finishing verses with book titles.[44] Reading forms part of the schoolgirl code, with the reading occasionally extending beyond the text to the particular edi-tion: Mary-Lou wears her hair in plaits which are described in several books as 'Kenwigses' for their resemblance to illustrations of the Kenwigs women in the edition of *Nicholas Nickleby* her form reads in class.

Reading bonds girls between schools and represents the power of knowledge when the girls at St Scholastica's take an idea for a magic cave from a novel for the annual sale they share with the Chalet School:

'. . . we got the idea out of one of her [Charlotte M. Yonge's] books,' explained Hilary.

'. . . It's the one called *The Three Brides*. . . .'

'We haven't got *The Three Brides*,' said Jo thoughtfully. . . .

'But', complained Cornelia at this point, 'if we haven't got it, how under the canopy am I to find out about the Magic Cave?'

'You can't. That was the great idea,' said Hilary calmly.[45]

With these values, the deprivation of reading, rather than the imposition of reading, is a punishment. Use of the school library is described as a privilege of community, and in three books non-conforming girls are threatened with the withdrawal of the right to borrow from its fiction section.[46] Two books introduce a new matron who, failing to understand the school's values and ethics, must depart prematurely; in both instances, her sins include stopping girls from reading in bed in the early mornings.[47]

Most Chalet girls explicitly enjoy reading, led by 'omnivorous' and 'insatiable' reader and series heroine, Jo Bettany; the series begins with twelve-year-old Jo engrossed in Scott's *Quentin Durward*, and Jo's reading is the broadest in the series. The few girls in the series who avowedly dis-like reading are either the less pleasant characters (Grizel Cochrane, typically described as 'hard'), or tomboys like Jack (Jacynth), who prefers working with motors. Most books refer to girls reading for pleasure. Mistresses also relax with light literature such as Richmal Crompton's *More William*.[48] Reading is an expected relaxation: Nina Rutherford, a budding musical genius, is advised to try handcrafts on the basis that as a professional pianist she will spend a great deal of time travelling, when 'no one can read all the time'.[49] Rereading favourite books from the Victorian period is common practice, with different girls rereading Dinah Craik's *John Halifax, Gentleman*, Richard Jefferies' *Bevis*, Dickens's *Dombey and Son*, A.L.O.E.'s *The Crown of Success*, and Juliana Horatia Ewing's *Six to Sixteen*, in the case of *Bevis* and *The Crown of Success* (a general Chalet School favourite) for the sixth time.[50] On the whole the girls enjoy what they read, and whatever books they find laborious are either imposed tasks or books of dubious suitability. Len Maynard struggles with John Ruskin's *Sesame and Lilies*, her set holiday reading, but the author hastens to make her add how much she likes his *King of the Golden River*;[51] when Naomi Elton is 'not enamoured' with *Humphry Clinker* (the reading of which Mary-Lou questions), she shows her delicacy and good taste in disliking a text full of scatological humour.[52] Unlike their counterparts in other school stories, the girls live surrounded by books. The common rooms, staff room, school secretary's office, headmistress's office, matron's room, and the few homes into which the reader is permitted a glimpse all contain low bookshelves filled with books described approvingly as 'gaily jacketed', the type to appeal to the relevant age group. For example:

> Opposite, bookcases filled with books of all sorts and in the three official languages of the school . . . offered an inviting selection to readers. . . . All in all, it was a really delightful room;[53]

> The room was a large, pleasant one, with pale yellow walls. . . . Along two of the walls ran low bookcases, crowded and crammed with books of all kinds that folk who had not yet reached the teen age would like.[54]

The presentation of reading draws in the actual reader in her teens or younger, at an age at which children read actively, involving themselves with their reading and identifying with a book's characters.[55] Girls who could aspire to an exclusive continental boarding school education only vicariously through the Chalet School titles[56] could identify with the Chalet girls by reading; to an extent by reading the same books, many of which are established classics. They could participate in the competitions involving books, which are described thoroughly. They could pick up the same literary allusions as the Chalet girls. Indeed, Brent-Dyer encourages reading by offering additional, superfluous literary allusions in her explanatory narrative, such as 'Mary-Lou who, like *Amy* of "Little

BOOKS, READING AND LIBRARIES IN THE GIRLS' SCHOOL STORY 189

Women" fame, was fond of delicacies', and 'Diana Skelton seems to be only step removed from Wordsworth's idiot boy'.[57] The actual reader is furthermore in a position to identify parallels between the Chalet School and other books. *Eustacia Goes to the Chalet School* is especially rich in this respect. The first sentence, 'There is no disguising the fact that Eustacia Benson was the most arrant little prig that ever existed', recalls the introductory sentence of Frances Hodgson Burnett's *The Secret Garden*: 'When Mary Lennox was sent to Misselthwaite Manor to live with her uncle, everybody said she was the most disagreeable-looking child ever seen.' Eustacia tells tales in similarly pompous language to Paul Bultitude in F. Anstey's *Vice Versa* ('I felt that you ought to know that the two girls in front of me are wasting their time in some babyish games instead of doing as they were bidden'), while an accident in which Eustacia hurts her back is reminiscent of Katy's accident in *What Katy Did*. Dr Jem advises Eustacia in a compound of Dr Carr's and Cousin Helen's words in Coolidge's text, and Eustacia learns to appreciate her aunt in illness as Katy did Aunt Izzie.[58] Elsewhere, Deira, furious with Head Girl Grizel for assigning her the position of Hobbies Prefect, burns Grizel's harmony book in a scene with shades of Amy burning Jo's book in *Little Women*.[59] It is hard not to regard Primula Mary Venables of *The New House at the Chalet School* as not having been named after Primula Mary Beton of Dorita Fairlie Bruce's Springdale series, or Dickie Carey's affectionate reference to her mother as 'Mother Carey' not to be based on 'Mother Carey' of Charlotte M. Yonge's *Magnum Bonum*.

That the Chalet girls are models for reading becomes especially clear in a consideration of titles read. In a fan club newsletter, Brent-Dyer recommends specific well-known children's classics by Lewis Carroll, Charles Kingsley, George MacDonald, Oscar Wilde, Louisa M. Alcott and Susan Coolidge, and anything by Andrew Lang, G. A. Henty, Noel Streatfeild and Rudyard Kipling. She moves into adult territory with titles by John Ruskin ('"hard going" but his writing is excellent'), and the works of John Buchan, Dorothy Sayers (specifically the 'Lord Peter' books), Jane Austen, Scott, Thackery, Dickens, 'the great poets' and 'the leaders in the best daily papers'.[60] Subsequently she adds Anthony Trollope, Angela Thirkell, Nancy Spain, Lord David Cecil's *Melbourne*, *Unforgettable, Unforgotten*, by Anna Buchan (alias O. Douglas), Robert Louis Stevenson, Juliana Horatia Ewing and Cynthia Harnett.[61] The choice is sweeping and eclectic, with books from different genres and periods, and the Chalet girls read most of the books or authors named.[62] Brent-Dyer states that there are 'hundreds more' to read,[63] and members of the Chalet School read extras too. Except for Shakespeare, the earliest text mentioned is Sheridan's *The Rivals* (1775). The Chalet girls read a range of works extending from the late eighteenth century to recent publications, a mixture of children's fiction (E. Nesbit; *Little Women*; Martha Finlay's Elsie book; Arthur Ransome; school stories and others) and general fiction (a great deal of Dickens; George Eliot; Scott; George du Maurier's *Trilby*; John Galsworthy's *The Forsyte Saga*), with a fair proportion of historical fiction with clear educational overtones, such as Edna Lyall's *In Spite of All* and Violet Needham's *The Boy in Red*. While some books are mentioned only once, others recur, notably the works of John Buchan, Kipling and Yonge.

The relevance for actual girls is underlined by the fact that although the Chalet girls are educated for much of the series in English, French and German, their recreational reading matter is almost entirely in English, the language of the targeted readers. When Gillian Linton borrows the fairy tale 'Le Chat de Madame Michel' (actually *Histoire de la Mère Michel et son chat*) from the school library it is specifically in order to improve her French,[64] and other foreign titles appear in the context of books in lessons. Despite the trilingual education and a high proportion of foreign pupils, the textbooks, like the books read for pleasure, have an English base: Shakespeare, Jane Austen and Dickens for English literature; standard readers for other languages, such as Mme de Ségur's *Les Malheurs de Sophie* (published in a school edition by Longmans in 1930) and Louis Énault's *Le Chien du capitaine*, which appeared for schools by 1890.

The books Brent-Dyer recommends by precept in her newsletter and by intertextual reading in the series are educational, being also those recommended for girls in professional literature for teachers and librarians.[65] They are part of a broader educative mission, whereby Brent-Dyer recounts local legends, describes towns and their history visited by the girls on excursions, festoons the text with (admittedly execrable) scraps of French and German vocabulary to encourage girls to learn, and presents domestic science lessons with step-by-step instruction for the preparation of food which teaches the reader as well as the Chalet School pupils. Chambers in its blurbs for Chalet School titles in the 1930s advertised them as being 'as instructive as they are entertaining'.[66] The appeal was to adults with purchasing power as much as to girls.

Fictional authorship is more prevalent in the Chalet School than in the standard school story. Four girls have fathers who are journalists or naturalists and have written acclaimed books, the school's music master has produced a monograph on music, Eustacia (now Stacie) Benson's books on Aeschylus are hailed as authorities, and Lavender Leigh's aunt in *Lavender Laughs at the Chalet School* (1943) has penned an entire series of geography readers popular with the Chalet girls. The main author is series heroine Jo Bettany. Jo serves as Brent-Dyer's fictional mouthpiece and representative. Like Brent-Dyer, Jo produces popular school, adventure, and guides stories and historical novels at a prodigious rate. Her books are invariably beloved of the Chalet School pupils, as Brent-Dyer's are by her fans, and having read and enjoyed Jo's books is a sign that a new girl will make good. Jo's books in the series, like Brent-Dyer's in fact, are awarded as prizes in competitions. Brent-Dyer advertised her books through her fan club, and through intertextual references within the series, often footnoted. Jo's authorship is an additional advertisement tool. *Nancy Meets a Nazi* equates with *The Chalet School in Exile*, while Jo's *The Lost Staircase* is an actual title by Brent-Dyer.[67]

The 'reality' of the Chalet School world blurs with the fiction of Jo's stories within it, as Jo builds pranks and adventures that occur in the Chalet School into her books. The symbiosis between 'fact' and fiction is at its greatest when a girl 'fell back in desperation on an episode she had read in one of her uncle's old school stories' to stick a teacher's drawer closed with cobbler's wax, and Jo reacts with: 'What a gaudy episode for my new school yarn! Thanks a million! It's just what I wanted!'[68] Jo hereby reflects her creator, who both based incidents in her fiction on activities in the Margaret Roper School she ran in Herefordshire between 1938 and 1948 and modelled elements of the Margaret Roper School on the Chalet School.[69] The relationship of the later Chalet girls to Jo, the successful writer, equates on one level that between fans and Brent-Dyer. The parallel enables readers to identify still more closely with the Chalet School.

The Chalet School follows the standard topos of presenting unrealistic intradiegetic schoolgirl fiction within the 'authentic' fiction. Much of this occurs when the school is being formed and its Continental pupils avidly read English girls' school stories as a point of reference.[70] It falls to Jo as an English girl from an English school to describe the stories as 'tosh' and to protest:

'But it says so in the books I have read,' persisted the elder girl.

'But that's only to make the story,' explained Jo. 'We don't really do such things – honest Injun, Gertrud!'[71]

Once the school has been established, the fiction recedes, to reappear only briefly as new girls must correct erroneous imaginings. The example of Rosalind Lilley, who fears snobbery on the basis of her reading, has been noted above. In a chapter entitled 'The Result of Too Many School Stories', Polly Heriot, who has read many school stories and assumed them to be mimetic, rings the fire bell in the middle of the night in imitation of *Pat, the Pride of the School* (not a real title), thereby rousing the entire valley. Jo consequently 'sat down that afternoon to review her own book, and with a stern hand she remorselessly removed any pranks there-from that might be supposed to incite brainless Juniors to imitation thereof'.[72]

Yet the inspiration of school stories is not always bad. In *Carola Storms the Chalet School* (the eponymous heroine of which is also imbued with school stories, and must adjust her perceptions), the prefects reform pupils' language by making them write down the true meanings of words they use as slang, an idea gained from a fictitious school story.[73] Brent-Dyer recommends certain school stories through the reading of her characters. Gwensi Howell in *The Chalet School Goes To It* has shelves full of the books of Dorita Fairlie Bruce, Winifred Darch and Elsie Oxenham as well as of the fictional Jo Bettany.[74] Bruce, Oxenham and, obliquely, Phyllis Matthewman appear elsewhere in the series. In a late book, *Adrienne and the Chalet School* (1965), Adrienne, like the Chalet School's earliest foreign pupils, reads school stories (in this instance Jo's) for guidance and learns from them the characteristics of the ideal schoolgirl:

> During the long and often wearisome convalescence, she had brought the girl school stories written by this sister of hers, Mme Maynard. Adrienne had never read any tales like this and it did not take her long to discover what kind of girl both the author and Soeur Cécile preferred. She must be truthful and honest, working and playing with all her might, faithful to her promises, kind, loyal, above talking maliciously about other girls. These were the main points to strike Adrienne – though later she was to find others.[75]

Adrienne is academically ambitious, an accepted 'slogger' and high achiever. Unlike Polly, she illustrates the quality of discerning reading, distilling qualities from plot and realising that what is to be imitated is the best of the values, not the incidents of mischievous girls. In this way books read – Jo's and, by implication, Brent-Dyer's – represent an inner truth. The reader learns to read in a way to derive moral benefit from school stories.

Reading has its times and places. It must not make girls unpunctual, as it does Eustacia.[76] Richenda Fry must learn not to read while dressing, Ruey Richardson not to interrupt her preparation time with novel-reading.[77] Within these constraints, failure to read when one is supposed to be reading is what repeatedly causes trouble. The possible dire consequences of being immersed in a book and so oblivious to one's surroundings are never mentioned. But because Madge Bettany falls asleep over her book instead of reading it, she fails to notice an impending storm and she and the girls under her care are trapped by it.[78] Recalcitrant girls plot silly deeds, such as running away, or evil ones, such as taking revenge on a

BOOKS, READING AND LIBRARIES IN THE GIRLS' SCHOOL STORY   193

classmate, instead of concentrating on the book before them, as in: 'The one idea of "showing them" filled her mind to the exclusion of everything else, and as she sat with *Henry Esmond* open before her, Grizel was busily making plans for the morrow'[79] and: 'Betty, sprawled on a near-by settee, pretended to be deep in Prester John', when listening to chatter which gives her a handle on how to 'pay off all scores'.[80] Reading is connected with tranquillity and with bodily safety; the pretence or neglect of reading with mental anguish and with physical danger.

Books may be acceptable in certain contexts, but not in others. Brent-Dyer recommends Dorothy Sayers and role-model schoolgirl Mary-Lou admits: 'I rather love a really good whodunnit, don't you?'[81] Yet detective stories are generally the butt of disparaging remarks, such as: 'That is what comes of reading so many detective novels . . . If you'd leave thrillers alone, all of you, and try something sensible, you wouldn't be so ready to look for the worst before it happened'; 'It's high time someone looked after your reading.'[82] *Redheads at the Chalet School* takes on elements of the detective story as evil forces attempt to kidnap the daughter of a detective who has harmed their gang. The detective story, 'real' as in Redheads or obviously fictitious, signifies too much danger to the safe, enclosed world of school. Ghost stories or innocuous legends become 'bad' reading when told to excitable children too close to bedtime, inducing nightmares. As distinctions are made, readers are expected to discriminate between appropriate and inappropriate reading matter. 'I wonder what she's been reading during the hols?' is a refrain when girls have impractical ideas.[83] While Miss Derwent vets books brought into school, staff acknowledge that they cannot influence what girls read outside the confinements of school and, towards the end of the series, that television and the cinema can also influence girls' minds. In providing so many suggestions of reading of her own – a greater quantity within the pages of the Chalet School series than in the fan newsletter – Brent-Dyer attempts to guide her readers' reading and to equip them to discriminate.

A report by the Board of Education in 1910/11 had commented on the need in any well-equipped school for a small fiction library of historical novels and books of adventure.[84] Within girls' schools generally, the existence of the school library is a status symbol. It is a quiet place where (mainly senior) girls work. Brent-Dyer makes it far more prominent. It is particularly salient in *Eustacia Goes to the Chalet School*, in which Eustacia, new and accustomed to solitude, seeks the library out when it is closed and suffers so bitterly from having it banned to her that she ultimately runs away. But it appears in most books. A standard ritual of the new school year is assignment of duties among the prefects, whereby one girl is always the library prefect, later assisted by a second girl for the junior library. All three of Brent-Dyer's major schoolgirl role models, Jo Bettany, her daughter Len and Mary-Lou Trelawney, are library prefects before progressing to become head girl. The library is noted as a good one, with regular donations of books or money by girls when they leave, and it contributes to the academic reputation of the Chalet School. When the school splits between England and Switzerland, a chapter is assigned to dividing books between the two branches, and *Summer Term at the Chalet School* devotes a chapter to the process of book selection, with each form suggesting the acquisition of three works of fiction and three of non-fiction.[85] These and a library stocktake which reveals certain implicitly popular books to be missing[86] provide the opportunity in a short space to mention and tacitly to recommend many actual titles, while the fact of the library is an additional link between the Chalet School and its readers.

Occasionally the library appears as a physical space. In *Redheads at the Chalet School*, it is from the library that Len Maynard spies the kidnapping villain snooping around, and enough of the library layout is described to explain how Len could observe without danger of being seen.[87] When the school celebrates its twenty-fifth anniversary, library architecture comes into play with a suggestion to erect a purpose-built library, which some girls think could allow a better overview and prevent books from being mistreated or going missing.[88] Brent-Dyer follows an actual trend, writing this as school libraries were becoming increasingly important.[89]

The library offers an added opportunity for the girls to demonstrate autonomy: they appear to do everything in the library, and the supervisory role of a mistress is shadowy. In another expression of female empowerment, the Chalet School offers one example of a pupil wanting to become a librarian and knowing about the training and the most prestigious positions:

'I want to be a librarian 'cos I love books so much. I'm going to Oxford first to get my B.A., and then I'll have to take special library training, and go in for the librarian exams. But it'll be well worth it. I'd like,' she added modestly, 'to get a post as librarian at the Bodleian, or else at Windsor Castle. Something like that, you know. Or the British Museum wouldn't be too bad.'

'You don't want much!' cried Daisy. 'The Bodleian, Windsor, or the British Museum! Upon my word, Bride, you don't lack for cheek!'[90]

None of Brent-Dyer's girls demonstrates the bibliophily of Antonia Forest's Nicola Marlow, who chooses the *Iliad* as a school prize for its appearance – 'two vellum-bound, gold-patterned volumes dated 1834, printed in Greek with the notes in Latin: utterly fabulous and gloriously incomprehensible' – and who exchanges her share in a donkey for a facsimile of Shakespeare's First Folio, entranced by the type and the preliminaries.[91] But Brent-Dyer does discuss the treatment of books. Library books require repair; older girls mourn the rough treatment of books by younger ones, which may result in the loss of pages or the tearing of the spine;[92] Eustacia defends her handling of a book by her knowing how to treat books respectfully; books may be out of bounds not just for content, but for their value.[93] All books have a life thereby and are to be respected. Jo's proofs, the first form of her books, recur, described in their physicality as 'paper eels'.[94] The rounded presentation of books as artefacts as well as carriers of content raises appreciation for the printed word.

Successful as she indubitably was, few would describe Elinor Brent-Dyer as a skilful writer, especially in her later Chalet School books with their worn plots. Yet she transforms the school story by turning the games-mad institution to one with an intellectual emphasis, while retaining readers. She advertises her books skilfully through her characters' love of reading, portrays the unportrayable solitary activity as an enjoyable, often communal, one, and guides her readers to broad, sound reading through the reading of her characters. She instils a respect for books into her readers. Repeated references to reading in particular situations, to bookshelves, to library duties and to certain authors and titles contribute to the series element which above all renders the Chalet School books enduring.[95] Brent-Dyer uses reading in her books as an educational vehicle which gains adult approval without deterring her target audience. She adroitly blends self-promotion with an altruistic mission. This is a legacy of which to be proud.

Notes

1. Sue Sims and Hilary Clare, *The Encyclopaedia of Girls' School Stories* (Aldershot: Ashgate, 2000), pp. 14, 10.

2. Sheila Ray, *The Blyton Phenomenon: The Controversy Surrounding the World's Most Successful Children's Writer* (London: Deutsch, 1982), p. 195.

3. See Sims and Clare, *Encyclopaedia*, which includes a bibliography for each writer treated.

4. See especially Rosemary Auchmuty, *A World of Girls* (London: Women's Press, 1992); Judith Humphrey, *The English Girls School Story: Subversion and Challenge in a Traditional, Conservative Literary Genre* (Bethesda, MD: Academica Press, 2009); Rebecca Knuth, *Children's Literature and British Identity: Imagining a People and a Nation* (Lanham, MD: Scarecrow Press, 2012), pp. 121–3.

5. The exception is Sheila Ray, 'The Literary Context', in *The Chalet School Revisited*, ed. by Rosemary Auchmuty and Juliet Gosling (London: Bettany, 1994), pp. 97–138. Ray concentrates on critical attitudes towards school stories and then on literary references in the first seventeen Chalet School titles.

6. Dorita Fairlie Bruce, *The Senior Prefect* (Oxford: Oxford University Press, 1921), ch. 28. For the ubiquity of such a view, see Sims and Clare, *Encyclopaedia*, pp. 8–9.

7. Terms used by Bruce W. Tuckman, 'Developmental Sequence in Small Groups', *Psychological Bulletin*, 63 (1965), 384–99.

8. See ch. 4, 'The School Story', in M. O. Grenby, *Children's Literature*, second edn (Edinburgh: Edinburgh University Press, 2014), pp. 87–116.

9. See Pat Pinsent, 'Theories of Genre and Gender: Change and Continuity in the School Story', in *Modern Children's Literature: An Introduction*, ed. by Kimberley Reynolds (Houndmills: Palgrave Macmillan, 2005), pp. 8–22.

10. For example, Winifred Darch, *Margaret Plays the Game* (London: Oxford University Press, 1931), ch. 5.

11. Irene Mossop, *Well Played, Juliana!* (London: Sampson Low, Marston, 1928), ch. 16.

12. Gwendoline Courtney, *At School with the Stanhopes* (London: Nelson, 1951), ch. 8.

13. See, for example, Betty Laws, *The New Head – and Barbara* (London: Cassell, 1925), ch. 8.

14. Antonia Forest, *The Cricket Term* (London: Faber, 1974; repr. Harmondsworth: Puffin, 1979), ch. 5.

15. Winifred Darch, *The Upper Fifth in Command* (London: Oxford University Press, 1928).

16. Elinor M. Brent-Dyer (henceforward EBD), *The Rivals of the Chalet School* (1929), ch. 20. London: Chambers is the imprint of all Chalet School books.

17. For a discussion of such intertextuality, see Heather Julien, 'Learning to be Modern Girls: Winifred Darch's School Stories', *The Lion and the Unicorn*, 32 (2008), 1–21 (pp. 10–12).

18. Phyllis Matthewman, *The Intrusion of Nicola* (London: Lutterworth, 1948), ch. 16.

19. Matthewman, *Intrusion*, ch. 7.

20. Matthewman, *Intrusion*, ch. 3.

21. See also Winifred Darch, *The New School and Hilary*, about *Schoolgirl's Chum* (a fictitious title): 'really the adventures were so impossible and the jokes so awfully silly. Besides, all the common kids read it'; 'I prefer original tricks myself, not things out of a penny magazine' (London: Oxford University Press, 1926) (ch. 6).

22. For treatments of snobbery, see Clare Hollowell, 'For the Honour of the School: Class in the Girls' School Story', *Children's Literature in Education*, 45 (2014), 310–23 and, with respect to Winifred Darch, Julien, 'Learning to be Modern Girls', pp. 4–9.

23. For a biography of Brent-Dyer, see Helen McClelland, *Behind the Chalet School*, second edn (London: Bettany, 1996).

24. EBD, *Ruey Richardson, Chaletian* (1960), ch. 12.

25. Julien, 'Learning to be Modern Girls', p. 4. Winifred Darch, a professional teacher like Brent-Dyer, shares this emphasis; however, Darch, unlike Brent-Dyer, is writing about day-schools and high schools.

26. Noted also by Juliet Gosling, '"School with Bells On!": The School at the Chalet and Beyond', in Auchmuty and Gosling, *The Chalet School Revisited*, pp. 139–71 (p. 144).

27. EBD, *Challenge for the Chalet School* (1966).

BOOKS, READING AND LIBRARIES IN THE GIRLS' SCHOOL STORY 197

28. EBD, *Theodora of the Chalet School* (1959), ch. 9.

29. Sports which are described are those requiring individual prowess: regattas when the Chalet School is situated at St Briavel's; obstacle races and so forth in Switzerland.

30. EBD, *The School at the Chalet* (1925), ch. 15; *The Head Girl of the Chalet School* (1928), chs. 8 and 12; *Rivals*, ch. 16; *Trials for the Chalet School* (1959), ch. 4 respectively. Further occurrences of mistresses reading to girls appear in: *The New House at the Chalet School* (1935), ch. 17; *Gay from China at the Chalet School* (1944), ch. 15; *Tom Tackles the Chalet School* (1955), 'story poems', ch. 15; *A Leader in the Chalet School* (1961), chs. 3 and 6; *The Feud in the Chalet School* (1962), ch. 13, *Prefects of the Chalet School* (1970), ch. 10 (a travel book).

31. EBD, *The Chalet School and the Island* (1950), ch. 4. Single girls often recommend books to others.

32. EBD, *Althea Joins the Chalet School* (1969), ch. 4.

33. EBD, *Jo of the Chalet School* (1926).

34. EBD, *The Exploits of the Chalet Girls* (1933), ch. 9.

35. EBD, *Adrienne and the Chalet School* (1965), ch. 6.

36. EBD, *Rivals*, ch. 4.

37. See Judy Simons, 'Angela Brazil and the Making of the Girls' School Story', in *Popular Children's Literature in Britain*, ed. by Julia Briggs, Dennis Butts and M. O. Grenby (Aldershot: Ashgate, 2008), pp. 165–81 (p. 172).

38. EBD, *The Chalet School Does It Again* (1955), ch. 3.

39. EBD, *Does It Again* (1955), ch. 3.

40. EBD, *Peggy of the Chalet School* (1950), ch. 10.

41. EBD, *Peggy*, ch. 12–13.

42. EBD, *Shocks for the Chalet School* (1952), ch. 15.

43. Brent-Dyer, *Leader*, ch. 5. *Das Buch von Trott* is actually André Lichtenberger's *Mein kleiner Trott*, a translation of *Le petit Trott*; Brent-Dyer almost always uses the German title and makes translating it a German exercise for Chalet pupils.

44. EBD, *Jane and the Chalet School* (1964), ch. 14; *Bride Leads the Chalet School* (1953), ch. 18; and *A Genius at the Chalet School* (1956), ch. 19.

45. EBD, *The Chalet School and the Lintons* (1934), ch. 17.

46. EBD, *The New Chalet School* (1938), ch. 13; *Bride*, ch. 12; *A Problem for the Chalet School* (1956), ch. 11.

47. EBD, *The Princess of the Chalet School* (1927), ch. 7; *The New House at the Chalet School* (1935), ch. 7.

48. Brent-Dyer, *Lintons*, ch. 13.

49. Brent-Dyer, *Genius*, ch. 5.

50. EBD, *Jo to the Rescue* ((1945), ch. 14; *Bride*, ch. 14.

51. EBD, *A Future Chalet School Girl* (1962), ch. 14.

52. EBD, *Trials*, ch. 10.

53. EBD, *The Chalet School in the Oberland* (1952), ch. 2.

54. EBD, *Leader*, ch. 1. I counted fourteen books with similar references.

55. For an exposition of reading at different ages, see J. A. Appleyard, *Becoming a Reader: The Experience of Fiction from Childhood to Adulthood* (Cambridge: Cambridge University Press, 1990).

56. See Gillian Avery, *Childhood's Pattern: A Study of the Heroes and Heroines of Children's Fiction 1770–1950* (London: Hodder and Stoughton, 1975), p. 207; P. W. Musgrave, *From Brown to Bunter: The Life and Death of the School Story* (London: Routledge & Kegan Paul, 1985), p. 232; Julien, 'Learning to be Modern Girls', p. 10.

57. EBD, *Carola Storms the Chalet School* (1951), ch. 16; *Bride*, ch. 13.

58. EBD, *Eustacia Goes to the Chalet School* (1930), ch. 6; ch. 25.

59. EBD, *Head-Girl*, chs. 6–7.

60. *Chalet Club News Letter*, 8 (1962), repr. in: *Chalet Club News Letters* (Coleford: Girls Gone By, 2004), p. 32.

61. *Chalet Club News Letter*, 12 (1964), repr. in: *Chalet Club News Letters*, p. 53.

62. The only novels they do not are by Kingsley, Wilde, Coolidge, Henty, Nancy Spain, Lord Cecil, Anna Buchan, Mrs Gaskell, Miss Read, *Villette* (but Nina Rutherford in the Chalet School reads *Shirley*), D. E. Stevenson and Miss Read. They read less of the poetry, and none of the recommendations in the *Newsletter* for younger readers.

63. *Chalet Club News Letter*, 8, p. 32.

64. EBD, *Lintons*, ch. 10.

65. Ray, 'Literary Context', pp. 98–9.

66. McClelland, *Behind*, p. 280.

67. EBD, *The Lost Staircase* (1946); cf EBD, *Lavender Laughs in the Chalet School* (1943), ch. 7 and *Jo to the Rescue* (1945), ch. 4.

68. EBD, *Challenge for the Chalet School* (1966), ch. 15–16.

69. McClelland, *Behind*, pp. 228–32.

70. EBD, *The School at the Chalet* (1925), ch. 5, 11, 18.

71. EBD, *School at*, ch. 5.

72. EBD, *Jo Returns*, chs. 9–10.

73. EBD, *Carola*, ch. 11.

74. EBD, *The Chalet School Goes To It* (1941), ch. 5.

75. EBD, *Adrienne* (1965), ch. 3.

76. EBD, *Eustacia*, ch. 8.

77. EBD, *The Chalet School and Richenda* (1958); ch. 4; *Ruey*, ch. 12.

78. EBD, *School at*, ch. 17.

79. EBD, *School at*, ch. 21.

80. EBD, *The Highland Twins at the Chalet School* (1942), ch. 13.

81. EBD, *Trials*, ch. 10.

82. EBD, *The Chalet Girls in Camp* (1932), ch. 9; *The Coming of Age of the Chalet School* (1958), ch. 14.

83. EBD, *Prefects*, ch. 3.

84. Musgrave, *From Brown to Bunter*, p. 225.

85. EBD, *Changes for the Chalet School* (1953), ch. 13; *Summer Term at the Chalet School* (1965), ch. 11.

86. EBD, *The New Mistress at the Chalet School* (1957), ch. 18. The missing books are by Buchan, Thirkell, Matthewman and MacDonald, as well as a geography reader; in this context, it is noteworthy that in 1951 Elinor Brent-Dyer published four geography readers.

87. EBD, *Redheads at the Chalet School* (1964), ch. 8.

88. EBD, *Summer Term*, ch. 8–9.

89. Sheila G. Ray, 'Library Work with Children and Young People', in *Five Years' Work in Librarianship 1961–1965*, ed. by P. H. Sewell (London: Library Association, 1968), pp. 377–87 (p. 383). The Ministry of Education had ordered schools to improve their libraries in the 1950s (Sims and Clare, *Encyclopaedia*, p. 21).

90. EBD, *Tom Tackles*, ch. 9. By the next time girls discuss future plans, Bride has joined the many who wish to teach. When later in the series a library prefect, Eve Hurrell, wants to become a librarian, no expansion is given.

91. Forest, *The Cricket Term*, ch. 9; ch. 10.

92. EBD, *Summer Term*, ch. 9.

93. Note an expensive art book with many plates, which Polly Heriot borrows unlawfully and accidentally drops, crumpling the plates; the incident provides seven pages of narrative (EBD, *Jo Returns*, ch. 8).

94. EBD, *Jane*, ch. 10.

95. Sue Sims, 'The Series Factor', in Auchmuty and Gosling, *The Chalet School Revisited*, pp. 253–81 (p. 279).

Bibliography of secondary literature

Appleyard, J. A., *Becoming a Reader: The Experience of Fiction from Childhood to Adulthood* (Cambridge: Cambridge University Press, 1990)

Auchmuty, Rosemary, *A World of Girls* (London: Women's Press, 1992)

Auchmuty, Rosemary and Juliet Gosling (eds), *The Chalet School Revisited* (London: Bettany Press, 1994)

Avery, Gillian, *Childhood's Pattern: A Study of the Heroes and Heroines of Children's Fiction 1770–1950* (London: Hodder and Stoughton, 1975)

Chalet Club News Letters (Coleford: Girls Gone By, 2004)

Gosling, Juliet, '"School with Bells On!": The School at the Chalet and Beyond', in *The Chalet School Revisited*, ed. by Rosemary Auchmuty and Juliet Gosling (London: Bettany, 1994), pp. 139–71

Grenby, M. O., *Children's Literature*, second edn (Edinburgh: Edinburgh University Press, 2014)

Hollowell, Clare, 'For the Honour of the School: Class in the Girls' School Story', *Children's Literature in Education*, 45 (2014), 310–23

Humphrey, Judith, *The English Girls School Story: Subversion and Challenge in a Traditional, Conservative Literary Genre* (Bethesda, MD: Academica Press, 2009)

Julien, Heather, 'Learning to be Modern Girls: Winifred Darch's School Stories', *The Lion and the Unicorn*, 32 (2008), 1–21

Knuth, Rebecca, *Children's Literature and British Identity: Imagining a People and a Nation* (Lanham, MD: Scarecrow Press, 2012)

McClelland, Helen, *Behind the Chalet School*, 2nd edn (London: Bettany, 1996)

Musgrave, P. W., *From Brown to Bunter: The Life and Death of the School Story* (London: Routledge & Kegan Paul, 1985)

Pinsent, Pat, 'Theories of Genre and Gender: Change and Continuity in the School Story', in *Modern Children's Literature: An Introduction*, ed. by Kimberley Reynolds (Houndmills: Palgrave Macmillan, 2005), pp. 8–22

Ray, Sheila, *The Blyton Phenomenon: The Controversy Surrounding the World's Most Successful Children's Writer* (London: Deutsch, 1982)

Ray, Sheila, 'Library Work with Children and Young People', in *Five Years' Work in Librarianship 1961–1965*, ed. by P. H. Sewell (London: Library Association, 1968), pp. 377–87

Ray, Sheila, 'The Literary Context', in *The Chalet School Revisited*, ed. by Rosemary Auchmuty and Juliet Gosling (London: Bettany, 1994), pp. 97–138

Simons, Judy, 'Angela Brazil and the Making of the Girls' School Story', in *Popular Children's Literature in Britain*, ed. by Julia Briggs, Dennis Butts and M. O. Grenby (Aldershot: Ashgate, 2008), pp. 165–81

Sims, Sue, 'The Series Factor', in *The Chalet School Revisited*, ed. by Rosemary Auchmuty and Juliet Gosling (London: Bettany, 1994), pp. 253–81

Sims, Sue and Hilary Clare, *The Encyclopaedia of Girls' School Stories* (Aldershot: Ashgate, 2000)

Chapter 11

The body in the library in the fiction of Agatha Christie and her 'Golden Age' contemporaries

K. A. Manley

A number of creators of amateur detectives – notably Agatha Christie, Dorothy L. Sayers and Michael Innes – were aware of the usefulness of a literary upbringing in an era when the average policeman acquired no more than elementary schooling. It is a characteristic of 'Golden Age' detective fiction (1920s–40s) that the well-educated private sleuth should be pitted against the lesser educated 'other', the plodding policeman who obeys the rules: Sayers's Lord Peter Wimsey, for instance, attended Eton and Balliol.[1] And with education come books and libraries. Agatha Christie may not have patented the body in the library, but she certainly lent it more life (or rather, death). Usually the library is merely a stage setting in detective fiction, but some writers considered books and libraries in more bibliographical detail.[2] This chapter considers the multiple ways in which books and libraries are deployed and represented in a selection of novels and stories by Christie and some of her Golden Age contemporaries.

Agatha Christie was a brisk, witty, easy-to-read writer, whose style was often criticised by contemporaries. Fellow-practitioner J. I. M. Stewart, alias Michael Innes, condemned her prose as 'flat and cliché-ridden and undistinguished', containing forgettable, precise details; but, he added grudgingly, the flatness was her own brilliant method of deflecting the reader's attention by deceit, citing *The Murder of Roger Ackroyd* (1926), where the narrator looks back at the study, 'wondering if there was anything I had left undone'.[3] Few critics and writers of the interwar period took crime novels seriously, though many enjoyed reading them.

Although Robert Graves criticised Christie's 'schoolgirlish' prose, he privately appreciated her writing, commenting that detective stories were not meant to be realistic, just as Watteau's paintings of shepherds and shepherdesses did not represent the realities of eighteenth-century sheep-farming.[4] Christie herself was proud to be a lowbrow writer read by highbrows: Samuel Beckett, Ludwig Wittgenstein, George Orwell, Graham Greene, all loved her books.

Post-war, Christie suffered from over-academisation.[5] Critical approaches range from the Marxist, with Ernst Bloch's condemnation of Hercule Poirot because he 'intuits the totality of the case in accordance with the increasingly irrational modes of thinking characteristic of late bourgeois society',[6] to the feminist, for example with Merja Makinen arguing that Christie was writing in a period of 'gender renegotiation' and was making women more dominant and men more passive.[7] Such criticisms are legitimate avenues of exploration, but may confuse the question of how crime novels might best be understood. Exploration of the use of books and libraries within the books resists possible over-intellectualisation while properly acknowledging authorial skill.

This use of books in Golden Age detective fiction reflects the historical period. Both Christie's major protagonists, Poirot and Miss Marple, are vestiges of the Great War: Poirot is a refugee and Marple's only known beau did not return from the Front. The underlying memory of the horrors of war haunts crime fiction of the period. Shocking as murder may be, Alison Light has referred to crime novels of this era as 'literature of convalescence' because its readers, psychologically affected by the cultural shocks brought on by war, sought books in which a solution is offered amidst the uncertainty of the times; this interpretation could apply to the aftermath of any unsettled period.[8] Christie, although her personal interest in crime fiction predated the First World War, read detective novels as a VAD in a Torquay hospital for escapism.[9] Fiction reflects the historical attitude: Wimsey was afflicted by shell shock, and read detective fiction as a refuge.[10] Escapism and nostalgia are more significant ingredients than readers' reactions to war.

Samantha Walton has emphasised the importance of psychology and the uneasy relationship between crime and sanity, or rather, insanity.[11] Christie was subversive; the possibility of an insane murderer often lurks below the surface. Although her novels may have familiar 'cosy' settings, the introduction of dead bodies into the home unsettles the reader by undermining and disturbing the normal social adhesion of their lives, or how they perceive their lives. Motives for murder often reveal dark family secrets or suspicions of insanity. By setting a murder in a library, Christie contrasted the improbability and sensationalism of the crime with a 'highly orthodox and conventional' location, whereby books and libraries symbolise civilisation and respectability. She liked to upset readers with the incongruous, and what is more upsetting to the ordered rhythm of life in the average village than the presence of a murdered person in the one domestic room which should be full of comfort, familiarity and above all, order? Readers were made to feel that there could be no hiding place from murder and that the murderer might belong to their own community.[12]

Christie's fictional engagement with libraries stems from voracious childhood reading, producing a fascination with rhymes and quotations from Shakespeare and the Bible.[13] In accordance with her utterance that: 'I couldn't possibly write about miners talking in pubs because I simply do not know what miners talk about in pubs',[14] her stories are often set in the upper middle-class milieu familiar to her from her 'coming-out' years in Torquay when she regularly visited the houses of the local gentry, all of which would have contained a family library. The books in Christie's library at Greenway (now owned by the National Trust), Christie's holiday home in Devon, offer clues to her character. Greenway's library shelves contain a cloth-bound working collection of the 'ordinary' books which most people read.[15] Mark Purcell has argued that the National Trust country house library enfolds different purposes including the scholarly, the entertaining, the self-improving and 'the repository of family memory'.[16] Greenway's library contains all those elements, but especially the last. At its core lie books collected by Christie's parents and those which provided her education; she never attended school. Her American father bought shelves of classic fiction, poetry and magazines. Books and religion were important to her mother: 'There was a picture of St Francis by her bed, and she read *The Imitation of Christ* [attributed to Thomas à Kempis] night and morning. That same book lies always by my bed.'[17]

Christie's parents ensured that she received suitable books, including gifts from her great-aunt Margaret (an inspiration for Miss Marple). Many of her father's books were kept in a room which Christie requisitioned and contained Lewis Carroll, Charlotte M. Yonge, G. A. Henty, schoolbooks and more novels. Henty's adventure stories were great favourites of other detective story writers and of her brother Monty, who joined the King's African Rifles. Christie was not the only crime writer to have read avidly while young. Rex Stout devoured his father's library of 1,200 books by the age of ten, while Dorothy L. Sayers, a vicar's daughter, endured a lonely childhood in the Cambridgeshire fens, only relieved by reading.[18] Young Christie acquired a circle of imaginary friends who read real books, and their imaginary signatures can be found in several volumes. According to her *Autobiography*, one friend was Sue de Verte,[19] but Greenway's copy of *Les Petites Filles Modèles* (1896) by the Comtesse de

Ségur is inscribed 'Sue de *Morte*'. Christie's memory let her down; the youthful Agatha Christie played with a companion called Death, a fact not revealed in biographies.

Greenway contains volumes owned by both of Christie's husbands, her son-in-law Anthony Hicks and her sister Madge, who married the Manchester textile merchant James Watts and lived in Abney Hall, Cheadle, with a large 'universal' library. Over half their books were housed in the billiard room, emphasising the Victorian male domain. At Greenway, as in any private house, the designated library was never the sole depository for books, which spread to Christie's bedroom with many books, and even to the kitchen and the imposing, long, narrow, first-floor mahogany lavatory.

Christie had fiction, as well as her own background, to inspire her when deploying libraries in her fiction. She was particularly fond of two American crime story writers whose amateur detectives lived in New York City and were book lovers with splendid libraries. Elizabeth Daly's antiquarian scholar and bibliophile, Henry Gamadge, boasted a Chesterfield sofa in his library as well as a round table in the window where he and his wife dined (a dumb waiter rose directly from the kitchen),[20] while the library of the young literary sleuth and writer, Ellery Queen, was also his living room with its oak-ribbed ceiling and 'massive furniture' of divans, footstools and leather cushions, 'a veritable fairyland of easy bachelordom'. The room was 'Dotted with books, massed with books', all 'well-used'. Entering his apartment 'an odour redolent of old leather and masculinity would assail the nostrils', according to *The French Powder Mystery* (1930), in which Queen unravels a murder after realising the significance of particular non-fiction books found on the library desk of the murdered woman's husband. The titles are invented, as are the names of the authors – Morrison, Wedjowski, Throckmorton, Freyberg and so on. Ellery eventually realises that the books – which are completely unlike the rest of the works in the library, whose owner preferred Jack London and the like – are significant because the first two letters of each author's names correspond to days of the week – Monday, Wednesday and so on. They are part of a code indicating meeting days of a drug syndicate; an ingenious bibliographical ruse.[21] Queen is present when a body, with an Etruscan dagger in its back, is discovered on the library floor in a house where he is a guest in *The Finishing Stroke*, published in 1958 but set in 1929. No books are identified, but the library setting is typical for the crime.

Libraries appear in Christie's fiction from her first published novel, *The Mysterious Affair at Styles* (1920), in which Hastings visits a country house in Essex, 'ransacking the library until I discovered a medical book which gave a description of strychnine poisoning' (ch. 4).[22] This was when a country house book collection encompassed every conceivable topic – the 'universal library' – just like the tomes in Lord Peter Wimsey's family home (see below). Fictional personal libraries, like Christie's actual library at Greenway, fit their owner's needs. In *The Sittaford Mystery* (1931), Emily visits the Dartmoor cottage of an amateur ornithologist 'but by far the greater part of the bookcases was given up to criminology and the world's famous trials'.[23] Christie collected similar material, and books on poisons, naturally. Her books are not arranged in any order; fussy Poirot castigates Captain Hastings when he misplaces a book: '"See you not that the *tallest books* go in the top shelf, the next tallest in the row beneath, and so on. Thus we have order, method, which, as I have often told you, Hastings – " "Exactly," I said hastily, and put the offending volume in its proper place.'[24] Poirot's fussiness is complemented by his secretary, the 'unbelievably ugly and incredibly efficient' Miss Lemon, a living machine whose purpose in life was to create a perfect filing system named after her.[25] The control and organisation of information is as important as the physical arrangement of books.

Many Christie stories feature apparently locked rooms.[26] Christie favoured the 'closed circle' genre, where the number of suspects is limited, as in *Murder on the Orient Express* (1934), *Death in the Clouds* (1935), set in an aeroplane, and *And Then There Were None* (1939), which takes place on an island. For Christie, country houses are the perfect setting for a 'closed circle' murder because they contain an entire community, with resident gentry, visitors and servants; a village in miniature, as Miss Marple realised, with petty spites and gossip. Christie thought that they were the best location for her stories because they were so recognisable. Libraries fit into this. Christie was familiar with Anna Katharine Green's American classic *The Leavenworth Case* (1878), read to her at the age of eight, in which the victim is shot dead in his locked library.[27]

The library is equally important whether inside or outside the home. In *After the Funeral* (1953) a woman is murdered (by hatchet) in her cottage while her housekeeper is in Reading, changing the victim's library books; the setting is all the more unsettling for being mundane. Libraries give ambience. The reading of the will is held in the library because the room 'had the proper atmosphere for that with its bookshelves and its heavy red velvet curtains'.[28] A library plays a subtle role in the play *Spider's Web* (1954). Christie gives instructions for a stage set of a drawing room with bookshelves but specifies a door leading to a library, only visible when a concealed switch is pressed. The main character, Clarissa, speculates on what she would do if she found a body in the library. At the denouement the police inspector conceals himself in that library; its hidden presence is central to the plot. Libraries are intended to be significant locations.

The well-loved domestic library reflects its owners' personality. At Gossington Hall in St Mary Mead, Colonel and Mrs Dolly Bantry's library:

> was a room very typical of its owners. It was large and shabby and untidy. It had big sagging arm-chairs, and pipes and books and estate papers laid out on the big table. There were one or two good old family portraits on the walls, and some bad Victorian water-colours, and some would-be-funny hunting scenes. There was a big vase of Michaelmas daisies in the corner. The whole room was dim and mellow and casual. It spoke of long occupation and familiar use and of links with tradition.[29]

This evokes the 'repository of family memory' style of library, but lying on the floor is a young, dead blonde girl – *The Body in the Library* (1942), the classic novel of this genre. 'Bodies are always being found in libraries in books', expostulates Colonel Bantry; 'I've never known a case in real life.' Dolly comments to Miss Marple: 'I only hope that Arthur won't take a dislike to the library. We sit there so much.' This is the library as comfort zone. It also reveals the body as theatre, displayed to contrast the hideous nature of murder with the 'other', the normal everyday life of the country house. The body is initially wrongly identified – deceit is a key element in any Christie novel. Miss Marple solves the crime, relying on village gossip and her knowledge of the evil that exists in a small community; her experiences act as a counter to the conventional thinking of the (male) police.[30]

In *Murder Is Easy* (1939), the murderer is the unpaid librarian of the public library in Wychwood-under-Ashe, endowed inside a former manor house. The body of a young boy is discovered by an elderly lady who is run down while on the way to Scotland Yard to report her suspicions. The stereotypical librarian is 'completely the country spinster . . . neatly dressed in a tweed coat and skirt . . . Her face was pleasant and her eyes, through their pince-nez, decidedly intelligent.'[31] Her motive is that she has been jilted: 'First of all I just thought of killing him. That's when I began to read up criminology – quietly, you know – in the library. And really I found my reading came in most useful more than once later.'[32] The advantages of working in a library!

Christie is not the only detective writer to show an interest in libraries and books, or to make the presence of a library in the home a statement of social class. Dorothy L. Sayers's wealthy and erudite detective Lord Peter Death Bredon Wimsey accumulated a large collection of antiquarian books with fine, calf bindings, housed in his flat in London's Piccadilly, as described in *Whose Body?* (1923).[33] The library overlooked Green

THE BODY IN THE LIBRARY IN THE FICTION OF AGATHA CHRISTIE   209

Park and was furnished with two leather-upholstered chairs, a huge Chesterfield sofa, Chippendale table, writing bureau and a baby grand piano for relaxation; the colour scheme was black and primrose.[34] The room's comfort contrasts markedly with the state of Wimsey's mind when he endures flashbacks to the Great War. His book collection included several incunabula such as Francesco Colonna's *Hypnerotermachia Poliphili* (Venice: Aldus Manutius, 1499), Apollonios Rhodios's *Argonautica* (Florence, 1496), Dante's *Divina Commedia* (1477, 1481, and a post-incunable edition of 1501), *The Golden Legend* (Wynkyn de Worde, 1494), Petronius's *Satyricon* (Venice, 1499), and Vitruvius's *De Architectura* (Rome, 1486), as well as manuscripts of John Donne, Catullus and more. In describing this collection Sayers transfers her own appreciation of scholarship to her literary hero; the focus on Dante, in particular, reflects the passion which led Sayers to translate the *Inferno* and *Purgatory* of his *Divine Comedy* for Penguin.[35]

On one side are books on crime, or, as Wimsey points out in *Unnatural Death* (1927), detected crimes. He collected the Notable British Trials series and naturally owned the collected works of Harriet Vane and his own publication, *Notes on the Collection of Incunabula*.[36] This is a serious collection, though the noble lord lived round the corner from the London Library; whether he patronised this well-stocked subscription library (or the convenient scholarly libraries of the Society of Antiquaries and the Royal Institution) is unknown. He did borrow (sending his manservant, Bunter) from The Times Book Club, one of the largest circulating libraries in the metropolis, situated in Oxford Street, later in Wigmore Street. Many of his creator's first readers would have borrowed their copies from such establishments.

Lord Peter was heir to Bredon Hall in the Norfolk village of Duke's Denver whose library belonged to his non-bibliophile brother, Gerald, the duke. Peter comments dismissively: 'My brother, being an English gentleman, possesses a library in all his houses, though he never opens a book. This is called fidelity to ancient tradition. The chairs, however, are comfortable.'[37] Peter and his new wife, Harriet, visit Bredon Hall. The library was of the 'universal' variety but: 'it isn't what it ought to be. It's full of the most appalling rubbish and the good stuff isn't properly catalogued.' Harriet inspects the library 'with its tall bays and overhanging gallery, . . . Harriet found it restful. She wandered along pulling out here and there a calf-bound volume at random, sniffing the sweet, musty odour of ancient books. . . .'[38] She encounters an elderly man in a dressing gown who smiles at her, bows, and continues reading a book. He was, according to Peter, a distant cousin of the duke. That is, the duke who lived in the reign of William and Mary.

Not all domestic libraries were full of earnest non-fiction, as the ingenious *The Murder of My Aunt* (1934) by Richard Hull (pseudonym of Richard Henry Sampson) shows. The narrator abhors his aunt's choices of literature:

> my aunt has nothing in the house fit to read. It's full of Surtees and Dickens and Thackeray and Kipling and dreadful hearty people like that whom no one reads now, while my aunt's taste in modern novels runs to the *Good Companions* [by J. B. Priestley], *If Winter Comes* [by A. S. M. Hutchinson], or that interminable man, Hugh Walpole. Of course I have made my own arrangements – partly with the Next Century Book Club and partly with an admirable little French Library I found behind the British Museum. Some very amusing stuff they send me at times.[39]

The aunt delights in suggesting he walk to the nearest town to collect a parcel of books with an obscured address label but meant for him, the only person in the neighbourhood to read such books. The sender would obscure the label, claims his aunt, because they 'don't want them back through the post in case, in making enquiries, the police read them'. Motives for murder are stacking up.

Motives for acquiring books can be confused. In Edgar Wallace's *The Books of Bart* (1923), an aspiring author owns an 'accidental' collection:

> One wall of the study was occupied by bookshelves, in which had assembled a whole tatterdemalion army of books, ranging from the costly volumes which Bartholomew purchased at sales, in moments of mental aberration, to the paper-covered novels which were the relics of innumerable railway journeys, and were now preserved because they contained 'ideas' which Bartholomew had indicated with conspicuous blue pencil marks, though he could never recall the ideas they suggested when he came to examine the books.[40]

It has already been seen how Lord Peter Wimsey's library reflects both the wealth and scholarship of its owner, and the French Inspector Gabriel Hanaud states concisely the library's importance in revealing its owner's character in A. E. W. Mason's *The House of the Arrow* (1920): 'I have always thought that if one only had the time to study and compare the books which a man buys and reads, one would more surely get the truth of him than in any other way. But alas, one never has the time.'[41] A book is missing from the library of a murdered professor but reappears the next day; inside, Hanaud discovers a reference to a poisoned arrow.[42]

A revelatory private library features in John Dickson Carr's short story, *The Shadow of the Goat* (1926). The owner's 'hobby was sorcery and the

THE BODY IN THE LIBRARY IN THE FICTION OF AGATHA CHRISTIE   211

deadly arts, in pursuit of which he had a library stuffed with forgotten books – the works of Hermes the Egyptian, Lillius, Geber, James Stuart, Cotton Mather, all of them. He belonged in a day when they burned such men.'[43] Lord Peter Wimsey believed that books revealed stages of a person's development 'like lobster-shells. We surround ourselves with 'em, and then we grow out of 'em.'[44] In *Clouds of Witness* (1926) the ownership of erotic books points towards a mystery's solution. A murder victim's books on Russian royalty in *Have His Carcase* (1932) explain the obsession which leads him to his death. In the rarely used library featured in *The Unpleasantness at the Bellona Club* (1928) occurs a death by shooting. This novel is replete with references to Lewis Carroll's *Alice* and the upside-down world of *Wonderland*.[45]

In the above examples, it is bibliographical or bibliophilic interest which provides the link between library and personality. This is not always the case. Miss Marple's nephew finds himself in a decayed domestic library in Agatha Christie's 'Greenshaw's Folly' (1956): 'From what he could see from a cursory glance, there was no book here of any real interest or, indeed, any book which appeared to have been read. They were all superbly bound sets of the classics as supplied ninety years ago for furnishing a gentleman's library.'[46] The reference to 'classics' being 'supplied' underlines the unpalatable truth that universal libraries could be acquired whole – bought by the yard – for show. The elderly houseowner, soon to be murdered, has hidden her will inside *Lady Audley's Secret*, Mary Braddon's once notorious potboiler from 1862 – no one reads it in Miss Marple's time. What the fact of the library indicates is decayed gentility.

It is not merely the entire library which provides a clue to its owner's character. Individual books, too, reveal much about their owners. In Christie's *Lord Edgware Dies* (1933), Captain Hastings finds the books of the dislikeable and 'vaguely effeminate' Lord Edgware are too revealing: 'There were the *Memoirs* of Casanova, also a volume on the Comte de Sade, another on mediæval tortures.'[47] Edgware is a deeply unpleasant and dominating man, especially to his wife and immediate circle, and so Lord Edgware dies – and in his own library (although unlocked). In *Murder in Mesopotamia* (1936) Poirot examines the books of the murdered archaeologist, Mrs Leidner, concluding from them that she 'had brains, and . . . was, essentially, an egoist'. They are real book titles about strong-minded women, and Poirot recognises that she was not a sensual woman but had intellectual interests and 'essentially worshipped *herself* and who enjoyed more than anything else the sense of *power*'.[48] Leidner was based on Katharine Woolley, the domineering, hypochondriac wife of Leonard Woolley, the excavator at Ur for whom Christie's future husband worked.

The significance of an individual book is a frequent puzzle. A characteristic example occurs in Elizabeth Daly's *The Book of the Dead* (1946), where a young lady approaches Henry Gamadge with a copy of Shakespeare lent from the library of a man she cannot trace. Passages in *The Tempest* are marked (including 'Burn but his books'), causing Gamadge to suspect that something unpleasant may have happened. The young lady is promptly murdered, and an attempt is made on Gamadge's life; he locks himself in his library. The murder is solved, and the result turns upside down everything that has gone before. In *Nothing Can Rescue Me* (1943) Gamadge visits a country house. The wife is writing a novel, but an unknown person has added threatening comments which Gamadge identifies as quotations taken from books in the library, including Edgar Allan Poe and George Herbert. Gamadge finds the owner dead from a blow from a statuette. A literary puzzle. Is the murderer insane? In *The Book of the Crime* (1951), a husband reacts furiously when he comes across his wife in the library, dusting two particular books. Gamadge works out that they both concern the Tichborne case. Can the husband have a related dark secret, such as impersonation with a view to defraud?

In the short story 'The Dragon's Head' (1926), Lord Peter Wimsey encourages his ten-year-old nephew to purchase antiquarian books (his public-school classmates only collect stamps), and he buys an unspecified edition of Sebastian Münster's *Cosmographia Universalis*. When a strange visitor and burglars call, Wimsey suspects there is more to the volume than meets his monocle. An illustration turns out to be a map indicating buried treasure, which they promptly retrieve.[49]

In these last few examples, the books themselves reveal the truth; these material artefacts do not lie, unlike many of their owners, but they often involve literary games. It can be the materiality of the book, irrespective of content, which provides a clue. A short story involving what lurks behind books is 'The Doom of the Darnaways' (1930) featuring G. K. Chesterton's Father Brown. He notices in their family library the spine titles of books on Pope Joan, Iceland and the religion of Frederick . . . ; Brown guesses that must be Frederick the Great. He also realises that the titles are fake. The (late) Lord Darnaway had invented fake books to disguise a hidden staircase, a priest's hole, leading to another room, where his murdered body is found.[50]

To an Oxford-educated academic such as J. I. M. Stewart (Michel Innes), a lecturer in English literature, latterly at Christ Church, Oxford, who wrote on Shakespeare (his second Inspector John Appleby book was *Hamlet, Revenge!*), the library was an obvious location for novels in which the police detective is not only educated and intelligent but enjoys a sense of humour. As Innes wrote: 'Detective stories are purely recreational

THE BODY IN THE LIBRARY IN THE FICTION OF AGATHA CHRISTIE   213

reading, after all, and needn't scorn the ambition to amuse as well as puzzle.'[51] Appleby's scholarly knowledge of old books stems, according to Julian Symons, from high spirits.[52] But there is a serious level, and *Death at the President's Lodging* (1936) inhabits a disturbing world in which the borderline between sanity and insanity is slim.[53] When the president of an Oxbridge-type college is shot dead, Appleby carefully examines the library where the body is found. About 9,000 books are contained in the bookcases which clothe the room and at one end jut forward to form four shallow bays. In three bays are revolving bookcases containing the *Dictionary of National Biography*, the *New English Dictionary* and the *Argentorati Athenaeus* in fourteen bulky volumes (presumably the 1801–7 Strasbourg edition).

> 'The *Deipnosophists*', Appleby was murmuring; 'Schweighäuser's edition . . . takes up a lot of room . . . Dindorf's compacter – and there he is.' He pointed to the corner of the lower shelf where the same enormous miscellany stood compressed into the three compact editions of the Leipsic edition. [Inspector] Dodd, somewhat nonplussed before this classical abracadabra, growled suspiciously: 'These last three are upside down – is that what you mean?'[54]

Would careful book owners shelve books upside down? Would Poirot?[55] Dodd suspects a classical joke but Appleby points to a mark of grease, suggesting an amateur burglar with a candle. Dodd puts his hand behind a row of books (actually dummies) and pulls a concealed lever to reveal a small steel safe with a combination lock. Policemen had already pushed the books back on every shelf to discover whether a weapon had been concealed. Appleby contemplates 'hundreds of heavy folios on the lower shelves' which causes him to posit a theory that the president committed suicide by hollowing out a book to conceal an automatic, shoots himself, and returns the book to its shelf before collapsing on the floor.

Dodd glances 'with new curiosity . . . at the vellum and buckram and morocco rows, gleaming, gilt-tooled, dull, polished, stained – the representative backs of perhaps four centuries of bookbinding'. But it is murder, and there are bones (Appleby 'picked up a fibula . . . and wagged it with professionally excusable callousness at Dodd'). The dummy shelf contains the backs of fifty volumes of the *British Essayists* with the last ten in the wrong order. Reading the volume numbers of these fake books *in reverse* reveals the combination of the safe.[56]

Appleby feloniously enters a suspect's rooms to examine his books:

> It was a severe library . . . Ancient philosophy, massed together. Modern philosophy, similarly massed. *The International Library of Psychology*,

Philosophy, and Scientific Method – uniform, complete, overwhelming. Academic psychology – what looked like a first-class collection. Medical psychology – a great deal of this, too. General medicine – something like the nucleus of a consultant's library. Criminal psychology. Straight criminology . . . And that was all.[57]

Criminology is a popular topic in the private library in crime fiction. Appleby realises that the death is a literary construct, and he and Dodd perceive the crime in terms of a Sherlock Holmes or Edgar Allan Poe mystery, with allusions to other works such as the Bible. Detection of a crime is subordinated to Innes's playful desire to create a literary puzzle, informed by the books in the library.[58]

In *The Long Farewell* (1958), another library owner has been shot. Eighteenth-century owners

had doubtless here surveyed with complacency their undisturbed rows of handsomely tooled and gilded leather. There was still a mass of stuff to delight any authentic student of bibliopegy who should be set browsing in the place . . . But in addition to being the sort of library that many country houses can show, this room was also the workshop of a scholar.[59]

'There was a smell of leather.' Appleby contends with a professor who believes he is an expert on bibliopegy, the study of bookbinding. As the latter remarks, the 'history of bookbinding is a trivial sort of lore, after all. An amusement for collectors, sir.'[60] The plot involves a missing book with marginalia, Cinthio's *Ecatommiti* (1565), a genuine source for Shakespeare; this copy is a forgery.

Innes's *Operation Pax* (1951; published in America as *The Paper Thunderbolt*) is set largely in the Bodleian Library, though Innes denied knowledge of underground passages where the denouement takes place. Appleby's sister, Jane, consults a tome in the Upper Reading Room, unfrequented by scholars (who are confined in Duke Humfrey's) or undergraduates (too many stairs). The library appeals to her auditory and olfactory senses, bringing the heroine close to the detective and the alert reader in the use of all her senses:

But she came, too, for the smell of old leather and vellum and wood that permeated the approaches to the place; for the sound, strangely magnified in the stillness, of a fly buzzing on a window-pane, or for the muted clanking of the Emett-like contrivance which, behind the scenes, drew its continuously moving train of books up through secular darkness from crepuscular repositories below. She came, in short . . . for atmosphere.[61]

THE BODY IN THE LIBRARY IN THE FICTION OF AGATHA CHRISTIE   215

An odd man is chased around the catalogue shelves, 'a sort of hide-and-seek round this monumental guide to universal knowledge'. The Bodleian was the epitome of the universal library. Minutes later, the man is found lying in the street and being transferred to an ambulance; the doctor is a fake.

The plot involves deaths, with clues inside books which involves Jane burglariously entering the Bodleian after dark to find two titles. There are a lot of books to search, but she finds her quarry, only to have a book snatched away by her lover who falls to his death, 'plunging down through a million books, rank upon rank of books, armies of unalterable law'. There really is a body in the library. Once again, Appleby is confronted by the possibility of insanity, while the author amuses with a bibliographical puzzle. And there is the smell of leather.

The Bodleian makes brief appearances in Sayers's *Gaudy Night* (1935) where one impression is uppermost in Harriet Vane's mind: 'Mornings in Bodley, drowsing among the worn browns and tarnished gilding of Duke Humphrey, snuffing the faint, musty odour of slowly perishing leather.'[62] That odour of leather is an abiding memory of library users in crime novels. No murders occur, just a series of silly pranks, though a book is found burning in a grate. But the just-erected New Library of Vane's college does feature. Before its official opening, books and shelves are tipped on the floor, but there is time to restore the room. Not all appreciate the library, and Annie, a servant, remarks to Harriet Vane:

'It's a very handsome room, isn't it, madam? But it seems a great shame to keep up this big place just for women to study books in. I can't see what girls want with books. Books won't teach them to be good wives.' 'What dreadful opinions!', said Harriet.[63]

Sayers's lower-class characters tend to be stereotypes, but her scholarly background make her references to libraries sympathetic.

The name of the prolific Edgar Wallace is indelibly associated with violence and gore, but *The Door with Seven Locks* (1926) is surprisingly different because it is a tale of love. Young detective Dick Martin is retiring from Scotland Yard with an inheritance but is asked to solve the theft of books from the Bellingham Library in London. This little-known institution (based on the London Library) was founded in the eighteenth century to provide scientific books not easily found elsewhere. 'No novel or volume of sparkling reminiscence has a place on the shelves of this institution.' Here, as in Innes's Bodleian, there is the smell of old leather. Luckily for the detective, the founder specified that the library should employ 'two intelligent females, preferably in indigent circumstances'.[64]

Dick recovers the missing tome from a mad scientist who does not understand the workings of a subscription library (namely, that borrowers should subscribe before borrowing) and restores the volume to one of those females with whom he has fallen in love, as happens to lady librarians. 'What is the social position of a detective?', the librarian asks her mother. 'About the same as a librarian, my dear', comes the reply. Privately, he investigates the disappearance of one of her relatives which involves the mad scientist. The love story is interrupted by murders, including one in a country house library, though bibliographical details are lacking. The villains die unpleasantly, while the detective and his young lady live happily ever after.[65] The heroine is a stereotypical female librarian (though she does not wear spectacles), but the library setting raises this pulp novel to a higher tone.

The library is a place of both concealment and drama; the books are (almost) irrelevant, but the location is what matters. In Robert Barr's 'Lord Chizelrigg's Missing Fortune' – part of his collection of spoof Sherlock Holmes stories *The Triumphs of Eugène Valmont* (1906) – a revised will is left between the pages of a book in the eccentric lord's library, which also possesses a forge and anvil. But which book? The library is acting as an instrument of concealment, and the safe is hidden behind a bookcase. A concealed safe appears in *The Black Stage* (1945) by Anthony Gilbert (pseudonym of Lucy Malleson), where a country house is disturbed at midnight by noises emanating from the library. Books are lying around which had previously hidden the location of a safe in which the diamonds were kept. 'Burglars aren't readers as a rule', says one character. 'They'll look behind pictures, but not much behind books.' Another character borrows a volume of Hakluyt's *Travels* for its adventure stories. The diamonds are missing, the lights suddenly go out, a shot is fired, and the body of a visitor is found on the library floor.[66]

The importance of libraries and the printed word is found in several of Christie's short stories. In 'The Strange Case of Sir Arthur Carmichael' (1933), Dr Carstairs stays in a country house to observe Sir Arthur, a young man in a poor mental state who only drinks milk and chases mice. Carstairs dreams that a cat beckons him to the library and points to a shelf of books. On awakening, a book is missing. After a shock, Sir Arthur reveals he had been dreaming he was a cat. There is a death, and the missing book turns out to be about whether a person can transform into an animal. This is one of Christie's creepy psychological tales, and another such story involves a different kind of printed material. In 'Philomel Cottage' (1924) a new wife discovers, in a drawer locked by her husband, press cuttings showing an old photograph of a serial killer who had escaped from jail; it looks remarkably like her husband.[67]

THE BODY IN THE LIBRARY IN THE FICTION OF AGATHA CHRISTIE   217

Murders in libraries often occur in Christie's short stories with little detail as regards the library, as in 'The Love Detectives' (1950) and 'The King of Clubs' (1923). *The Seven Dials Mystery* (1929) includes pistol shots in the library during the night; a masterpiece of confusion.[68] But in 'Three Blind Mice' (1948), Christie achieved her apogee. Monkswell Manor was a guest house with a wireless in the library and a log fire:

> Mrs. Boyle, in the library, turned the knobs of the radio with some irritation. . . . Twirling impatiently, she was informed by a cultured voice: 'The psychology of fear must be thoroughly understood. Say you are alone in a room. A door opens softly behind you – '
>
> A door did open. . . .
>
> The belt of the raincoat slid round her neck so quickly that she hardly realized its significance. The knob of the radio amplifier was turned higher.[69]

The library has ceased to be a place in which to linger, the opposite of 'cosy'. Whatever theories academics might concoct, it is Christie's gift of evoking unanticipated horror that made her popular. This story epitomises the archetypal 'body in the library'. It is sheer terror, presented far more convincingly than by any of her contemporaries. Christie knew what her readers demanded. In the world of Golden Age detective fiction, a dead body on the floor can only enhance a library, and Christie took an old and frequently used formula to a higher level. Books, individually, and en masse, both provide clues and obfuscate in the desire to read people and deeds. Senses are heightened through the smell of old leather, surely the 'correct' and expected odour of the traditional country house library. The reader both identifies with the familiarity of books and libraries per se, while remaining gloriously secure that the upper middle-class or institutional accumulation is comfortingly distant.

Notes

1. His *Who's Who* entry appears in Dorothy L. Sayers, *Gaudy Night* (London: Gollancz, 1935).

2. For discussion of those authors who use the library in their work, see George L. Scheper, 'Bodley Harm: Libraries in British Detective Fiction', *Popular Culture in Libraries*, 2 (1994), 1–20, discussing the library as a repository of the heritage of civilisation; see also Marsh McCurley, 'Murder in the Stacks: Defining the Academic Bibliomystery', in *The Great Good Place? A Collection of Essays on American and British College Mystery Novels*, ed. by Peter Nover (Frankfurt: P. Lang, 1999), pp. 143–52. For occasional references to books, if not libraries, in detective novels, see A. E. Murch, *The Development of the Detective Novel* (London: Peter Owen, 1958), pp. 219–22 and 237–42.

3. J. I. M. Stewart, *Myself and Michael Innes* (London: Gollancz, 1987), pp. 177–9.

4. *In Broken Images: Selected Letters of Robert Graves, 1914–1946*, ed. by Paul O'Prey (London: Hutchinson, 1982), p. 325; cf. J. C. Bernthal, *Queering Agatha Christie: Revisiting the Golden Age of Detective Fiction* (Switzerland: Palgrave Macmillan, 2016), p. 6; Robert Graves and Alan Hodge, *The Long Weekend* (Harmondsworth: Penguin, 1971), p. 297; LeRoy Panek, *Watteau's Shepherds: The Detective Novel in Britain 1914–1940* (Bowling Green, OH: Bowling Green University Popular Press, 1979).

5. For an up-to-date account of Golden Age scholarship, see *The Routledge Companion to Crime Fiction*, ed. by Janice Allan et al. (London: Routledge, 2020).

6. Ernst Bloch, *The Utopian Function of Art and Literature* (Cambridge, MA: MIT Press, 1988), p. 251.

7. Merja Makinen, *Agatha Christie: Investigating Femininity* (Basingstoke: Palgrave Macmillan, 2006), p. 7. For an interpretation of Christie as a 'quiet feminist', see Marion Shaw and Sabine Vanacker, *Reflecting on Miss Marple* (London: Routledge, 1991); cf. Anne Hart, *Agatha Christie's Marple* (London: Macmillan, 1985). More aggressive feminist interpretations appear in Susan Rowland, *From Agatha Christie to Ruth Rendell: British Women Writers in Detective and Crime Fiction* (London: Palgrave Macmillan, 2001); Sally R. Munt, *Murder by the Book? Crime Fiction and Feminism* (London: Routledge, 1994).

8. Alison Light, *Forever England: Femininity, Literature, and Conservatism between the Wars* (London: Routledge, 1991), p. 65; see also Gill Plain, *Twentieth-Century Crime Fiction: Gender, Sexuality, and the Body* (Edinburgh: Edinburgh University Press, 2001), ch. 2, 'Sacrificial Bodies: The Corporeal Anxieties of Agatha Christie'.

9. Murch, *Development*, p. 219.

10. Ariela Freedman, 'Dorothy Sayers and the Case of the Shell-Shocked Detective', *Partial Answers: Journal of Literature and the History of Ideas*, 8 (2010), 365–87 (p. 381); Terrance L. Lewis, *Dorothy L. Sayers' Wimsey and Interwar British Society* (Lewiston, NY: Edwin Mellen Press, 1994), ch. 1, 'The Effects of the Great War', pp. 1–13.

11. Samantha Walton, *Guilty But Insane: Mind and Law in Golden Age Detective Fiction* (Oxford: Oxford University Press, 2015).

12. Shaw and Vanacker, *Reflecting on Miss Marple*, ch. 1.

13. For Agatha Christie's life, see Janet Morgan, *Agatha Christie* (London: Collins, 1984; reprinted HarperCollins, 2017) and Laura Thompson, *Agatha Christie* (London: Headline Review, 2007).

14. Interview with Agatha Christie, *Birmingham Daily Post* (24 February 1958).

15. Agatha Christie's library was catalogued by the present author for the National Trust and the records can be viewed on Library Hub Discover, https://discover .libraryhub.jisc.ac.uk/.

16. Mark Purcell, 'The Country House Library Reassess'd: or, Did the "Country House Library" Ever Really Exist?', *Library History*, 18 (2002), 157–90.

17. Agatha Christie, *An Autobiography* (London: Collins, 1977), pp. 6, 12.

18. H. R. F. Keating, *The Bedside Companion to Crime* (London: Michael O'Mara, 1989), p. 47; cf. Catherine Kenney, 'Sayers (married name Fleming), Dorothy Leigh (1893–1967), *Oxford Dictionary of National Biography* (2004), https://doi.org.10.1093 /ref:odnb/35966 and Catherine Kenney, *The Remarkable Case of Dorothy L. Sayers* (Kent, OH: Kent State University Press, 1990).

19. Christie, *Autobiography*, pp. 87–8.

20. Elizabeth Daly, *The House Without the Door* (New York: Farrar and Rinehart, 1942; repr. [New York]: Felony & Mayhem, 2006), p. 125; *The Book of the Lion* (New York: Walter J. Black for the Detective Book Club, 1948), pp. 99, 106.

THE BODY IN THE LIBRARY IN THE FICTION OF AGATHA CHRISTIE   219

21. 'Ellery Queen', *The French Powder Mystery* (London: Victor Gollancz, 1930; repr. London: Hamlyn, 1981), p. 191.

22. Agatha Christie, *The Mysterious Affair at Styles* (London: John Lane, 1920), p. 52.

23. Agatha Christie, *The Sittaford Mystery* (London: Fontana Collins, 1978), p. 99.

24. 'The Adventure of "The Western Star"', in Agatha Christie, *Poirot Investigates* (London: Collins, 1924), p. 20.

25. This description of Miss Lemon appears in Agatha Christie, *The Labours of Hercules* (London: William Collins, 1947), p. 232. For further discussion of Miss Lemon, see Meg Boulton, 'The Encyclopedic Palace of the World: Miss Lemon's Filing System as Cabinet of Curiosities and the Repository of Human Knowledge in Agatha Christie's Poirot', in *The Ageless Agatha Christie: Essays on the Mysteries and the Legacy*, ed. by J. C. Bernthal (Jefferson, NC: McFarland, 2016), pp. 98–113.

26. Cf. Robert Adey, *Locked Room Murders and Other Impossible Crimes: A Comprehensive Bibliography* (rev. edn, Minneapolis, MN: Crossover, 1991; 2nd edn ([New York]: Locked Room International, 2018).

27. Christie, *Autobiography*, p. 198. See also Ngaio Marsh's closed-circle novel *Singing in the Shrouds* (1958) in which Inspector Alleyne travels incognito with a suspected murderer onboard a little ship with a similarly little library containing a volume in the *Notable Trials* series and a few crime novels. A row breaks out over those books, with Alleyne enjoyably listening to the small group of passengers discoursing over the kind of crimes for which he might be about to arrest them (Ngaio Marsh, *Singing in the Shrouds* (New York: Pyramid, 1974), pp. 141–2).

28. Agatha Christie, *After the Funeral* (London: Fontana Collins, 1956), p. 14.

29. Agatha Christie, *The Body in the Library* (London: Collins, 1942), p. 14.

30. Russell H. Fitzgibbon, *The Agatha Christie Companion* (Bowling Green, OH: Bowling Green State University Popular Press, 1980), p. 32; Alistair Rolls, 'An Ankle Queerly Turned; or, The Fetishised Bodies in Agatha Christie's *The Body in the Library*', *Textual Practice*, 29 (2015), 825–44; Berna Köseoğlu, 'Gender and Detective Literature: The Role of Miss Marple in Agatha Christie's *The Body in the Library*', *International Journal of Applied Linguistics & English Literature*, 4 (2015), 132–7.

31. Agatha Christie, *Murder is Easy* (London: Fontana Collins, 1964), pp. 43–4. The television adaptation of 2008 changes the characters; the librarian is no longer the murderer and Miss Marple is intruded.

32. Agatha Christie, *Murder is Easy*, p. 174.

33. For Wimsey's class, see Lewis, *Wimsey*, ch. [2], 'Lord Peter and the Ruling Classes', pp. 15–29.

34. Philip. L. Scowcroft, 'The Layout of Wimsey's Flat', *Sidelights on Sayers*, 23 (July 1987), 14–17.

35. Themes noted in this paragraph are pursued by R. B. Reaves and Margaret P. Hannay in *As Her Whimsey Took Her: Critical Essays on the Work of Dorothy L. Sayers* ed. by Margaret P. Hannay (Kent, OH: Kent State University Press, 1979). Similarities between Sayers and Wimsey are discussed in Barbara Reynolds, *Dorothy L. Sayers: Her Life and Soul* (London: Hodder & Stoughton, 1993), pp. 178–9. Further biographies of Sayers, including discussion of Wimsey, are: Catherine Kenney, *The Remarkable Case of Dorothy L. Sayers* (Kent, OH and London: Kent State University Press, 1990); Nancy M. Tischler, *Dorothy L. Sayers: A Pilgrim Soul* (Atlanta, GA: John Knox, 1980).

36. Christine. R. Simpson and Philip Scowcroft, 'Some Books in Lord Peter's Library', *Sidelights on Sayers*, 26 (August 1988), 8–11.

37. Dorothy L. Sayers, *Murder Must Advertise* (London: Gollancz, 1933), ch. 11.

38. Dorothy L. Sayers, *Busman's Honeymoon* (London: Gollancz, 1937), 'Epithamalion', ch. 2.

39. Richard Hull, *The Murder of My Aunt* (London: British Library, 2018), pp. 20–1; cf. Anthony Slide, *Lost Gay Novels* (London: Routledge, 2011), pp. 98–100.

40. Edgar Wallace, *The Books of Bart* (London: Ward Lock, 1923), part I, ch. 1.

41. A. E. W. Mason, *The House of the Arrow* (Harmondsworth: Penguin, 1960), p. 49.

42. Mason, *House of the Arrow*, pp. 71–4.

43. J. D. Carr, *It Walks by Night* (London: British Library, 2019), p. 235.

44. Dorothy L. Sayers, *The Unpleasantness at the Bellona Club* (London: Gollancz, 1928), ch. 18.

45. [C. R. Simpson], 'Other Readers and Book Collectors', *Sidelights on Sayers*, 26 (August 1988), 3–7; Aoife Leahy, *The Victorian Approach to Modernism in the Fiction of Dorothy L. Sayers* (Newcastle-upon-Tyne: Cambridge Scholars, 2009), pp. 25–56.

46. Agatha Christie, *Miss Marple and Mystery: The Complete Short Stories* (London: Harper, 2008), p. 661.

47. Agatha Christie, *Lord Edgware Dies* (London: Collins, 1954), p. 33.

48. Agatha Christie, *Murder in Mesopotamia* (London: Fontana Collins, 1985), pp. 164–5.

49. Dorothy L. Sayers, *The Dragon's Head: Classic English Short Stories* (Oxford: Oxford University Press, 1988), pp. 180–207.

50. G. K. Chesterton, *The Penguin Collected Father Brown* (Harmondsworth: Penguin, 1981), pp. 424–43.

51. Stewart, *Myself and Michael Innes*, p. 118.

52. Julian Symons, *Bloody Murder* (London: Faber & Faber, 1972), p. 126.

53. Walton, *Guilty But Insane*, pp. 80–3.

54. Michael Innes, *Death at the President's Lodging* (London: Penguin, 1958), pp. 33–4.

55. In Sayers's short story, 'The Professor's Manuscript', Montague Egg realises that the professor is a fake because the books were not arranged by subject and were too neat (the same sizes were together) and too tight on the shelves; a library for show. There is no murder but there is deceit (Dorothy L. Sayers, *In the Teeth of the Evidence and Other Stories* (London: Victor Gollancz, 1972), pp. 100–13).

56. Innes, *Death*, pp. 34–6, 184. Cf. Christie's short story 'Strange Jest' (1941), in which the safe is hidden behind the sermons in the library of the elderly victim, as the last books behind which a burglar would look (*Three Blind Mice and Other Stories* (New York: Dodd, Mead, 1985), p. 100).

57. Innes, *Death*, pp. 85–6.

58. Andrew Green, 'Death in a Literary Context: Detective Novels of the Golden Age as Enacted Criticism', *Clues*, 39/2 (2021), 41–50.

59. Michael Innes, *The Long Farewell* (London: Penguin, 1971), p. 68.

60. Innes, *Long Farewell*, pp. 59–61.

61. Michael Innes, *Operation Pax* (Harmondsworth: Penguin, 1975), p. 173.

62. Dorothy L. Sayers, *Gaudy Night* (London: Victor Gollancz, 1935), p. 169.

63. Sayers, *Gaudy Night*, p. 93.

64. Edgar Wallace, *The Door with Seven Locks* (London: Hodder & Stoughton, 1926), ch. 2.

65. Wallace, *Door with Seven Locks*, chs 12, 20 & 21.

66. Anthony Gilbert, *The Black Stage* (Harmondsworth: Penguin, 1955), pp. 60–74.

67. Agatha Christie, *The Collected Short Stories* (London: HarperCollins, 2002), pp. 43–64, 193–211.

68. Agatha Christie, *Three Blind Mice*, pp. 230, 236; Agatha Christie, *The Under Dog and Other Stories* ([New York]: W. Morrow, 2012), p. 167.

69. Christie, *Three Blind Mice*, pp. 58–9.

Bibliography of secondary literature

Adey, Robert, *Locked Room Murders and Other Impossible Crimes: A Comprehensive Bibliography*, 2nd edn ([New York]: Locked Room International, 2018)

Allan, Janice et al. (ed.), *The Routledge Companion to Crime Fiction* (London: Routledge, 2020).

Bernthal, J. C., *Queering Agatha Christie: Revisiting the Golden Age of Detective Fiction* (Switzerland: Palgrave Macmillan, 2016)

Bloch, Ernst, *The Utopian Function of Art and Literature* (Cambridge, MA: MIT Press, 1988)

Boulton, Meg, 'The Encyclopedic Palace of the World: Miss Lemon's Filing System as Cabinet of Curiosities and the Repository of Human Knowledge in Agatha Christie's Poirot', in *The Ageless Agatha Christie: Essays on the Mysteries and the Legacy*, ed. by J. C. Bernthal (Jefferson, NC: McFarland, 2016), pp. 98–113.

Christie, Agatha, *An Autobiography* (London: Collins, 1977)

Fitzgibbon, Russell H., *The Agatha Christie Companion* (Bowling Green, OH: Bowling Green State University Popular Press, 1980)

Freedman, Ariela, 'Dorothy Sayers and the Case of the Shell-Shocked Detective', *Partial Answers: Journal of Literature and the History of Ideas*, 8 (2010), 365–87

Graves, Robert, *In Broken Images: Selected Letters of Robert Graves, 1914–1946*, ed. by Paul O'Prey (London: Hutchinson, 1982)

Graves, Robert and Alan Hodge, *The Long Weekend* (Harmondsworth: Penguin, 1971)

Green, Andrew, 'Death in a Literary Context: Detective Novels of the Golden Age as Enacted Criticism', *Clues*, 39(2) (2021), 41–50

Hart, Anne, *Agatha Christie's Marple* (London: Macmillan, 1985)

Keating, H. R. F., *The Bedside Companion to Crime* (London: Michael O'Mara, 1989)

Kenney, Catherine, *The Remarkable Case of Dorothy L. Sayers* (Kent, OH: Kent State University Press, 1990)

Kenney, Catherine, 'Sayers (married name Fleming), Dorothy Leigh (1893–1967), *Oxford Dictionary of National Biography* (2004), https://doi.org.10.1093/ref:odnb/35966

Köseoğlu, Berna, 'Gender and Detective Literature: The Role of Miss Marple in Agatha Christie's *The Body in the Library*', *International Journal of Applied Linguistics & English Literature*, 4 (2015), 132–7.

Leahy, Aoife, *The Victorian Approach to Modernism in the Fiction of Dorothy L. Sayers* (Newcastle-upon-Tyne: Cambridge Scholars, 2009)

Lewis, Terrance L., *Dorothy L. Sayers' Wimsey and Interwar British Society* (Lewiston, NY: Edwin Mellen Press, 1994)

Light, Alison, *Forever England: Femininity, Literature, and Conservatism between the Wars* (London: Routledge, 1991)

Makinen, Merja, *Agatha Christie: Investigating Femininity* (Basingstoke: Palgrave Macmillan, 2006)

McCurley, Marsh, 'Murder in the Stacks: Defining the Academic Bibliomystery', in *The Great Good Place? A Collection of Essays on American and British College Mystery Novels*, ed. by Peter Nover (Frankfurt: P. Lang, 1999), pp. 143–52.

Morgan, Janet, *Agatha Christie* (London: Collins, 1984; repr. HarperCollins, 2017)

Munt, Sally R., *Murder by the Book? Crime Fiction and Feminism* (London: Routledge, 1994)

Murch, A. E., *The Development of the Detective Novel* (London: Peter Owen, 1958)

Panek, LeRoy, *Watteau's Shepherds: The Detective Novel in Britain 1914–1940* (Bowling Green, OH: Bowling Green University Popular Press, 1979)

Plain, Gill, *Twentieth-Century Crime Fiction: Gender, Sexuality and the Body* (Edinburgh: Edinburgh University Press, 2001)

Purcell, Mark, 'The Country House Library Reassess'd: or, Did the "Country House Library" Ever Really Exist?', *Library History*, 18 (2002), 157–90.

Reaves, R. B. and Margaret P. Hannay in *As Her Whimsey Took Her: Critical Essays on the Work of Dorothy L. Sayers*, ed. by Margaret P. Hannay (Kent, OH: Kent State University Press, 1979)

Reynolds, Barbara, *Dorothy L. Sayers: Her Life and Soul* (London: Hodder & Stoughton, 1993)

Rolls, Alistair, 'An Ankle Queerly Turned; or, The Fetishised Bodies in Agatha Christie's *The Body in the Library*', *Textual Practice*, 29 (2015), 825–44

Rowland, Susan, *From Agatha Christie to Ruth Rendell: British Women Writers in Detective and Crime Fiction* (London: Palgrave Macmillan, 2001)

Scheper, George L., 'Bodley Harm: Libraries in British Detective Fiction', *Popular Culture in Libraries*, 2 (1994), 1–20

Scowcroft, Philip. L., 'The Layout of Wimsey's Flat', *Sidelights on Sayers*, 23 (July 1987), 14–17.

Shaw, Marion and Sabine Vanacker, *Reflecting on Miss Marple* (London: Routledge, 1991)

[Simpson, Christine R.], 'Other Readers and Book Collectors', *Sidelights on Sayers*, 26 (August 1988), 3–7

Simpson, Christine. R. and Philip Scowcroft, 'Some Books in Lord Peter's Library', *Sidelights on Sayers*, 26 (August 1988), 8–11.

Stewart, J. I. M., *Myself and Michael Innes* (London: Gollancz, 1987)

Talbot, David, Interview with Agatha Christie, *Birmingham Daily Post* (24 February 1958)

Thompson, Laura, *Agatha Christie* (London: Headline Review, 2007)

Tischler, Nancy M., *Dorothy L. Sayers: A Pilgrim Soul* (Atlanta: John Knox, 1980)

Walton, Samantha, *Guilty But Insane: Mind and Law in Golden Age Detective Fiction* (Oxford: Oxford University Press, 2015)

Chapter 12

'Very nearly magical': books and their readers in Terry Pratchett's Discworld series

Jane Suzanne Carroll

At the beginning of Terry Pratchett's twenty-fifth Discworld novel *The Truth* (2000), a freelance reporter William de Worde describes engraving as 'a sort of very nearly magical way of getting lots of copies of writing'.[1] If engraving is 'very nearly magical', it follows that printed books are closer still to magic in Pratchett's Discworld. Through the forty-one Discworld novels, numerous shorter texts – including short stories 'Troll Bridge' (1992), 'Theatre of Cruelty' (1993), 'The Sea and Little Fishes' (1998) – plays, picture books, graphic novels and secondary texts about the Discworld,[2] Pratchett 'uses fantasy as a fairground mirror, reflecting back at us a distorted but recognisable image of twentieth-century concerns'.[3] The Discworld functions as a complex microcosm that enables Pratchett to write with warm cynicism and biting humour about all kinds of real world – or Roundworld – concerns. Through the series, Pratchett returns again and again to certain key themes: duty, justice, privilege, power and powerlessness, the futility of violence, and what it means to be human. Perhaps the most important of these recurring themes is the power of stories. In the Discworld, stories are driven by 'narrativium', a core element akin to earth, air, fire, or water.[4] Narrativium gives everything a purpose, it 'is an attribute of every other element' and so: 'Iron contains not just iron, but also the story of iron, the history of iron, the part of iron that ensures that it will continue to be iron and has an iron-like job to do.'[5] Narrativium does the same for people as for iron: the stories people tell and the fictions they tell about themselves are the mechanism by which they shape their identities, and remind themselves of who they are. Given the foundational and elemental power of stories, then, it is no surprise that the written word plays an important role in the Discworld books.

The Discworld is thick with texts. The smallest are the mine signs of the dwarfs, single enigmatic glyphs scrawled on the walls of their excavations, and the sacred 'chem' that are placed inside the otherwise empty heads of the golem. The chem are written in ancient Cenotine, taken from passages from ancient holy books that contain 'relevant texts that are the focus of belief'.[6] For the golems, who have no thoughts other than the commands in their heads, these sacred texts are synonymous with belief and with action: a golem 'can't disobey the words in its head'[7] and without its chem, a golem is nothing more than a lifeless statue. More commonly, the texts in the Discworld take the form of printed and bound books. The Discworld wiki 'L Space' lists 141 separate Discworld publications that are written by, read by or mentioned by characters.[8] The mass production and mass circulation of texts in the form of pamphlets, periodicals (including *Bows & Ammo*, *Total Pins*, *Golem Spotter Weekly* and *What Gallows?*), newspapers (*The Ankh-Morpork Times*; *Pseudopolis Herald*; the *Tanty Bugle*), annual publications like the *Almanack and Booke of Dayes*, flyers, handbills and mail-order catalogues indicates a largely literate or semi-literate population in this fantasy world.

Powerful books

In the Discworld, books are powerful. This is especially true of the books that are gathered together in the library of the Unseen University, the largest collection of books within the Discworld. As Jim Shanahan summarises: 'Books are knowledge, and knowledge is power; power is energy, and energy is mass; and mass distorts time and space.'[9] The power of books to manipulate the fabric of reality is an acknowledged fact in the Discworld. The result of this warped space and time is L-space, a quantum space wherein all books and all collections of books are connected. In *The Science of Discworld II: The Globe*, Ian Stewart, Jack Cohen and Pratchett explain that:

> It is via L-space that all books are connected (quoting the ones before them, and influencing the ones that come after). But there is no time in L-space. Nor is there, strictly speaking, any space. Nevertheless, L-space is infinitely large and connects all libraries, everywhere and

everywhen. It's never further than the other side of the bookshelf, yet only the most senior and respected librarians know the way in.[10]

Through L-space the Library in the Unseen University becomes infinite. Because it is connected to every other collection of books in the universe, the power and reach of its collection is multiplied and magnified exponentially.

Because of the potential power of the collections, many of the books in the Unseen University Library are, quite sensibly, kept out of reach of readers. In describing the fittings and function of the Library, Pratchett draws on images of the chained library, common enough in academic and religious institutions in England between the late Middle Ages and the early modern period, when books were highly valued. As Richard Gameson notes, the chains used to lock books to medieval lecterns were not intended to impede reading, but to 'ensure that they were not removed'.[11] In his survey of chained libraries, which seems a likely source for Pratchett's Library, Burnett Hillman Streeter explains wryly:

> In the Middle Ages books were rare, and so was honesty. A book, it was said, was worth as much as a farm; unlike a farm it was portable property that could easily be purloined. Valuables in all ages require protection. Books, therefore, were kept under lock and key. This was done in two ways. Either they were shut up in a cupboard . . . or a chest, or they were chained, sometimes four or five together to a desk, often in the choir.[12]

However, the practice of chaining books in the Unseen University Library seems deliberately calculated to impede and even prevent reading. This is because the books in this particular library are not just valuable commodities, but potentially dangerous ones too. Pratchett writes: 'All books of magic have a life of their own. Some of the really energetic ones can't simply be chained to the bookshelves; they have to be nailed shut or kept between steel plates.'[13] These precautions are not merely to protect the books from the readers, but also to protect the readers from the books. In *The Light Fantastic* (1986), the librarian, Dr Horace Worblehat, is transformed into an orangutan simply because the *Octavo*, a sentient book that contains the Eight Great Spells that were used in the creation of the Discworld, has been opened.[14] In *Guards! Guards!* (1989) a book purloined from the University Library gives its readers the power to summon dragons from another dimension, though, significantly, it does not confer on them the power to control these dragons. Even the apparently ordinary books in the University Library are potentially dangerous. As Pratchett explains in *Soul Music* (1994): 'It would be a mistake to think that [mundane books] weren't also dangerous, just because reading them didn't make fireworks go off in the sky. Reading them sometimes did the more dangerous trick of making fireworks go off in the privacy of the reader's brain.'[15]

It is unsurprising, therefore, that in spite of widespread literacy many characters in Discworld regard reading and printed books with distrust and even distaste. The Nac Mac Feegle, a race of enthusiastically violent pixies, are deeply superstitious about the written word, believing that once a person's name is written down, the person can be sent to prison. They fear that learning to read irreparably alters the way a person's mind works. Big Yan explains that:

> When a man starts messin' wi' the readin' and the writin' then he'll come doon with a dose o' the thinkin' soon enough. I'll fetch some o' the lads and we'll hold his heid under water until he stops doin' it, 'tis the only cure. It can kill a man, the thinkin'.[16]

For the Feegles, thinking is a disease transmitted through the written word and one that, left untreated, will prove fatal. Although the Feegles' beliefs about reading being fatal are not widespread, relatively few characters in the Discworld are described as avid, or even basically competent, readers. Among human characters, although literacy is widespread, reading is not widely celebrated. Glenda Sugarbean, a young woman with a keen interest in romance novels, 'read the way a cat eats: furtively, daring anyone to notice',[17] suggesting that even for a fluent reader like herself, there is something shameful in the act of reading. Fred Colon, a member of the City Watch, who is described as *'functionally* literate', thinks 'of reading and writing like he thought about boots – you needed them, but they weren't supposed to be fun, and you got suspicious about people who got a kick out of them'.[18]

While the suspicion of reading is pervasive in the Discworld series, the root cause of this unease is not often expressed. It is only in *Monstrous Regiment* (2003) that Sergeant Jackrum is able to articulate the discomfort that he and many others feel when confronted with the written word. He complains that: 'You can't trust the people who do that stuff [reading and writing]. They mess around with the world, and it turns out everything you know is wrong.'[19] Here it is not clear whether Jackrum means 'readers' or 'books' when he says 'they mess around with the world', but in a sense it does not really matter what he means, because for Jackrum as for many other Discworld characters, readers and books are synonymous. That readers, like books, can 'mess around with the world' implies that there is some power contained within books that, in turn, rubs off onto their readers. William de Worde, one of the most ably literate characters in the

BOOKS AND THEIR READERS IN TERRY PRATCHETT'S DISCWORLD SERIES

series, recognises that the power of books is rooted in the shifting and movable nature of type. As he gazes at a typesetter's tray, he realises that the metal blocks that make up words – and make up whole texts – have the potential to become anything at all:

> William stared down at the box of letters again. Of course, a quill pen potentially contained anything you wrote with it. He could understand that. But it did so in a clearly theoretical way, a safe way. Whereas these dull gray blocks looked threatening. He could understand why they worried people. Put us together in the right way, they seemed to say, and we can be anything you want. We could even be something you don't want. We can spell anything. We can certainly spell trouble.[20]

Here Pratchett reminds the reader that the power of the printed word comes from possibility. Books are not immutable or permanent, but are composed of moving parts. The astute reader, aware that books are born from movable type and are inherently flexible, should be open to the possibilities of various, varied and variable readings.

The mutable nature of books is highlighted throughout the Discworld series. Pratchett demonstrates that even supposedly holy books are flawed and open to interpretation and misinterpretation. The best expression of this is the *Book of Nuggan*, the holy book of the Nugganites who follow the small god Nuggan. The *Abominations* lists at least 6,668 things that Nuggan has prohibited, including chocolate, false teeth, umbrellas, mechanical devices for measuring time, girls knowing how to write, shirts with six buttons, babies and the colour blue.[21] As the list of abominations is continually updated by Nuggan, a god who grows increasingly deranged, his followers keep their holy book in loose-leaf binders so that new abominations can be added and old ones can be removed.[22] That the holy book is open to change renders it unstable, implying that Nuggan himself is unstable, and that the whole religion founded around him can be called into question. While power might seem to rest with the godhead and his priests, Pratchett allows the reader and some key characters to understand that power does not really stem from the god's words, but from the faith that his believers place – or rather misplace – in him. In *Carpe Jugulum* (1998) the realisation that faith in holy books is misplaced even dawns on the Quite Reverend Mightily Oats, a devout Omnian priest. When he is desperate to kindle a fire that will drive away the darkness and the wet and the threat of vampires, he initially turns to the *Book of Om* for comfort and guidance, and despairs when he cannot read the book by the feeble light of his matches. It is only when he 'listened to his own mind'[23] that he realises that the *Book of Om* will help him build the fire he needs: he just needs to set the whole book on fire first. Here

Pratchett underscores the idea that no book in the Discworld is inherently holy or meaningful and that books are made to serve their readers.

The mighty text

If knowledge is power and books are knowledge, it should follow that because of the proliferation of books within the Discworld, power is everywhere and accessible to everyone, circulating through the entire population and open to all kinds of readers. Yet we must remember that different books hold different kinds of power. The magical force contained within the pages of the *Octavo* differs from the political and social power of the *Ankh-Morpork Times*. This is not only because one text is magical and the other mundane, but because one has the power of institutional authority and the other has the power of subversive potential. On the one hand, there are what we might term 'authoritative texts'. These are produced by, or sanctioned by, those in possession of religious, educational or governmental power. The power wielded by these institutions is typically privileged, legitimate and patriarchal. This power comes from the top of the social ladder. The texts draw their power from established institutions and in turn bolster the power of these institutions. Other texts operate beyond these established sites of institutional authority and so their power rests in enabling otherwise disempowered characters to challenge the established world order.

That these mundane books can empower their audiences is especially important when we consider that books are often associated with people who are outside of the traditional models of power such as women, children and outcasts. Some of these unsanctioned texts, such as Nanny Ogg's scandalous 'cookbook', *The Joye of Snacks*, are chaotic and playfully subversive. Others, like The *Ankh-Morpork Times*, the Discworld's first newspaper, disrupt social order and speak truth to power. These texts draw their power from their potential to disrupt the orders imposed by institutions. They may not have authority but they do have might. Writing in relation to children's literature, Clémentine Beauvais distinguishes between authority and might. She explains that:

> Because the implied child reader of children's literature *might* be taught by the children's book something that the adult *does not yet know*, that child is powerful in some sense of the word power – a sense that I call 'might'. The adult authority is not – or not just, and certainly not always – an omnipotent, manipulative, authoritarian, repressive, oppressive entity. Authoritative, yes – but not authoritarian.[24]

BOOKS AND THEIR READERS IN TERRY PRATCHETT'S DISCWORLD SERIES   231

Like the child readers Beauvais discusses, the mundane texts produced by characters within the Discworld novels possess a 'potent, latent future to be filled with yet-unknown action'.[25] Their power rests in a sense of their mighty possibility: nobody knows what could happen to the readers of these texts, nobody is fully certain of the impact they could have on the world. This is especially true of a book called *Where's My Cow?*, one of the few children's books mentioned in Pratchett's series.

Where's My Cow? is, on the surface, an innocuous and simple picture book in which the narrator tries to find his lost cow. Its format and plot is familiar to any Roundworld reader who has ever read Fiona Watt's 'That's Not My . . .' series.[26] In his efforts to locate the cow, the narrator encounters and is momentarily bamboozled by various other familiar animals:

> Eventually, the cow would be found. It was that much of a pageturner. Of course, some suspense was lent by the fact that all other animals were presented in some way that could have confused a kitten, who perhaps had been raised in a darkened room. The horse was standing in front of a hatstand, as they so often did, and the hippo was eating at a trough against which was an upturned pitchfork. Seen from the wrong direction, the tableau might look for just one second like a cow.[27]

Although it seems to pale in comparison with the magical world-shaping force of a book like the *Octavo*, this children's book has enormous subversive might. In Pratchett's speech 'Straight from the Heart, Via the Groin', delivered in 2004, he mentions that *Where's My Cow?* was the starting point around which the plot of *Thud!* revolved; that he was absolutely certain that: 'there's going to be a moment where Vimes is reading through it for the umpteenth time . . . and in the back of his mind is this terribly complex crime, and somehow that little book is going to become pivotal to the solution'.[28] Although it is a 'little book', *Where's My Cow?* holds its own in a terribly complex world. It is a mighty text that can shape lives, thwart demons and make its readers into powerful and potentially dangerous people.

Clues, cows and karabasis

Samuel Vimes, the commander of the city watch, is, perhaps, the most dangerous reader in the Discworld. He appears as the central figure in the Watch sub-series of novels, *Guards! Guards!* (1989), *Men at Arms* (1993), *Feet of Clay* (1996), *Jingo* (1997), *The Fifth Elephant* (1999), *Night Watch* (2002), *Thud!* (2005) and *Snuff* (2011) and the very short story 'Theatre of Cruelty' (1993), and as a minor character in many other Discworld novels.

232   JANE SUZANNE CARROLL

Unlike many characters, Vimes shows no difficulty with reading or writing: as a child he had the honour of being a 'blackboard monitor'[29] in his class, which suggests that he was favoured by his teacher, perhaps even favoured because of his academic promise, and, as an adult, makes his living reading – and reading into – all kinds of things. As a detective, Vimes is a kind of professional reader, 'an authorial figure who strives to apprehend and contain the criminal plot and thus appropriate the entire story'[30] by interpreting the clues left at crime scenes and reconstructing the evidence into a sort of narrative. Although Vimes evidently dislikes reading the reports compiled by the watchmen under his command and loathes the *Ankh-Morpork Times*, he is an enthusiastic reader of other texts and one of the only fluent readers of the city space itself.

In Pratchett's work, Ankh-Morpork functions as a vast figurative text intelligible only to a select few who have learned to interpret its moods and weathers and to navigate its mazy streets. Through his long experience as a watchman and because he has spent virtually his entire life within the bounds of Ankh-Morpork, Vimes is keenly attuned to the city and its moods. In addition to his encyclopaedic knowledge of the citizens – particularly those citizens who are inclined towards crime or misdemeanour – he has a deep and embodied knowledge of the city streets. A recurrent motif in the novels about Vimes is his preference for cheap, thin-soled boots, the kind worn by some of the poorest people in the city. These cheap boots let in water and cold, but they have the advantage of bringing the soles of his feet into almost direct contact with the ground, enabling him to know by the shape of the cobblestones where exactly in the city he is, even in the dark. In *Night Watch*, Vimes's comprehensive knowledge of the city streets is displayed for the reader:

> after a lifetime of walking them, he did feel the streets. There were the cobblestones: catheads, trollheads, loaves, short and long setts, rounders, Morpork Sixes, and the eighty-seven types of paving brick, and the fourteen types of stone slab, and the twelve types of stone never intended for street slabs but which had got used anyway and had their own patterns of wear, and the rubbles, and the gravels, and the repairs, and the thirteen different types of cellar covers, and twenty types of drain lids – He bounced a little, like a man testing the hardness of something. 'Elm Street,' he said. He bounced again. 'Junction with Twinkle. Yeah.'[31]

Here Pratchett emphasises the embodied nature of this knowledge, calling attention to how these different surfaces feel beneath Vimes's feet, to the action of bouncing on the balls of his feet, an action that allows Vimes to renew his contact with the ground and reawaken his senses. Through

BOOKS AND THEIR READERS IN TERRY PRATCHETT'S DISCWORLD SERIES   233

the thin soles of his boots, Vimes comes into contact with the city and knows it phenomenologically as well as intellectually. Significantly, in *Feet of Clay* his ability to navigate the city through touch is described as a kind of literacy, as an ability to 'read the street'.[32] By reading with his whole being, by being able to read texts that others cannot, Vimes is a character endowed with more than usual literacy.

Vimes's ability to read all kinds of texts comes to the fore in *Thud!*, a narrative which involves the intersections between a variety of texts: mundane and mystical, personal and political. The plot revolves around Vimes's efforts to solve the murder of Grag Hamcrusher, a fundamentalist dwarf who had riled up interracial tensions among the dwarfs and the trolls in the city through preaching hatred and violence. Vimes identifies Hamcrusher's hatred as being founded in 'some holy book, apparently'[33] and his dismissal of the dwarfs' holy book – the *Book of Tak* – brings him momentarily closer to the other Discworld characters who are suspicious of any kind of text. But Carrot, who was raised by dwarf parents, reminds Vimes that dwarfs 'think the world was written. . . . All words have enormous power. Destroying a book is worse than murder to a deep-downer.'[34] Carrot's analogy links books to life, a connection that becomes crucial later in the novel. While the *Book of Tak* seems to be the root cause of all the trouble in the beginning of the novel, it is another kind of text made by dwarfs, a mine sign, that brings real danger into the city.

Mine signs are a sort of graffiti made by delving dwarfs. Most of these signs are innocuous; small glyphs scratched into the walls and supporting beams of a mine to show other dwarfs the way or to label the excavations. But other mine signs are mystical and extremely powerful. Carrot explains that: 'Some deep-downers believe that the dark signs are real . . . Like they exist somewhere down in the dark under the world, and they cause themselves to be written.'[35] In the course of investigating Hamcrusher's murder, Vimes accidentally brushes up against one of the mine signs and it leaps from the wall of the mine into his body. The sign Vimes touches is the Summoning Dark, a glyph 'drawn in the dark . . . by a dying dwarf'[36] that brings with it the power of a demonic entity. The Summoning Dark possesses Vimes and though he is unaware of its presence, it manipulates him into leaving the city space and to travel to Koom Valley, the site of an ancient battle between dwarfs and trolls.

In counterbalance to the Summoning Dark and the religious texts of the dwarfs, Pratchett sets the picture book *Where's My Cow?* This is an important book to Vimes because he reads it to his son, Young Sam, every single night at six o'clock. Vimes believes that reading a book with his son before bedtime is more important than anything else in the world. The danger, action and violence of Vimes's professional life is thrown into sharp relief by his domestic family life through these moments of reading. Pratchett's decision to give over significant amounts of narrative space to the scenes about reading *Where's My Cow?* communicates the central importance of this nightly ritual to readers, establishing the profound connection Vimes has with his child and the deep importance of his commitment to read to his child every night. There is great tenderness and intimacy in Pratchett's descriptions of the bedtime routine.

> Young Sam pulled himself up against the cot's rails, and said, 'Da!' The world went soft. . . . It was funny, really. He spent the day yelling and shouting and talking and bellowing . . . but here, in this quiet time . . . he never knew what to say. He was tongue-tied in the presence of a fourteen-month-old baby. All the things he thought of saying, like 'Who's Daddy's little boy, then?' sounded horribly false, as though he'd got them from a book. There was nothing to say, nor, in this soft pastel room, anything that needed to be said.[37]

There is a palpable sense of their closeness here, and in the contrast between the soft, safe world of the nursery and the cruelty and violence of the world outside the door. It is interesting to note that Vimes feels that any trite or clumsy words sound like words 'from a book' which suggests that he, too, has internalised some of the dislike of the written word that is so pervasive in the Discworld. In spite of this slight unease about books, Vimes makes *Where's My Cow?* a core element of his son's bedtime routine and, by extension, a core element of his parenting. Thus, the book and the nightly ritual of reading the book to his child becomes an anchor-point for Vimes's identity. He reflects: 'I'm not the sharpest knife in the drawer. Hell, I'm probably a spoon. Well, I'm going to be Vimes, and Vimes reads *Where's My Cow?* to Young Sam at six o'clock. With the noises done right.'[38] Through reading to his son, Vimes forges a new parental identity that is founded on duty, honesty and tenderness.

Through shared reading, Vimes encultures in Young Sam the kinds of power that reading has brought to him. In one key scene he demonstrates the flexibility of texts, supplementing the usual plot of the picture book for one in which the narrator looks for his daddy in the streets of Ankh-Morpork and meets a disreputable assortment of city dwellers, beggars and thieves. While Vimes reverts to the official version of the story the next day, this playful reworking of the text demonstrates to Young Sam that stories can be changed: that readers have the power to resist the force of narrativium and to create their own narratives. Vimes shows his son that while books are important, their potency is derived from the power the reader invests in them. In showing Young Sam an alternative version of his favourite story, Vimes shows his son that texts can be resisted and played with and brought to heel rather than slavishly obeyed. It is especially significant that he uses a picture book meant for child readers in order to do this. Children's books, and particularly picture books, are not simple texts with which to train novice readers, but dynamic texts that demand playful and nimble reading.[39] As Beauvais explains:

> sophisticated picture books, or iconotexts (Hallberg 1982), are characterised by a gap between pictures and text; between words and images. Gaps . . . encourage creativity in the young reader, leading the child to 'fill them in' with their own interpretation, since no clear meaning is given in either text or picture.[40]

The way the verbal and visual narratives may run in parallel or at cross-purposes, and may complement or contradict the meanings on offer, forces picture book readers to engage in multiple, complex interpretive acts from the very outset. As a picture book, *Where's My Cow?* is the perfect kind of book to demonstrate the mutability of text and to show Young Sam that no book is complete without a reader.

Of course, the flexibility of texts does not mean they cannot become sacred, and *Where's My Cow?* certainly becomes a sacred text within *Thud!* Because he reads the same book every night, Vimes has committed it to memory and can recite it in its entirety: 'He recited it tonight, while wind rattled the windows and this little nursery world, with its pink and blue peace, its creatures who were so very soft and woolly and fluffy, seemed to enfold them both. On the nursery clock, a little woolly lamb rocked the seconds away.'[41] The act of recitation is significant. This conscious recurrence, wherein the words of the text are repeated faithfully, imbues the book with a ceremonial quality. In this moment of reading, Vimes slips outside of the ordinary, profane time of the outside world – hinted at through the woolly lamb marking the passage of time – and enters into a space where time seems to stand still. The nursery becomes both a space and a time outside of the ordinary business of the world. Here Vimes and his son enter into a kind of mythic time that revolves around repetition, recurrence and renewal. Through daily repetition, through the ritual of shared reading, *Where's My Cow?* becomes a sacred text for Vimes and his son. The words of the book are enmeshed with 'the deeply ingrained, almost magical, habit of sanity and normal fatherhood'.[42] This 'almost magical' habit of reading echoes the 'almost magical' quality of engraving and printing mentioned throughout Pratchett's corpus. *Where's My Cow?* is a magic book, though not a book of magic.

Pratchett allows the reader to see exactly how much the bedtime story means to Vimes and Young Sam and how crucial it is to their identities as parent and child when, later in *Thud!*, Vimes is prevented from getting home on time to read to Young Sam. Both father and son are deeply affected by the loss of their shared reading routine. The boy is devastated, left staring at the nursery door and wailing, no matter how many other people try to comfort him. Vimes, on the other hand, turns berserk. As he moves through the caves in Koom Valley, he bellows out the words of the bedtime story, learned by heart through endless repetition as he faces down and kills the people who have prevented him from getting home on time to read the story. This scene is fantastically strange, with both horror and humour rising out of the juxtaposition between the image of the mighty avenging hero and the ridiculousness of him screaming the words of *Where's My Cow?* to the confusion and horror of everyone else in the cave system. The scene recalls katabatic narratives, 'a journey of the Dead made by a living person in the flesh who returns to our world to tell the tale':[43] here, too, is a voyage into the underworld and the realm of the dead whence the hero returns victorious. Thus, the words of *Where's My Cow?* serve a mythic as well as mundane function: the words of the picture book bring Vimes back from the underworld – both a literal underworld of the cave system and a metaphorical one of death – and call him home to his son. It seems that Vimes is a man doubly possessed, once by the malevolent spirit of the Summoning Dark and once by the picture book *Where's My Cow?*

In recalling the hero from the underworld, *Where's My Cow?* becomes one of the most powerful texts in the Discworld. It enacts literal magic. The shared love Vimes and Young Sam have for the book make it an intensely meaningful one to them personally, and that Vimes has internalised and memorised the text means that it becomes part of him. Vimes's endless oral repetition of this text recalls its status as a ritual text for father and son, and he repeats it, like a prayer or a mantra, at the point of death. Throughout *Thud!*, two books account for almost all of the thirty-nine instances of the word 'book' in the text: one of these is the Book of Tak, the other is *Where's My Cow?* In balancing these two against one another – a holy book and a mundane one, a book of authority and a book of might – Pratchett suggests that these books are equal and complementary forces, held in perfect equilibrium. The choice of book is the thing that saves Vimes from doom: he does not believe in the spirit of the Summoning Dark, but he does believe in reading to his child at bedtime. The picture book, in this moment of extreme suffering and pain, is mightier than the holy book, and enables its devotee to rise from darkness and death to fulfil the promise of reading to Young Sam at bedtime. Its potency comes not from any godhead or authority, but from the shared faith Vimes and his son have in the book and from the ritual repetition of its words.

In Terry Pratchett's Discworld both magic and mundane books have power and pass that power on to their readers. Pratchett himself recognised the 'might' of stories, and in his Katharine Briggs Memorial Lecture explained that all stories present the possibility of futures and that, through listening or reading, an audience can participate in the power of a story: 'those sitting in the circle of firelight while the story is told are not passive listeners, but believe they have some rights in the story and that the story itself is a window into another world with a quasi-existence of its own'.[44] The reader of a book is not 'passive' but active, and can be inspired to take further action. Crucially, Young Sam is not a passive listener to the bedtime story *Where's My Cow?*, but an active participant in the story. He participates vocally, through coos and babble, and emotionally: he is invested in the shared reading time with his father, every bit as much as Vimes himself is invested. Young Sam loves reading and loves this book in particular with a fierce and enthusiastic love. It is his insistence on this story that recalls his father from the world of the dead, it is his joy in the picture book that makes it a mighty text, it is his participation as a child reader that enables *Where's My Cow?* to enact the promise of the 'very nearly magical' power of the printed word, securing its place among the most powerful books in the Discworld.

Notes

1. Terry Pratchett, *The Truth* (London: Transworld, 2000), p. 26.

2. Terry Pratchett, *The Science of Discworld* (London: Ebury, 1999); Terry Pratchett, *The Art of Discworld* (London: HarperCollins, 2004); Terry Pratchett and Jacqueline Simpson, *The Folklore of Discworld: Legends, Myths and Customs from the Discworld with Helpful Hints from Planet Earth* (London: Doubleday, 2008).

3. 'Terry Pratchett's Discworld', Fabulous Realms, 23 Mar. 2012, https://ashsilverlock .wordpress.com/2012/03/16/a-visit-to-discworld, accessed 1 April 2023.

4. 'Narrativium', https://wiki.lspace.org (2012), accessed 27 January 2024.

5. Ian Stewart, Jack Cohen and Terry Pratchett, *Science of Discworld III: Darwin's Watch* (London: Random House, 2011), pp. 1–2.

6. Terry Pratchett, *Feet of Clay* (London: Corgi, 1997), p. 136.

7. Pratchett, *Feet of Clay*, p. 39.

8. 'Category: Discworld Publications', https://wiki.lspace.org/Category:Discworld_ publications (2012), accessed 29 November 2022.

9. Jim Shanahan, 'Terry Pratchett: Mostly Human', in *Twenty-First-Century Popular Fiction*, ed. by Bernice Murphy and Stephen Matterson (Edinburgh: Edinburgh University Press, 2017), pp. 31–40 (p. 33).

10. Ian Stewart, Jack Cohen and Terry Pratchett, *The Science of Discworld II: The Globe* (London: Random House, 2011), p. 38.

11. Richard Gameson, 'The Medieval Library (to c.1450)', in *The Cambridge History of Libraries in Britain and Ireland, Vol. I, To 1640*, ed. by Elisabeth Leedham-Green and Teresa Webber (Cambridge: Cambridge University Press, 2008), pp. 13–50 (p. 29).

12. Burnett Hillman Streeter, *The Chained Library: A Survey of Four Centuries in the Evolution of the English Library* (Cambridge: Cambridge University Press, 1931; repr. 2011), p. 3.

13. Terry Pratchett, *Eric* (London: Victor Gollancz, 1990), p. 8.

14. Terry Pratchett, *The Light Fantastic* (New York and London: Harper Collins, 1986), pp. 8–9.

15. Terry Pratchett, *Soul Music* (London: Random House, 2009), p. 152.

16. Terry Pratchett, *A Hat Full of Sky* (London: Doubleday, 2004), pp. 98–9.

17. Terry Pratchett, *Unseen Academicals* (London: HarperCollins, 2009), p. 30.

18. Terry Pratchett, *The Fifth Elephant* (London: Random House, 2008), p. 127. Italics in original.

19. Terry Pratchett, *Monstrous Regiment* (London: Corgi, 2004), p. 257.

20. Terry Pratchett, *The Truth*, p. 39.

21. Pratchett, *Monstrous Regiment*, p. 289.

22. Pratchett, *Monstrous Regiment*, pp. 27–8.

23. Terry Pratchett, *Carpe Jugulum* (London: Corgi, 1999), p. 318.

24. Clémentine Beauvais, *The Mighty Child: Time and Power in Children's Literature* (Amsterdam: John Benjamins, 2015), p. 16.

25. Beauvais, *The Mighty Child*, p. 19.

26. The 'That's Not My . . .' series with Usborne has seventy-six texts following the same formula. See Usborne, https://usborne.com/books/browse-by-category/baby-books, accessed 15 January 2023.

27. Terry Pratchett, *Thud!* (London: Transworld, 2005), p. 125.

28. Terry Pratchett, 'Straight from the Heart, Via the Groin'. Speech given at Noreascon 2004, Worldcon, in *A Slip of the Keyboard: Collected Nonfiction* (New York: Doubleday, 2014), pp. 44–64 (p. 59).

29. Pratchett, *The Fifth Elephant*, p. 225.

30. Lisa Surridge, '*Detection and Its Designs: Narrative and Power in Nineteenth-Century Detective Fiction* by Peter Thoms (review)', *University of Toronto Quarterly*, 69(1) (1999/2000), pp. 250–5 (p. 251).

31. Terry Pratchett, *Night Watch* (London: Transworld, 2002), pp. 99–100.

32. Pratchett, *Feet of Clay*, p. 16.

33. Pratchett, *Thud!*, p. 32.

34. Pratchett, *Thud!*, p. 144.

35. Pratchett, *Thud!*, p. 144.

36. Pratchett, *Thud!*, p. 195.

37. Pratchett, *Thud!*, p. 149.

38. Pratchett, *Thud!*, p. 219.

39. I borrow this term from Roderick McGillis's *The Nimble Reader: Literary Theory and Children's Literature* (New York: Twayne, Prentice Hall International, 1996)

40. Beauvais, *The Mighty Child*, p. 72.

BOOKS AND THEIR READERS IN TERRY PRATCHETT'S DISCWORLD SERIES   239

41. Pratchett, *Thud!*, p. 152.

42. 'Book: Where's My Cow?', https://wiki.lspace.org/Book:Where%27s_My_Cow%3F, 2023, accessed 1 April 2023.

43. Raymond J. Clark, quoted in Keira Vaclavik, *Uncharted Depths: Descent Narratives in English and French Children's Literature* (New York: Routledge, 2017), p. 3.

44. Terry Pratchett, 'Imaginary Worlds, Real Stories'. The Eighteenth Katharine Briggs Memorial Lecture, November 1999, *Folklore*, III (2000), 159–68 (p. 159).

Bibliography of secondary literature

About Discworld & Terry Pratchett Wiki (2012), https://wiki.lspace.org/Main_Page

Beauvais, Clémentine, *The Mighty Child: Time and Power in Children's Literature* (Amsterdam: John Benjamins, 2015)

Gameson, Richard, 'The Medieval Library (to c.1450)', in *The Cambridge History of Libraries in Britain and Ireland, Vol. I to 1640*, ed. by Elisabeth Leedham-Green and Teresa Webber (Cambridge: Cambridge University Press, 2008), pp. 13–50

McGillis, Roderick, *The Nimble Reader: Literary Theory and Children's Literature* (New York: Twayne, Prentice Hall International, 1996)

Pratchett, Terry, 'Imaginary Worlds, Real Stories'. The Eighteenth Katharine Briggs Memorial Lecture, November 1999, *Folklore*, III (2000), 159–68

Pratchett, Terry, 'Straight from the Heart, Via the Groin'. Speech given at Noreascon 2004, Worldcon, in *A Slip of the Keyboard: Collected Nonfiction* (New York: Doubleday, 2014), pp. 44–64

Shanahan, Jim, 'Terry Pratchett: Mostly Human', in *Twenty-First-Century Popular Fiction*, ed. by Bernice Murphy and Stephen Matterson (Edinburgh: Edinburgh University Press, 2017), pp. 31–40

Streeter, Burnett Hillman, *The Chained Library: A Survey of Four Centuries in the Evolution of the English Library* (Cambridge: Cambridge University Press, 1931; repr. 2011)

Surridge, Lisa, '*Detection and Its Designs: Narrative and Power in Nineteenth-Century Detective Fiction* by Peter Thoms (review)', *University of Toronto Quarterly*, 69(1) (1999/2000), 250–5

'Terry Pratchett's Discworld', Fabulous Realms, 23 Mar. 2012, https://ashsilverlock.wordpress.com/2012/03/16/a-visit-to-discworld

Vaclavik, Keira, *Uncharted Depths: Descent Narratives in English and French Children's Literature* (New York: Routledge, 2017)

Index

A

adventure romance/adventure fiction, 10, 163–80, 193, 205, 216
Alcott, Louisa May, 4
Little Women, 4, 187, 188, 189, 190
American Library Association (ALA), 112, 118, 120
Anstey, F. (Thomas Anstey Guthrie)
Vice Versa: A Lesson to Fathers, 189
Austen, Jane, 6–7, 75–94, 108, 182, 186, 189, 190
Mansfield Park, 6, 65, 67–9
Northanger Abbey, 6–7, 75–9, 82–9, 126
Pride and Prejudice, 82, 186
Sense and Sensibility, 82

B

Ballad-books, 45, 176–7
Balzac, Honoré de, 148, 157
Barham, R. H.
Ingoldsby Legends, 163
Barr, Robert
'Lord Chizelrigg's Missing Fortune', 216
Barrie, J. M.
The Little Minister, 187
Baudelaire Charles, 145, 153–5, 158
'Le Balcon', 153–5
Les Fleurs du Mal, 158
Beattie, James, 77
Beddoes, Thomas, 80
Bentinck, Hans Willem (First Earl of Portland), 51
Bewick, Thomas
A History of British Birds, 1–2, 12
Bible/bibles, 7, 9, 125–44, 145, 149, 150–51, 159, 160n11, 163, 164–5, 175–7, 179, 182
Family, 133
Imperial Family Bible, 135–6
New Testament, 4, 9, 125–40
Old Testament, 133, 163
Bible Society, 133, 135
Bodleian Library, 214–15
Boethius
Da Consolatione Philosophiae, 26
bookbinding/bookbindings, 28, 126–32, 135–8, 176–7, 213–14
women in, 132, 137–8
bookcases, 1–2, 7, 67, 172, 188, 207, 213, 216. *See also* bookshelves
book collectors (fictional), 50, 113, 208–10, 212–14
books

destruction of, 5, 13, 114, 129–30, 152, 173, 174–6, 189, 215, 233
illustrations in, 1–2, 52, 99, 174, 187 (*see also* picture books)
manuscript, 13, 28, 30–32
materiality of, 2, 9, 10, 22, 25, 28, 125–40, 166–7, 174–6, 212
non-codical forms, 27–8, 32–3, 165–7, 226, 233
order of, 11, 12, 132–4, 207, 213–14
physical engagement with, 24–5, 26–7, 125–6, 129–32, 135–9. *See also* reading, embodied
physicality of, 2, 4, 20, 22, 33, 125–6, 129–33, 135, 140, 195
smell of, 11, 169, 206, 209, 214–15, 217
bookshelves, 13, 60, 188, 192, 195, 205, 207, 210, 213, 215, 220n55, 227. *See also* bookcases
Bradbury, Ray
Fahrenheit 451, 13
Braddon, Mary
The Doctor's Wife, 8
Lady Audley's Secret, 211
Brent-Dyer, Elinor, 184–99
Chalet School series, 10, 183, 184–95
British Museum, 112
British Museum Library, 11, 12, 194
Brontë, Charlotte
Jane Eyre, 1–2, 3–4, 7, 14n2
Bruce, Dorita Fairlie, 192
The Senior Prefect, 181–2
Buchan, John, 189, 190
John Burnet of Barns, 168–9
Mr Standfast, 4
Salute to Adventurers, 164
Buchan Anna (O. Douglas), 189, 198n62
Bunyan, John
The Pilgrim's Progress, 3–4
Burnett, Frances Hodgson
The Secret Garden, 189
Burney, Fanny, 182
Evelina, 64, 186
The Wanderer, 72n29

C

Carroll, Lewis, 189, 205, 211
Cavendish, Margaret, 6, 42–56
'Assaulted and Pursued Chastity', 42–3, 45–50, 52–3
'Heaven's Library', 52, 55n52
Natures Pictures Drawn by Fancies Pencil to the Life, 52–3

242 INDEX

Cavendish, Margaret (*continued*)
  'She Anchoret', 52, 55n32
  The Unnatural Tragedy, 55n32
  The Worlds Olio, 55n30, 55n32
censorship, 106–7, [118], 186
Cervantes, Miguel de, 5
  Don Quixote, 5, 77, 81, 98, 105 (see also quixotism)
Chambers, Jessie, 146, 151–3, 156
  D. H. Lawrence: A Personal Record, 146, 151–2
chapbooks, 165
Chaucer, Geoffrey, 21–6, 27, 32
  the *Book of the Duchess*, 23–4, 25, 26
  Parliament of Fowls, 24–6
  Troilus and Criseyde, 21–3, 28–9
Chesterton, G. K., 127
  'The Doom of the Darnaways', 212
Christie, Agatha, 203–8, 211, 216–17
  After the Funeral, 207
  And Then There Were None, 207
  Death in the Clouds, 207
  'Greenshaw's Folly', 211
  Lord Edgware Dies, 211
  Murder in Mesopotamia, 211
  Murder is Easy, 208
  Murder on the Orient Express, 207
  'Philomel Cottage', 216
  Spider's Web, 207–8
  'Strange Jest', 220n56
  The Body in the Library, 208
  'The King of Clubs', 217
  'The Love Detectives', 217
  The Murder of Roger Ackroyd, 203
  The Mysterious Affair at Styles, 206–7
  The Seven Dials Mystery, 217
  The Sittaford Mystery, 207
  'The Strange Case of Sir Arthur Carmichael', 216
  'Three Blind Mice', 217
codex/codices, 27, 32
Codrington, Robert, 44, 47, 48, 50
  The Second Part of Youths Behaviour, 45
Collins, Wilkie, 106, 187
  'The Unknown Public', 106
  The Woman in White, 187
conduct books, 5, 41–3, 44–9, 52–3, 60, 61, 82
contents tables, 31
Coolidge, Susan, 189
  What Katy Did, 189
Co-operative Women's Guild, 146, 147
Courtney, Gwendoline
  At School with the Stanhopes, 182

D

Daly, Elizabeth, 206
  Nothing Can Rescue Me, 212
  The Book of the Crime, 212
  The Book of the Dead, 212
Darch, Winifred, 192, 196n25
  Heather at the High School, 184
  The New School and Hilary, 196n21
  The Upper Fifth in Command, 183
Daudet, Alphonse
  Lettres de mon Moulin, 157
  Tartarin de Tarascon, 157
de la Fayette, Madame
  La Princesse de Clèves, 88
de Ségur, Comtesse
  Les Malheurs de Sophie, 190
  Les Petites Filles Modèles, 205–6
detective fiction, 10–11, 171, 193, 203–24, 232
Dickens, Charles, 100, 106, 151, 189, 190, 210
  Dombey and Son, 188
  Great Expectations, 137
  Hard Times, 100
  Nicholas Nickleby, 187
Dickson Carr, John
  The Shadow of the Goat, 210–11
dreams/dreaming, 10, 12, 33, 62, 167, 173, 193, 216. *See also* dream-vision poems
dream-vision poems, 9, 23–33
du Bosc, Jacques
  L'Honneste Femme, 41, 43, 45, 46, 50

E

e-books, 33
Edgeworth, Maria
  Belinda, 5–6
education, 43–6, 98, 100–101, 106–8, 146–7, 160n3, 161n13, 164, 186, 188, 193, 195, 199n89, 203, 205. *See also* reading, as/for education
  women's, 43–6, 48–9, 51–3, 84, 134–7, 146
Eliot, George, 151
  Adam Bede, 136–7
  Middlemarch, 137
  The Mill on the Floss, 7
Énault, Louis, 190
Ende, Michael
  Die unendliche Geschichte (*The Neverending Story*), 12
Enfield, William, 68
  The Speaker, 68–9
Essay in Defence of the Female Sex [anon], 48
Ewing, Juliana Horatia, 188, 189

INDEX 243

F

fantasy, 49, 63, 66, 76, 81. *See also* fantasy fiction
fantasy fiction, 11, 12–13, 225–37
fictio, 29
fiction-reading, 5, 59–67, 75–89, 95–6, 100–101, 105–8, 151–2, 153, 159, 163, 170, 183, 186–7, 192, 193, 198n62, 210, 228
  opposition to, 44, 61–4, 66–7, 76, 95–6, 106–8
  positive representations of, 6–7, 65–6, 75–8, 82–3, 86–9
Flaubert, Gustave
  Madame Bovary, 8
Fordyce, James, 60
  Sermons for Young Women, 60, 82
Forest, Antonia
  The Cricket Term, 183, 194–5
frontispieces, 52, 166, 174–5

G

Garnett, Edward, 161n15
genre, 4–5, 6, 10–13, 42–50, 171–2
ghost stories, 12, 163, 193
Gilbert, Anthony (Lucy Malleson)
  The Black Stage, 216
Gisborne, Thomas, 61
Gissing, George
  New Grub Street, 12
Goethe, Johann Wolfgang von
  Faust, Part I, 96–9, 101–4
  Faust, Part II, 97, 99
Gogol, Nikolai, 107
  Dead Souls, 107
Goncharov, Ivan, 107
Goodreads, 108
Gothic novels, 82–5, 87–8
Green, Anna Katharine
  The Leavenworth Case, 207
Greuze, Jean-Baptiste, 62
  Lady Reading the Letters of Heloise and Abelard, 62–3

H

Haggard, Henry Rider, 10, 151
  King Solomon's Mines, 163, 166–7, 170, 172, 177n2
  She, 165–6, 168
handwriting, 24–5
Hardy, Thomas
  Jude the Obscure, 9–10, 125–44
  Tess of the D'Urbervilles, 128
Hebert, Rev. Charles, 134
Henryson, Robert
  The Testament of Cresseid, 9, 27–9, 32

Henty, G. A., 189, 205
Heyer, Georgette, 186
Hickes, George, 44
Hill, Aaron, 65–6
historical novels/fiction, 153, 190, 191, 193
histories/history books, 44, 45, 46–8, 53, 55n32, 56n52, 165
Hood, Thomas, 145
  'Fair Ines', 154, 155–6
Horace, 164
Household Words, 100, 106
Huet, Pierre Daniel
  Traité de l'origine des romans, 52
Hull, Richard (Richard Henry Sampson)
  The Murder of My Aunt, 210

I

Inchbald, Elizabeth
  Lovers' Vows, 67–9
incunabula, 209
information, 8–9, 111–20, 207. *See also* information literacy
information age, 33, 111, 120
information literacy, 111–12, 114, 116–20
Innes, Michael (J. I. M. Stewart), 203, 212–13
  Death at the President's Lodgings, 213–14
  Operation Pax, 214–15
  The Long Farewell, 214
interiority, 10, 20–21, 62, 67, 86
intertextuality, 3–4, 98, 99, 172, 186, 190–91

J

James, Henry
  The Portrait of a Lady, 7–8
James, M. R. 12
  'Casting the Runes', 12
  'The Tractate Middoth', 12
James I of Scotland
  The Kingis Quair, 9, 26–7, 28, 32
Jowett, Benjamin, 126
Joyce, James
  A Portrait of the Artist as a Young Man, 148

K

Kingsley, Charles, 189
Kipling, Rudyard, 185, 189, 190, 210
Knox, Vicesimus, 61
  Elegant Extracts, 69–70

L

Lang, Andrew, 178n18, 189
LaPorte, Charles, 126

244   INDEX

Lawrence, D. H., 145–62
  Sons and Lovers, 9–10, 145–62
Laws, Betty
  The New Head—and Barbara, 183
Lennox, Charlotte,
  The Female Quixote, 79, 80–81, 88
Lewes, G. H., 97
librarians/librarianship, 12–13, 194, 208,
  216, 227
libraries, 7, 10–13, 50–51, 56n52, 146,
  151–3, 161n15, 168–9
  authors', 97, 205–6, 218n15
  chained, 227
  circulating/subscription, 61, 78, 82,
    146, 209, 216
  country house, 205, 206–7, 214, 216, 217
  in detective fiction, 10–11, 203–17
  family, 205–6, 208–9, 212
  in fantasy fiction, 11, 12–13, 226–8
  in ghost stories, 12
  Mechanics Institute, 146, 151–2, 160n3
  personal (fictional), 5, 7, 29, 113, 172,
    206–7, 208–11 (*see also* book collec-
    tors (fictional))
  school, 187, 193–5
  in school stories, 187, 190, 193–5
  women's, 45
literacy, 106–7, 111, 150, 226, 228, 233.
  See also information literacy
Lodge, David
  The British Museum Is Falling Down,
    11–12
London Library, 209, 215
Lydgate, John, 30
  'Fifteen Joys and Sorrows of Mary',
    30–32

M

MacDonald, George, 12, 185, 189
  Lilith, 12–13
Mackenzie, Henry, 61
Maistre, Xavier de
  Voyage autour de ma Chambre, 157–8
Makin, Bathsua, 48
male readers, 71n6, 82, 84–5
Manley, Delarivier, 6, 42–56
  The New Atalantis, 42–4, 46, 50–53
Mannyng, Robert
  Handlyng Synne, 19–20
maps, 166, 173–5, 212
Marlowe, Christopher
  Doctor Faustus, 98
Marsh, Ngaio
  Singing in the Shrouds, 219n27
Martineau, Harriet, 60
Mason, A. E. W.
  The House of the Arrow, 210

mathematics/mathematical books, 6, 45,
  47–9, 53, 168
Matthewman, Phyllis, 192
  The Intrusion of Nicola, 183–4
Mérimée, Prosper
  'Columba', 157
metafiction/meta-poetics, 2–3, 42–3,
  49–50, 52–3, 67, 75–6
metanarrative, 99, 115–16
moral philosophy. *See* philosophy/
  philosophical books
Mossop, Irene
  Well Played, Juliana!, 182

N

natural philosophy, 46, 168–9
newspapers, 117, 146–7, 150, 189, 226,
  230, 232
novel-reading. *See* fiction reading

O

O'Brien, Sean
  The Silence Room, 12
Oliphant, Margaret
  'The Library Window', 12
orality, 117, 164, 166, 169–71, 173, 175,
  177, 236
Orwell, George,
  Nineteen Eighty-Four, 13
Ovid, 50, 62, 167
  Metamorphoses, 23, 148
Oxenham, Elsie J., 181, 192

P

*Palgrave's Golden Treasury of Songs and
  Lyrics*, 146, 155, 157, 160n4
paper, 11, 126, 135–6, 166–7, 174–6
Pepys, Elizabeth, 45
Pepys, Samuel, 48
philosophy/philosophical books (*see also*
  natural philosophy), 7, 44, 47, 213–14
phonographs, 116, 118
picture books, 225, 231, 233–7
Piozzi, Hester Thrale, 135–6
playbooks, 6, 44–5, 47–9, 53, 84, 151, 174,
  186. *See also* plays
plays, 44, 48, 55n34, 67–70
poetry, 33, 44, 62, 69–70, 84, 100–101,
  147, 148, 153–8
Pratchett, Terry, 11
  Carpe Jugulum, 229
  Discworld series, 11, 225–37
  Feet of Clay, 231, 233
  Guards! Guards!, 227, 231
  Monstrous Regiment, 228
  Night Watch, 231, 232

Soul Music, 227–8
The Light Fantastic, 227
The Truth, 225
Thud!, 231, 233
Where's my Cow?, 231, 233–7
prefaces/prefatory material, 4, 43, 53, 65, 68–9
Price, Leah, 9, 126, 138,

Q

Queen, Ellery, 206
The Finishing Stroke, 206
The French Powder Mystery, 206
quire/quires, 9, 27–9, 32
quixotism, 5–8, 77, 82, 88–9

R

Radcliffe, Ann, 83–5, 87
The Mysteries of Udolpho, 64, 84–5, 87
The Romance of the Forest, 83, 85
reading
aloud, 20, 65, 102–4, 147, 148–9, 153–4, 157, 185, 233–4 (*see also* recitation)
child, 1–2, 10, 12, 43, 61–2, 66, 84, 101, 168, 172–4, 181–95, 205–6, 230–31, 233–7
communal, 9–10, 20–22, 33, 62–6, 98–9, 102–3, 108, 111–12, 116–120, 145–7, 148–9, 151–4, 159, 182, 185–7, 195, 219n27, 234–7
dangers of, 5–6, 41–4, 50–53, 59, 61–6, 69–70, 79–82, 95–6, 98–9, 103–9, 114, 166, 193, 227–8, 233 (*see also* reading, negative representations of)
devotional, 30–32
digital, 32–3
distracted, 8, 62, 112, 167–8
domestic/home, 21–2, 60, 62–70, 78 (*see also* reading, family)
as/for education, 4, 5, 7, 9–10, 41, 43–5, 47–53, 84, 98–100, 107–8, 146–7, 160, 189–90, 193
embodied, 9, 24, 26–7, 83–5
as empowerment, 7, 52, 116, 119–20, 230
envisioned/imagined, 3, 9, 19–39
family (*see* domestic/home)
future of, 32–3
history of, 2, 26, 59–60
identification with, 5–6, 8, 10, 61–2, 63–4, 70, 83–6, 95, 98–9, 103–5, 151–2, 153, 188 (*see also* quixotism)
intradiegetic, 75–94, 183–4, 191–2
metaphors of/for, 61–2, 66, 152
negative representations of, 8, 76, 80–81, 88, 95–110, 182–4, 228 (*see also* reading, dangers of)

non-codical, 25–8, 32–3, 117–18, 226
as performance, 60, 65, 66–70 (*see also* recitation) physical sensation of, 66, 85, 102–3, 170–71, 172 (*see also* reading, embodied)
prohibitions on, 44, 101, 107
shared (*see* reading, communal)
silent, 20, 64–5, 85, 108, 147–8, 170–71
social (*see* reading, communal)
solitary, 20–21, 61–4, 114, 147–8, 159, 167, 170–71
visceral, 78–9, 82–6, 89 (*see also* reading, embodied)
and visionary experience, 20–32
visual representations of, 62–3, 71n11
and writing, 22, 25, 113–15, 117–18, 163, 168, 171, 173, 183–4, 228, 232
reading publics, 106–9, 120
recitation, 68–70
Reeve, Clara, 77
Richardson, Samuel, 64–6, 87
Clarissa: Or, The History of a Young Lady, 140
Pamela in Her Exalted Condition, 64
Pamela: Or Virtue Rewarded, 65–6
Ricoeur, Paul, 77–8, 79, 86
Freud and Philosophy, 77
Time and Narrative, 77, 88
romance/romances, 22, 23, 41, 43–6, 49–50, 77, 80–81, 87. *See also* adventure romance/adventure fiction
Roman de Thèbes, 22. *See also* Statius
Ruskin, John, 188, 189

S

Sayers, Dorothy L., 189, 193, 203, 205, 208–9
Clouds of Witness, 211
Gaudy Night, 215
Have His Carcase, 211
'The Dragon's Head', 212
'The Professor's Manuscript', 220n55
The Unpleasantness at the Bellona Club, 211
Unnatural Death, 209
Whose Body?, 187, 208–9
school stories, 10, 181–202, 205
science fiction, 13
Scott, Sir Walter, 82, 145, 151–3, 155–6, 189, 190
Ivanhoe, 153
'Marmion', 7
Quentin Durward, 187
The Bride of Lammermoor, 153
The Lady of the Lake, 147
Shaftesbury, Seventh Earl (Anthony Ashley-Cooper), 135

246   INDEX

Shakespeare, William, 82, 84, 163, 186, 189, 190, 195, 212, 214
  Hamlet, 68, 82
  Macbeth, 146
  The Tempest, 212
Sharp, Granville, 133
Sheridan, Richard, 182
  The Rivals, 60–61, 189
Sidney, Sir Philip, 46
  Arcadia, 45
Smith, Charlotte
  Emmeline: or The Orphan of the Castle, 64–5
Smollett, Tobias, 182
  The Adventures of Roderick Random, 79–80, 88
  The Expedition of Humphry Clinker, 188
social media, 33, 108
Spurgeon, Charles, 125
Statius
  Thebaid, 22
Stendhal (Marie-Henri Beyle)
  Le Rouge et le Noir, 8
Stevenson, Robert Louis, 10, 151, 171
  'A Gossip on a Novel of Dumas's', 170–71
  'A Gossip on Romance', 167
  'A Penny Plain and Twopence Coloured', 174
  Kidnapped, 164–5, 167, 170, 172
  'Popular Authors', 174
  'Rosa Quo Locorum', 172
  'Talk and Talkers', 173
  Treasure Island, 167, 171, 172–7
Stoker, Bram
  Dracula, 8–9, 111–22
Swan, Annie S., 145, 149, 160n10

T

Tennyson, Alfred, Lord, 146
  Idylls of the King, 156
  'The Beggar Maid', 161n16
Thackeray, William Makepeace, 4, 189, 210
  Vanity Fair, 95

Times Book Club, 209
Tissot, Samuel Aguste, 80
Turgenev, Ivan, 95–105, 107
  A Sportsman's Sketches, 100
  Faust, 8, 96–105, 107–9
  and Goethe, 97–8
type/typography, 2, 11, 165, 195, 229
typewriting, 116
typology, 11, 133

U

Uncial, 165–6

V

von Arnim, Bettina, 97
  Goethes Briefwechsel mit einem Kinde ('Goethe's Correspondence with a Child'), 97
von Schurman, Anna, 48

W

Walker, Patrick, 165
  Biographia Presbyteriana, 165
Wallace, Edgar
  The Books of Bart, 210
  The Door with Seven Locks, 215–16
Wilde, Oscar, 189
  The Portrait of Dorian Gray, 95
Wolfreston, Frances, 45
Wollstonecraft, Mary, 62–3
women readers, 5–8, 41–53, 60–66, 80–89, 98–105, 118
Woolf, Virginia
  To the Lighthouse, 148
Woolley, Hannah
  The Gentlewomans Companion, 48
Wordsworth, William, 145, 154–6, 157, 158, 189
  'Lucy Gray', 155
  Lyrical Ballads, 155
  'The Solitary Reaper', 154, 155, 156

Y

Yonge, Charlotte M., 187, 189, 190, 205

www.ingramcontent.com/pod-product-compliance
Lightning Source LLC
Chambersburg PA
CBHW060827260325
24073CB00007B/15